The Traveller on the Hill-top

Mary Howitt
The Famous Victorian Authoress

Joy Dunicliff

Published by
CHURNET VALLEY BOOKS
43 Bath Street, Leek, Staffordshire. 01538 399033

© Joy Dunicliff and Churnet Valley Books 1998
ISBN 1 897949 50 2

Printed in Malta by Interprint Limited

DEDICATION

**To my husband who accompanied me on my many research visits,
for all his support and encouragement**

Acknowledgments

I should like to express my thanks to Australia House for their help in tracing information regarding Alfred Howitt, and the New Zealand Press who put me in contact with my N.Z. sources. I am grateful to the National Library of NZ, Alexander Turnbull Library, NZ Collection, the Canterbury Public Library, Canterbury Museum, and the NZ National Archives in Christchurch for their considerable help in tracing the life of Charlton Howitt. I am also most grateful for the information supplied to me by Mr Michael Todhunter concerning Charlton.

For help with information about the Botham family themselves I have to thank Michael Shaw, and for information supplied for the Howitt family trees, Mr Clarence Smith and the late Mr R F Mole.

All rights reserved. No part of this publication may be reproduced, stored in a retrieval system or transmitted, in any form or by any means, electronic, mechanical, photocopying, recording or otherwise, without permission of the publisher in writing.

PREFACE

An elderly lady in Uttoxeter lent me a book many years ago entitled *My Own Story*. It was a little book about a person called Mary Howitt, or rather Mary Botham at the time of the narrative, about her life up to the age of about 9 years.

I became very interested in the descriptions she gave of the town of my adoption, Uttoxeter, and she helped inspire my interest in the local history of her market town. I became concerned that the local people knew so little about their internationally recognised writer and particularly that the Town Council did nothing to perpetuate her name except name a road after her. The Johnsonian Society holds an annual celebration as a reminder of Samuel Johnson's penance which took place in Uttoxeter Market Place, but the centenary of Mary Howitt's death has passed unnoticed. In 1988 the occupier of Mary's old home paid herself for the plaque which now stands above the front door.

One year we took our children to Denmark where we visited Hans Christian Andersen's birth place in Odense. Here I learnt more about Mary Howitt than I had previously known. Our local library has none of her books and the only biography they list, *Laurels & Rosemary,* is not on the shelves. There, in Odense, were numerous letters and books written by her and in this museum I learned of Mary's relationship with the famous fairy tale author himself.

As time went by I became more interested in Mary herself. To me she became a fascinating person, achieving so much at a time when many women were either slaves or decorations to men. A person who fought with her religion, who was interested in making the world a better place to live, a person who believed in the equal rights of all. A person, also, who had first brought the delights of Hans Andersen's imagination to English children, which I so enjoyed as a child. And a person whose most remembered work, *The Spider and the Fly*, was often credited to 'Anon' in the 1930s.

Mary had an unusual childhood. Like so many women writers, she had a cross to bear during her young life, and that was the clothes her father's religion imposed upon her. I admired what her husband allowed her to do compared with other wives of the period. He knew what he wanted out of life and I felt sorry he was not allowed to follow the career of his choice. The two male offspring of this union were extraordinary men, in whom I have also developed an interest.

I hope the reader will find Mary as fascinating a person as I have done.

Joy Dunicliff 1999

Abbreviations used in this book in relation to quotes.

L & R	Laurel & Rosemary	GW	Good Words
VS	Victorian Samplers	SG	In Their Several Generations
TP	Todhunter Correspondence		

CONTENTS

Introduction		5
Chapter 1	FAMILY BACKGROUND	7
	The Bothams	7
	The Woods	10
	Mary's Parents	13
	Forest of Dean	15
Chapter 2	CHILDHOOD INFLUENCES	21
	Home	21
	The Napoleonic War	23
	Uttoxeter	25
Chapter 3	FURTHER EARLY INFLUENCES & INSPIRATIONS	31
	Education	39
Chapter 4	COURTSHIP & MARRIAGE	45
	William and the Howitt family	47
	Marriage	48
	Charles	55
	After Samuels Death	58
Chapter 5	LIFE IN NOTTINGHAM	61
	Death of Byron	61
	Slavery	63
	Nottingham Riots	65
	Early Writings	67
Chapter 6	WIDENING THE EXPERIENCE OF LIFE	71
	Esher	71
	Financial Problems	71
	Heidelberg	76
	Translating	76
	Claude	77
	Hans Christian Andersen	79
	Reunions and Inspirations	80
Chapter 7	WRITING FOR CHILDREN & OTHERS	87
	Emma	87
	Emma's Life in U.S.A.	88
	Clapton	93
	Mr Tegg & the Baker's Dozen	95
	The 19th Century Novel & The Howitts	100
	Household Words	102
Chapter 8	NATIONAL PROBLEMS & THE HOWITTS	105
	Journals & Bankruptcy	106
	The Confidence Trick	108
	The Women's Movement	110
	Spiritualism	111
	Artistic Renewal	111
Chapter 9	LINKS WITH THE ANTIPODES	115
	The Australian Visit	116
	Mary's Problems	120
	Alfred Howitt	122
	West Hill Lodge & Annie Howitt	127
	Charlton Howitt in New Zealand	127
	Restlessness	141
	Meggie Howitt	144
Chapter 10	THE TYROL AND ROME	147
	Franco-Prussian War	147
	Rome	148
	Golden Wedding Anniversary	148
	Family Deaths	149
	Conversion	150
	Farewell	151
	Obituaries	152
Acknowledgements and Bibliography		154
Family Histories		157

INTRODUCTION

Mary Howitt, née Botham, was a prolific, well-known and well-loved 19th century writer of stories and poems, many of which were for children, but her books would be difficult to find now. She was also a skilled translator of works still loved today, but not bearing her name.

Mary and her husband William between them wrote over 180 books which were published in 700 editions and issues. The Americans classed Mary as the second most popular living foreign poet to Mrs Hemans by 1835 and second to none by 1845. Mary continually increased her readership in the States until the Civil War period. As far as William was concerned, the Americans considered him to be the principal writer of the day on the subject of traditional rural life in England.

Between them they launched many classical writers such as Mrs Gaskell and John Keats by finding a publisher for their works, or by publishing their articles in one of the many journals in which William was involved. Mary was also the first to translate Hans Christian Andersen, including his famous fairy stories, and they helped published and promote his works in England. Mary also changed the style of children's writing, making it brighter and more readable.

Later, Mary's two sons, Charlton and Alfred, contributed in no small way to the opening up of the new countries of Australia and New Zealand, as well as sending botanical specimens to England, and writing about their experiences. Alfred can be considered the instigator or founder of anthropology in Australia.

Both William and Mary were active politically through their articles, letters and committees with a view to social change in accordance with their religious faith.

Although Mary Howitt was not born in Uttoxeter, a market town in Staffordshire, she spent her formative years in the town. Her father, Samuel Botham, was an Uxonian as were her two sisters and her brother. In all she spent nigh on twenty years in the town and often returned to it after her marriage.

Mary came from an unusual background, and to understand her it is necessary to first learn a little about her parents who came from very different and seemingly incompatible backgrounds.

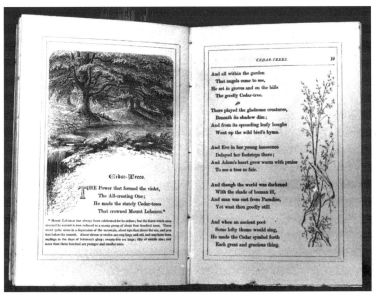

The Traveller on the Hill-top

Whitecliffe the site of Samuel Botham's ironworks in 1798.

The house in Whitecliffe near Coleford, Forest of Dean, where the Bothams lived for about 2 years and where Mary was born in the bad winter of 1799.

Howitt Place, the Botham's home in Uttoxeter, Staffordshire. Mary lived here until she was married. Painted by Francis Redfern.

CHAPTER ONE
FAMILY BACKGROUND

The Bothams

Samuel Botham's father, John (c1725-1807), was one of three sons and two daughters born to John Botham of Apesford, near Leek in the North Staffordshire Moorlands. He came from a long line of farmers whose documentation goes back to Richard III's time, and living there when Bonnie Prince Charlie and his troops passed through on their way to Derby in 1745 and on their return journey, when the Bothams nursed a wounded soldier back to health.

The family had little education and attended the Leek Quaker Meeting on what they called First Day morning (Sunday morning). They had become members of the Society of Friends, more often known as Quakers, in the early days of the movement and knew the founder, George Fox, personally. They suffered religious persecution when it was illegal to meet for a religious service other than in the Church of England. Most dissenters, the Quakers amongst them, usually met in houses or barns; soldiers sometimes raided such meetings, burning buildings and breaking up the gatherings. Imprisonment was commonplace, as was ridicule. Because the Quakers felt no obligation to the Church of England, they refused to pay tithes (rates paid to the parish church for the upkeep of the church and towards the vicar's stipend). After the Tolerations Act of 1689 the Quakers still refused to pay tithes to the parish and although prosecutions were fewer, many still went to prison. The Friends went so far as not to call the Parish Church a church; they used all sorts of names such as 'the parish meeting house', 'the church so called', 'daw house' or even 'steeple house'. Quakers, like other non-conformists (dissenters), were unable to hold public office or enter the professions. To hold such an office a certificate to say the person had attended communion in the Church of England had to be produced. To the Bothams, who were hill farmers, this may not have mattered, but they were still at risk of having their barns destroyed.

The remote Staffordshire Moorlands was a Quaker stronghold. One of the family, the widow Mary Botham, is mentioned in *Bess's Sufferings of Friends* (1753) in a list of fines and jail sentences, and being put in stocks, inflicted on Quakers in Bedfordshire. This Mary travelled the country as a minister of the Society of Friends, carrying her Testimonials, as did all early Friends when travelling around evangelising. The Friends, unlike other denominations at the time, allowed women to preach to meetings and to spread the 'Truth'.

John Botham junior inherited the farm on the death of his father but he was a restless man and did not want to settle down to farming. He moved to Uttoxeter in 1750 at the age of twenty-six. He worked as a herbalist, preparing his own herbs, vegetable drugs and salves. He was famous for his own Botham snuff. He believed himself to be a heaven-appointed minister for the Quaker community's physical and spiritual well-being, and this was given credence by his being an accredited minister of the Society from the age of 24 years. He was listened to as an oracle of wisdom in Quaker farming circles, and was consulted on all manner of topics.

He attended the Quaker Meeting house in Carter Street, Uttoxeter, and there he met and married Rebecca Summerland in 1755, a wealthy widow with two grown-up sons. He was 29 and she was considerably older. Rebecca was a member of the Shipley family and owned much property and a malting business in the town. She was a successful businesswoman herself, *"pious and prudent"*. She was Clerk to the Yearly Meeting in 1750, and highly respected within the Quaker movement. She had had many suitors in her widowhood and turned them all down, so when she married John, the Summerland family was taken by surprise.

Rebecca's first husband had been wealthy and this second marriage meant that all the Summerland money would go to her new husband, and not to the adult sons of the first marriage, upon their mother's death. The sons had expected to inherit a ready-made business and substantial wealth, and this, their considered birthright, was lost to the usurper John Botham. There was friction with the Summerland family for many years, and the resulting estrangement was to have a profound effect on the new son, young Samuel.

John Botham was popular. He travelled around the countryside with his medicines and often treated his patients for nothing. Later he became interested in animal magnetism and studied the works of Mesmer and Cagliostro. But he neglected his family and business, leaving his wife to bring up their sons, James (b.1756) and Samuel (b.1758). Rebecca was able to give the Botham boys a good education and then good apprenticeships, which annoyed the Summerland family further. James was apprenticed to a West India merchant in Manchester, and he married another Rebecca, Rebecca Topper, in 1787. She must have also been a Quaker as they did not marry outside their religious fraternity at this period - if they did they were dismissed from the Society. James died six weeks after the marriage, and Rebecca eventually moved to be nearer her family in Chelmsford, where his posthumous daughter, another Rebecca, was born.

The second son, Samuel, was educated at a Friends' School at Hartshill in Warwickshire, then at 14 years of age was apprenticed to a well-known and respected land surveyor, William Fairbank of Sheffield. In those days the training, practical and theoretical, of a land surveyor included road and bridge building, architecture, and the knowledge of forestry. Sadly, his mother, Rebecca, died somewhere between 1771 and 1775, before he had completed his training. Samuel never forgot the kindness shown by Mrs Fairbank at the time and every year afterwards he sent presents of hares and partridges to his *"honoured friend Mary Fairbank"*, and later took his wife and family to see her.

Samuel returned to Uttoxeter to find that his father had mortgaged nearly all his deceased mother's property; and nearly all the rent from lettings was needed to pay the interest. Fortunately under the terms of his mother's will the house in Balance Street had been left to Samuel. The house had been in the Shipley family for three generations, built in the reign of Queen Anne by a John Shipley, Rebecca's ancestor. This further strained the relationships between the Botham, Summerland and Shipley families, they felt that they had been robbed of their inheritance. Samuel decided to pay off the mortgage, so he moved himself and his father from Balance Street to a more humble dwelling, two cottages joined into one in Carter Street. The parlour had bare whitewashed walls with a projecting fireplace. Samuel who had natural artistic skills, painted what he considered an ornamental cornice on the stone work. His father was very critical and strongly disapproved of this friviolity - *"lest it should indulge the lust of the eye"*. The episode, and many others similar, had a marked effect on Samuel's life, and later on those of his children. He feared the magical and frightening effect that music and art had on himself, and might have on his children and grandchildren.

In 1784/5 Samuel set up his own business as a surveyor in Uttoxeter. Soon after, he was asked to survey the enclosure of the Uttoxeter Heath and in time, with brother James's help, he paid off the mortgages and returned to their house in Balance Street. Samuel's qualities as a surveyor were such, it was said of him that *"he measured land as if it were gold"*. His reputation established, he travelled to various parts of the country in his work and while he was working in South Wales for Lord Talbot of Ingestre he met his wife, Ann Wood. The French Revolution had made the English landed gentry nervous and throughout the Country they wanted their estates measured and valued. Together with the enclosure acts, this ensured a plentiful supply of work for good surveyors.

The Traveller on the Hill-top

Whenever there were problems at home, Father John went off on his wanderings. Later, when his brother James died, Samuel had many things to sort out, including the future of James's young pregnant widow, Rebecca. Samuel rarely spoke of this period of his life but he did reveal that when he had not known which way to turn, he had sought the advice of an old witch in a remote cottage on the Weaver Hills. He never revealed what had been said, but he *"left her dwelling with deep abasement";* he felt that he *"had been in the abyss of evil."*

Samuel was a dedicated Quaker. Their founder George Fox believed that the 'Truth' would be sent to them by God. *"We call all men to look to the Light within their own conscience,"* said Samuel Fisher in 1660. In 1656 George Fox said *"Conscience was above the scriptures and the scriptures ought to be tried by it, and not that by the scriptures. Not the letter nor the writing of the Scripture, but the ingrafted Word is able to save your soules."* Church-going was unimportant because God dwelled in men and women's hearts; the church was *"noe more holy than another piece of ground".*

Samuel did not believe in the use of the Bible; he wanted Friends to be instructed by God and not led by the instructions of other men. It was the duty of Friends to take the 'Truth' to all who were prepared to listen to them. Many of these people were traders or merchants who took the message and their written 'convincements' with them on their business journeys. Friends were much more mobile than many other people of the period.

This was one of the 'anti-popery' periods and the Quakers called for the removal of small images of popery, crosses, etc. The Quakers wanted to get rid of everything that reminded them of Roman Catholicism. They removed the word Saint from place names - St Ives and Bury St Edmunds were Ives and Bury Edmunds, and Chalfont St Peter, Peter's Chalfont. They even went to the extent of not using the names of days of the week because they are named after pagan gods; likewise the months of the year from January to September. Sunday was the First-day, Monday, the Second-day, and so on. The day date was preceded by the month number, so the 1st April would be written 4mo 1 followed by the year.

Their speech was archaic replacing 'you' with 'thou' as they considered all people equal. Thou was normally only used by others amongst very close friends or relations - and even this practice was dying out - and to address someone socially superior thus was an insult to most people. The Friends had a code of conduct for bringing up their children; a new born baby was considered completely innocent, and to keep them that way, to enable them to receive the 'Truth' from God, they were not allowed to mix with other children who might 'pollute' them. George Fox felt that people should not be vain, nor draw attention to themselves. Theirs was a life of simplicity, lacking in ornamentation in language, furniture, architecture, dress and gardens. At Meetings the congregation was warned against the like of striped or floral silks, wigs, 'broidered hairs', pearls, gold or any costly array.

Quakers believed in people helping themselves, and they put their children into apprenticeships so that they in turn would help their parents. They had their own workhouse and poor-law system with 'out-relief'. They helped their fellow Quaker businessmen in financial difficulties and supported each other through their problems. Purification was through works performed and not, as in the Roman Catholic Church, through justification and propitiation. There was no room for culture, no time for frivolity or the self-indulgence of painting, drama, sculpture, music or dance. Self-censorship and self-discipline was taught.

However in the 18th century some meetings became more structured with a dais and men and women seated on opposite sides as in the Anglican Church, something the founder members had been escaping from. Quakerism developed a ruling class, with special meetings; Yearly Meeting, Meeting for Sufferings, Second Day Morning Meeting, Six Weeks Meeting, Quarterly Meeting, Monthly Meeting. There were also women's meetings. In Leicester it got to the stage where a number of local families ran the system which was passed on from father to son, and grandson, a select Quaker leadership. Some people even considered them to be copying Church courts with visitors and visitations. Marriage to *"those of the world"* was always an anathema and one of the functions of these meetings was to discourage such relationships as well as acting as arbitratory courts for debts, property, wills, business deals, arguments and disputes between friends.

So by the time our Mary was born there were two types of Quakers, those who were "plain Quakers" adhering to extremes of dress and speech, (even in excess of George Fox's ideas), and "wet Quakers" who were more lax. Samuel was a "plain Quaker" who dressed in the costume of George Fox's period a hundred years earlier, and expected his family to adhere to his beliefs and requests - something any wife would have had to do in those days anyway.

Samuel had a spirit of mysticism, something Mary followed later in her life. He enjoyed discussions with his friends, amongst whom were William Warner, a young lawyer, and Thomas Hart, a wealthy young man who was later a banker at Bank House in Church Street, Uttoxeter. Both were staunch Anglicans. In their discussions they sought a new beginning. This was the time of the French Revolution and the Napoleonic Wars. They talked of freedom from popery, and universal brotherhood. Samuel even thought the times might precede the second coming of Christ. At one time the three men joined in a newspaper venture, but Samuel was upset by articles relating to bloodshed and fear, and withdrew. He was accused by his friends of backing out, but nevertheless they respected his Quaker convictions, and he maintained his friendship with Warner and Hart and their families throughout their lives.

As a child, Samuel used to play with his cousin, Ann Shipley, who was about his age. He was very happy in her company and it was thought that they would marry one day. Ann, however, had other ideas and wanted to marry her first cousin, Morris Shipley not a Friend. Such a marriage was not allowed within the Society of Friends, and Morris and Ann ran away to Gretna Green. The Society disowned them, but later they were reinstated. About 1790 they emigrated to America and the famous Shipley bankers were their descendants.

The Woods

Ann Wood, Mary's mother, was able to trace her family back to a General Francois Dubois, who, having been warned by a friend, escaped from France before the Massacre of St Bartholomew in 1572. He had taken his wife and infant son to Shrewsbury where, like many other Huguenots, he traded as a ribbon weaver, although he did not belong to the Guild of Mercers. They later moved to Wolverhampton where Francois' grandson William was born in 1609. The Dubois family had its own crest, a mailed arm upholding a mitre. At this time they changed their name to the English form, Wood.

None of this, however, can be substantiated. The Huguenot Society says that according to a privately published work "An interim report on the Wood family genealogy" by M.H.Wood in 1963, there is no definite proof of the Huguenot connection and puts its origin down perhaps to Victorian romanticism, and particularly David Agnew's "French Protestant Exiles", 1874 edition, which tells the story of William Wood and his Dubois forbears. The Society says it is difficult to prove the genealogy of any Huguenots who settled outside a Huguenot community - and Shrewsbury was not a Huguenot settlement.

Ann Wood's forbears owned many ironworks by the end of the 17th century. Another William, born 1671, a metallurgist, was a friend of Robert Walpole, and became a political victim through the selfish cunning of Dean Swift who at that time was in exile. He pilloried Walpole into dropping his halfpenny scheme saying no trader would take them and the Irish would starve.

The Traveller on the Hill-top

"The Halfpence are coming the nation undoing,
There is an end of your ploughing and baking and brewing,
In that you must all go to rack and to ruin".

Wood had been asked to make the Irish halfpenny coins, which were afterwards not used - he was known as the "Irish Patentee". The patent had cost £10,000 from the Duchess of Kendal and after much argument, when the whole project had fallen through, William was awarded a pension of £3,000 per annum for eight years, paid to him under the name of Avedale. This is where the local tale of old Mr Botham counting his halfpennies in the front of his Balance Street house probably originates. On his marriage William inherited Bermondsey forges and there he made railings for St Paul's Cathedral yard. He had fifteen children, and eight surviving sons. Amongst them were:

Francis: Mary Howitt based Uncle Nabob on him in her book *Wood Leighton*, the account of a town modelled on Uttoxeter. He shared his retirement with a locked teak chest but when it was opened after his death there was no treasure, only the mummified body of a Hindu woman!

Richard: Remained unmarried.

John: Was left 1/- in his father's will (the reason undisclosed) and owned the Wednesbury Iron Works. He had nineteen children. At the age of eighty he had a son, Benjamin, by his young second wife who inherited all his wealth and then squandered it.

Charles: The fifth son and Mary's maternal grandfather, an assay master in Jamaica. He was once brought an unidentified metal which on investigation he found to be platinum. This was unknown in Europe at the time and through a friend, Brownrigg, he introduced it to this country. He had also studied medicine, and made ointments for wounded slaves. His first wife and the elder children never understood his, or anyone else's, abhorrence of the cruelty of the slave trade. His Cynfarthfa foundry made canons for the American War of Independence, during which he sided with the so-called rebels. He also cast St. Paul's Cathedral railings. After twenty years in Jamaica, Charles came home and married for the second time, to his friend's younger sister, Jemima. She was the widow of Captain Lynden, an Irishman and captain of the slave ship Dolphin. They had two sons, Roger and Charles, the latter of whom was lost at sea.

Samuel: The sixth son, a serious man who became a Quaker and had a big influence on his niece Ann. He was described as a "man of good property". One of his daughters ran away from home with a highwayman, Jack Shepherd. He carried her away riding pillion. Nothing is told about what became of her after that.

Mary's mother, Ann, was daughter of Charles. He used to talk of when the family had moved from Cumberland to start the first ironworks in Merthyr Tydfil, when Ann was still a little girl. Born in 1762, she was his youngest daughter, and his favourite. She spent much of her time with him while he talked of all sorts of things, and she came to enjoy his company more than that of her mother and sisters. She recalled that he enjoyed music, poetry and literature, a joy he handed on to her. He had Quaker leanings and he told of the horrors of the slave trade that he had witnessed in Jamaica. She learnt to detest slavery. He inspired her with the desire to resist tyranny, and infused in her an admiration of George Washington. When her father died, Ann lost, whilst still a child, a friend, tutor, counsellor, provider and protector. He understood her better than anyone else, and his passing was affected her profoundly.

The foundry at Cyfarthfa continued to function under the direction of Ann's brother, William Wood, and half-brother, Roger Lyndon, but the family was broken up. Mary Wood, Ann's eldest sister, was adopted by her childless Uncle Brownrigg, and went to live in Cumberland. Amongst her many admirers was William Wilberforce, but she turned him down as she thought *"she could do better for herself",* and chose a cleric instead. Ann's other sister, Dorothy, educated at a fashionable ladies' school, was vivacious and her mother's favourite.

Ann became a lonely soul within her own home. As she grew up, she determined to remain independent, which meant leaving home and finding a job at a time when this was not a respectable thing for a young lady to do. The low paid positions of governess or companion were all that was open to her, positions usually filled by women with no income, either from impoverished "respectable" homes, or penniless widows. Ann's family mixed with many well-known people. At eighteen years of age she decided to be a governess and through her mother's cousin, Lady Esmond, she obtained a position in the household of Dr George Glasse, a chaplain to George III. She later became companion to a well-travelled old lady who gave many society dinners and parties. She met Dr Samuel Johnson two or three times, and many other notable people. By 1786 the elderly lady had died and Ann became companion to the daughters of Dr Horne, the Dean of Canterbury.

When Ann was staying with her Aunt Isabella Cox, née Wood, in London, she got involved against her will with a street mob. A young army lieutenant, Robert Wilson, saved her and escorted her back to her aunt's house. Later, she accompanied her cousin Bella to see a fashionable fortune teller. The fortune teller took Ann's palm, and said *'in measured accents'*, *"You will not marry your present lover. You will change your religion and marry another."* To Bella she said, *"Where is your wedding ring?"* adding solemnly, *"You have done the worst day's work you ever did. You will repent it as long as you live."* And so ended the interview. Bella had been forbidden to marry a soldier, an Irish Roman Catholic, but she had secretly married him! The marriage lasted only a few years before she left him. Her father, John, was said never to have smiled again.

When Ann's eldest sister got married, she had to give up her work and travels and returned home to live with her mother. In 1790, at the age of twenty-six, she was having a battle of religious conscience and at one time she considered becoming a nun. But as a child she had accompanied her father to a public meeting of the Society of Friends at Merthyr Tydfil, and although she could not remember what the preacher had said, he had made a marked impression on her. When her mother became aware of her interest in the Society, she revealed that her husband's dying request had been that if any of their children should want to join the Society she should not stop them as he had adopted the Society's religious opinions. Ann often stayed at Falmouth with the Foxes, a notable Quaker family, and in later years Mary Howitt wrote that she felt her mother showed particular pleasure when talking of her times in Cornwall. She found mental peace and tranquillity there amongst the rugged scenery and it nurtured her love of poetry. She also had good friends in Neath, where she spent much time with Evan and Elizabeth Rees.

Ann eventually joined the Society of Friends, a completely new way of life for her, a relearning of everything she had known. As one Quaker of the period said, the first thing to be done after conversion was to go the tailors to comply with the Quakers' strict code of dress. It had been assumed that Ann would marry Robert Wilson on his return from war, but when he tried to see her again she could not face him, and asked her Quaker friend, Sarah Fox of Falmouth, to go into the room instead of her. Sarah *"alarmed no doubt to find herself conversing intimately with the 'man of war', when he was leaving asked 'and if thou had a wife, how wouldst thou propose to maintain her?' 'By this,' putting his hand upon his sword, was the reply. 'A sword brought us together [thinking of how he had saved her from a London mob] and a sword has parted us.' So saying, Robert Wilson left the house."* [L&R]

Ann was to love Robert for the rest of her life. He remained unmarried and when she read of his death in 1839 at the age of seventy-seven, she wept.

Mary's Parents

During a visit to Evan and Elizabeth Rees in 1795, Ann Wood met another of their friends, Samuel Botham. A respected Friend advised her that if Samuel should propose marriage to her, she should not refuse. When Samuel asked Ann to marry him she felt it was *"Divine Providence"* and accepted. Everything Samuel did was guided by his interpretation of the scriptures, what he considered to be Divine Providence. Mary Howitt felt her father had, *"as a result of family quarrels and his environment, narrowed his outlook and become a stern self-repressing man. He was artistic, drew well, loved beauty and music. The latter frightened him by the feeling of power it had over him. He was fearful of evil and he mistrusted himself."*

Mary described her mother as having a *"clear, intelligent mind, her culture and refinement chastened and subdued by her new spiritual convictions and painful social surroundings. She had a very different mind, manners, speech, tone of voice, and her style of dress had been very different before the plain dress of Uttoxeter Quakers was enforced by her husband. She was of middle height, not handsome, but of a singularly intelligent countenance with well-cut features, clear grey eyes; the whole expression being that of a character strong and decisive but not impulsive."*

When Ann met Samuel she made a good assessment of him; she saw him as a timid person, fearful of evil and it was said of them that *"beneath the external life of this grave couple, with their often frustrated schemes, there ran a hidden current of spiritual struggle, a struggle of hopes and fears mixed with hope and peace, like a golden weft, with a web of coarser material, which beautifies the whole."*

Ann Wood married Samuel Botham on 6th December 1796 in South Wales, when she was thirty-two and he was thirty-eight years old. She wore a soft silk gown of neutral tints which was later folded away on the shelves of her wardrobe because her husband disapproved of silk. At the time of Samuel and Ann's marriage it was normal to wear a dress suitable for general best use for one's wedding usually in grey, mauve or other pastel shade. Her trousseau consisted of four silk dresses in delicate shades of grey and brown, which were never worn but were put in a drawer occasionally to be taken out, loved, refolded and put away again.

In George Fox's time there had been strict codes in dress according to status, each rank of society had different types of fabrics from which their clothes might be made. Presumably the Uttoxeter Quakers still adhered to the materials used for the 'humbler' levels of society of their Founder's period. Mary as a young adult said of her mother that *"she normally wore a dark coloured dress, usually of some shade of brown made of silkbine, a fabric made of a mixture of silk and wool. The long dress was worn, even in the house, drawn up on each side through the pocket-holes."* Mary felt the effect of such a dress was good but *"would have been really graceful if the material had been soft and pliable, but the thread of both silk and wool was spun with a close twist, which produced a stiff and harsh fabric."* She wore a *"thin double muslin kerchief"* which covered the bust, and a *"transparent white muslin cap"* of the ordinary Quaker make, raised somewhat behind, leaving the back hair visible rolled over a small pad. No buttons or trimmings were allowed, only hooks, eyes and cord and no ribbon on her bonnet. Ann used to go to Stafford to get her Quaker bonnet; there were specialists making Quaker bonnets in areas where there were enough Friends to support the trade.

Such restriction and self-discipline imposed on the family whilst Mary was a child made her aware that she was different from other people and this caused much rebellious thought and secretive action as she grew up. This was not unusual amongst Quaker children. An early Quaker, John Crook, recalled that the first converts suffered from outward, as well as inner, turmoils, *"in Gestures, and Postures, and Language, and Behaviour, divers from all People; which made them become a Gazing-stock to Men and Angels, and to be hated of their own*

Mother's Son, and near Relation." Another early Quaker, William Edmondson, said *"the Lord raised him up and made him as a BATTLE-AX [sic] in his Hand, and a ROD to correct stubborn Children."* This restrictive religion later made Mary doubt many times if it was the right religion for her, particularly when she was first married.

Immediately after their marriage in South Wales, Ann and Samuel returned to his house in Uttoxeter where he had been born, and where old John Botham was still living. The house in Balance Street, known today as Howitt Place, was built by John Shipley, in the reign of Queen Anne. The house had by then obtained its present shape. It is built in an 'L' shape and the forecourt is still paved with brown and white pebbles in a geometric pattern just as it was when Ann first arrived. Mary described the house as being *"one of great comfort, though it was old-fashioned, with low rooms and small windows."* She also explained that it,

> like all old-fashioned houses, had no regularity in its floors; we went down a step into one
> room, and up a step into another. The rooms were low and rather dark, and were papered
> with dingy, old, large-patterned papers, which made them look lower and less than they
> were. There were plenty of rooms in the house, most of them well carpeted and well
> furnished; but others there were with blocked-up windows, for this was in the time of the
> heavily-laid-on window tax, and people, for economy's sake, managed with as little light as
> possible; and these mysterious dark rooms had in them nothing but lumber or a couple of
> chairs, turned one upon another, and a bedstead without hangings, which looked dismal and
> skeleton like. These rooms, from which cobwebs were always fetched if anybody had cut
> themselves severely, and the blood would not staunch, had always in them a certain horror
> to my mind, and the established threat of putting any naughty children into the lumber-room,
> or the dark garret, never failed to produce a very subduing, if not a very salutary, effect.

The parlour and bedroom, reached by a separate staircase facing the street, were given to Samuel's father John. The domestic offices filled the middle space. On the garden side the common and best parlours with comfortable chambers above were for Ann and Samuel. In 1805, the house had new windows put in and the floors levelled. There was a cellar, about which Mary's description will be given later, through which ran a small stream that still existed a few years ago, not an unusual occurrence in Uttoxeter houses. The constant temperature meant no water pipes froze there, even when they did in the rest of the house.

Ann experienced loneliness once again, a spiritual isolation caused by the lack of understanding of her as a person. Samuel never realised or understood the depth of her knowledge and experience or how difficult it was for her to accept Quaker ideals in everyday life, let alone the narrowness of the Uttoxeter Friends, although she remained faithful to the Society all her life. Whether Ann ever regretted joining the Society, or her marriage, is not known. She must often have wondered how different her life would have been had she married Robert Wilson! If Samuel had understood his wife better how different Mary and her sisters' and brother's young lives could have been. Ann seems to have withdrawn within herself, a state which these days would be covered by the term 'depression'. When Mary was verifying her information for her autobiography, she wrote to her sister Anna:

> Dearest Mother seems to me to have had as it were two characters. She was so silent and
> shut up when our dear Father was at home and when alone with us how bright and cheerful!
> I question - but this I ask in all humility - do you think dearest Mother was really a Friend
> at heart?...I don't want to sit in judgment on our dear parents I love my mother - love her
> more tenderly when I think of all the hard and cruel passages in her life and my father and,
> dearest Anna, I am sorry from all my inmost heart for him when I think of all the
> mortifications he had to go through all his life.

Mary then wonders whether her sister and brother, who died young, ever had any pleasure in their lives. Mary's sister Anna often longed to question her father about numerous things that puzzled her, but she said,

he was a busy man, very silent and uncommunicative, even love for him was that of reverence and the most entire trust. Our mother was the reverse of this, but so influenced by our father, so loyal in her affection to him that his will was law in the household. I thought my parents the best people in England and according to my limited knowledge the Society of Friends perfect and the rest was the vain world.

Ann was not well received in Uttoxeter and the Friends nick-named her 'The Duchess', especially the Ellis and Shipley families. The elder members particularly thought her proud, therefore they did not mix with her. It is not surprising that the very conservative attitudes taken by the Uttoxeter Meeting should cause them to see Ann in this light, because of her very different background. Thankfully, she did have one sympathiser; John Shipley, Samuel's cousin, had married a woman from Kendal. Her husband's relatives, who comprised most of the Meeting, did not like her carriage and manners and called her the 'Kendal Woman'. She readily welcomed Ann Botham and supported her in her rejection.

John Botham continued to be an eccentric who made his herbal medicines. He had a bay at the side of the Balance Street house in which the medicines were made and stored. The dust and smells from the herbalist's work made Ann ill; she suffered with intense headaches and her eyesight was affected, but John Botham had no sympathy for her.

When Ann's first baby arrived on 10th September 1797, John Botham was again awkward, insisting the baby be called Rebecca after his wife. Samuel wanted her to be named Ann, which she also did not want. The baby's name was only decided upon when a Friend visited the house and suggested that she should be named Anna after Ann's old friend Anna Price of Neath. Anna meant 'graces' according to the Friends and was an acceptable compromise, but grandfather Botham always insisted on calling the baby Rebecca.

It was this little family who set off for Coleford in the Forest of Dean in 1798, Samuel relinquishing his good surveying job to go. It is possible that he chose to undertake his new venture because he was aware that Ann was distressed by her father-in-law, and because of her allergic reaction to his herbs.

The Forest of Dean

In 1798 the family moved to Whiteleeve, Whitecliffe near Coleford in the Forest of Dean where Samuel had undertaken a partnership in building and engineering in an ironworks. According to Mary's autobiography, her mother's memorandum says, *"After I had been married about a year my husband received a proposal from his partners, the Brothers Bishton..."* but according to Ann's record, written several years later and quoted by Amice Lee (a descendent) in her book *In Their Several Generations,* she said *"After I had been married rather more than a year my husband was prevailed upon to undertake the building and engineering ironworks.... An undue faith in James Bell the banker and James Blair the lawyer, (both Uttoxeter men) projectors of the scheme, induced him to fall in with their plans."*

Ann was unhappy about the venture and did not want to go, but Samuel, with his usual boy-like faith and energetic enthusiasm, put all his money into the project and moved his family to Coleford. The house was down the hill from the mine. It has since been demolished but a very similar one which was next door still stands. Raph Anstis, in his book *Around the Forest,* states that this was a hamlet which around 180 years ago was very noisy with two or three coke-fired furnaces hissing and steaming from the top hole at the base of a furnace. The fumes and the noise would have made it an unpleasant place to live at times.

Everything seemed to go wrong in Coleford. The Bishton brothers did not play fair and withheld their finances. Then the winter of 1798/9 was unusually severe with deep snow, the

16

The back of the childhood home of Mary in Balance Street, Uttoxeter, now known as Howitt Place, with its garden leading down to the Muckle Brook and facing the Bank Closes.

Ann Botham née Wood, Mary's mother, aged 80, and Mary's only brother, Charles. The silhouettes were cut-outs which were popular at the time and frequently done by travelling artists.

worst for sixty years, followed by heavy flooding. The frost started on 17th December 1798, and it kept freezing through until February 1799. The snow drifted with the strong winds, which blocked the roads so that people were unable to get fuel. Likewise the rivers used for transport were frozen over. The turnips were frozen in the ground and there was little if any food for livestock. It was the coldest winter for a hundred years, the coldest temperature ever recorded in England -3°F (-20°C). Mary comments in *My Own Story*, in 1844, that winters were not as cold or snowy as when she was a child.

On 11th February there was a rapid thaw brought about by heavy rain. The swollen streams and rivers poured down the hill to Whitecliffe. It was reported in the 18th February 1799 edition of the *Staffordshire Advertiser*:

> *Thaw with rain caused floods. London Mail due in at 5 pm arrived after 12 p.m. On Monday last it overturned in Hockliffe Holloway because of a combination of flood over snow heaps....two gentlemen and one lady were completely under water and extricated with difficulty.*

This winter claimed many many lives. On 25th February, a man was drowned at Wolseley trying to prevent ice damage to a bridge. A Coroner's inquest on a blacksmith, who a couple of weeks before had set out from Cannock to Rugeley and got lost - his body was found ten days later - found the verdict "starved to death". An entry 2nd March reported an inquest at Hill Ridware on Mary Mills who perished in the snow after leaving home on 31st January and whose body was "only recently found". A drunken boatman who tried to ride across the flood between the two bridges at Wolseley was washed away and drowned. The papers had many such reports. The washing away of Samuel Botham's forge, which had lain between the steep sided hills, was not surprising. The family, in their house just down the road, must have felt very frightened by the floods, especially as Ann was just about to have her second baby.

The loss of the forge left the Botham family in a bad financial state. But this was not the first time that Samuel had lost everything he owned. In *My Own Story* Mary states that before his marriage he had been *"engaging in the coal mines of the neighbour-hood"* in Kidwelly in South Wales. He had all his coal stacked on the beach when overnight there was a very severe storm and he had only escaped from his accommodation *"mid-leg"* deep in water, the waves beating against the house. People in the village had awakened him and he had been forced to break a window to escape. He helped save children, horses and cattle and managed to climb to higher ground. In the morning he looked down onto the houses to find many of them and their inhabitants washed away. Mary wrote *"The whole shore was swept of everything upon it"* and he *"had to sell his horse to provide himself with money to buy food."* In both cases Samuel, besides losing his business, had lost the results of months of work. Such trials and tribulations were called 'baptisms' by the Friends.

On 12th March, 1799, following the floods, Ann gave birth to a daughter. The baby was called Mary, which means 'bitterness', because of all their misfortunes. Ann was not well after the confinement; she described it as a *"sad recovery"*. After the disaster in Coleford, Samuel had a dream in which he returned to Uttoxeter where there was a job waiting for him. He admitted to Ann, still in bed under the nurse, that she had been right about not wanting to go to Coleford. The next morning he received a letter from Tom Trusted asking him to measure his estate. Samuel felt this was Divine Providence again.

Mary was only a few weeks old. New mothers were confined to bed for several weeks and this would have caused some delay in returning to Uttoxeter. There has been speculation as to how old Mary was when she came to Uttoxeter for the first time. Ann wrote that the family was not absent from Uttoxeter for more than three years. Whatever period they were away, their parents moved *"a year after"* their marriage to Coleford and Mary was still a baby when she came to Uttoxeter.

After the floods and the decision to return to Staffordshire the auctioneers came in. In three weeks the house and furniture were sold, and they sent their beds, linen and silver, packed in hogs-heads and boxes, by the River Severn and the Staffordshire and Worcestershire Canal to Great Haywood and thence by packhorse to Uttoxeter. They were left with £60 out of the £1,500 they had started with. Samuel went to the Monthly Meeting at Ross and found temporary accommodation for his wife and family, then returned to uttoxeter alone.

Once the family was back in Uttoxeter things started to improve. They moved into the two small cottages belonging to John Botham until the partners from the Coleford venture paid up allowing Samuel to take his family back to Balance Street. He bought more of the Bank Close fields, paying off a £300 mortgage. They now looked out across their back garden over a little bridge on the Hockley brook, then known as the Muckle brook, to fields on the other side which were their own.

The Uttoxeter Quakers treated Samuel and his family badly on their return, saying that if he had not married Ann things would have been different for him. Some unkind person had actually written to him in that vein when they had been in Coleford. The Summerland family drove past the Bothams when they were out walking without acknowledging them.

There was a time after their return when Samuel found he could not read his maps, a serious problem for a surveyor, and Ann went out and bought some spectacles but could only get cheap ones. He chose two pairs and said they would do until the better ones arrived.

Then in 1800 the Crown Commissioners wrote to Samuel offering him the post of surveyor for the enclosure of the Chase of Needwood, known also as the Forest of Needwood, bounded by Uttoxeter, Tutbury, Burton and Abbots Bromley. The forest stretched for ten miles, and grew magnificent oaks, limes, holly trees and other *"majestic"* and *"lordly"* trees. The *"undergrowth was luxuriant"* and there were *"gigantic"* holly trees amongst which lived *"20,000 head of deer"*. The forest was divided into five wards, of which Uttoxeter Ward was one, and four lodges leased from the Crown. Lieutenants, rangers, axe bearers and keepers of the forest were employed. A Woodmote Court was held. The Uttoxeter Ward of the forest had been enclosed many years earlier when it had grown the best trees in the forest according to Sir Oswald Mosley. He describes the forest in some detail in his History of the Town of Tutbury. He gives his reactions to the enclosure of the rest of the forest.

Upon Christmas Day 1802, the forest was disafforested, and a scene of melancholy devastation rapidly ensued; the trees which had hitherto clothed it in all the rich luxuriance of unrestrained nature, were felled in every quarter with little regard to size, although the act provided that none should be cut down under six inches in girth. The coverts and underwood were quickly cleared away, and a dreary waste appeared of lopped branches strewed in various directions, and relieved only by a few picturesque groups of charcoal burners and woodmen. Troops of idle peasants, now restrained no longer by the terrors of the law, chased the affrighted deer from their accustomed haunts, and destroyed them without mercy; some more fortunate than the rest escaped into adjacent parks, and intermingled with the herds already reared there while a few were found during several subsequent years lurking in the woods of Foremark and other distant places, where the yells and shouts of their ruthless pursuers had driven them, but could no longer assail their ears.

Mosley mentions the *"shameful devastation which the keepers of the various wards and parks had been committing for many years"* at a time when wood was the only fuel in the area, and that people possibly cut down young timber trees for fuel.

In the assignment of wood to the tenants for the reparation of their houses and hedges, and the supply of their fuel, much damage was occasionally committed; for if the king's rights or woodmen were not proof against a bribe, much better trees might have been nominally appropriated for these uses than the occasion required.

> THE
>
> NATURAL HISTORY OF TUTBURY.
>
> BY
>
> SIR OSWALD MOSLEY, Bart., D.C.L., F.L.S.
>
> TOGETHER WITH
>
> THE FAUNA AND FLORA
>
> OF
>
> THE DISTRICT SURROUNDING TUTBURY AND
> BURTON-ON-TRENT.
>
> BY
>
> EDWIN BROWN.
>
> WITH AN APPENDIX.
>
>
>
> LONDON:
> JOHN VAN VOORST, PATERNOSTER ROW.
> MDCCCLXIII.

He is also critical of people who cut assarts and built their cottages there, often extending their assarts in future years. He says they were "particularly expert" in deer poaching.

.....the tenants ought to have in Needwood, as commoners there [had the use of], all stool wood, hoar lynt [Hoar lynt is the white wood of the linden or lime tree, after the bark has been picked off to make ropes of], blackthorn, and windfallen wood lying upon the ground, provided it did not exceed half a load, and all the browsing wood and gorse, (furze or whin), and also wood for their bonfires by ancient custom.

At various times politicians had threatened to fell the forest of Needwood - Cromwell in May 1650, and later King Charles. Both failed, the 1650s effort because the people appealed to Cromwell saying they would be losing their rights to the forest. Cromwell was for the ordinary people and therefore dropped his claim. Charles's claim failed because again the people objected. In 1778 a bill was produced to Parliament and was rejected. Mosley states:

During the last fifty years, a kind of inclosing mania prevailed throughout

the kingdom; every spot of ground which was supposed capable of growing a blade of corn must be converted into tillage for the support of an increasing population, and to this prevailing notion Needwood amongst other forests that have shared a similar fate at length became a victim. The following inventory related to Tutbury Ward in 1650:

	£	s	d
2,775 acres at 3s. per acre,	232.	10.	0.
Upon improvement at 5/6d per acre			
per annum	426.	5.	0.
Lodge with 38 acres	6.	12.	0.
Dotards & fire trees 8,995	1,340.	11.	4.
Timber trees 1,456	976.	3.	4.
Barton ward containing 1,400 acres @ 2/6d each			
	175.	0.	0.
Upon improvement @ 4/6d per acre	315.	0.	0.
Lodge with 30 acres	6.	0.	0.
Timber trees 2,408	1,857.	0.	0.
Fire trees 4,735	689.	3.	4.
100 dotards @ 2/6d. each	12.	10.	0.
Yoxall ward 1,650 acres @ 2/6d. each	206.	5.	0.
Upon improvement @ 4/6d. an acre	372.	5.	0.
Fire trees 4,256	654.	6.	8.
Timber trees 3,770	3,542.	0.	0.
Lodge with 32 acres	8.	16.	0.
50 dotards appertaining thereto @ 2/- each			
	5.	0.	0.
Marchington ward 1,800 acres @ 4/- per acre			
	360	0	0.
Upon improvement at 7/- per acre	630.	0.	0.
Timber and other trees 12,838	4,010.	3.	4.
Dotards and fire trees 9,900	2,590.	3.	4.
Total value of land and lodges	996.	3.	0.
Upon improvement	1,746.	17.	0.
Whole number of deer 120	60.	0.	0.

Dotards - old and dying trees

After the Act of Enclosure was passed in June 1801, Samuel was appointed surveyor along with Mr Wyatt. Samuel was respected as a fair and honest man, an ideal which was supposed to mark Quakerism. It took nine years before the ancient woodland was destroyed and the final award was signed on 9th May 1811. The work involved measuring and felling trees, converting much of the land into farmland with assessment of claims and compensation for the people who claimed rights to the forest. Some of them lived in turf cottages on the waste lands and these had to be moved, leaving the occupants to find other places to live. On certain days, the Bothams' house would be crowded with people claiming allowances for their ancient privileges and forest rights, peasants whose forefathers had built turf cottages, others whose rights included venison, game or timber. Samuel, a man who would not allow gift or word to influence his decisions, was also a man who hated crowds or coach travel, he preferred to ride around on his own or in the company of his family.

CHAPTER TWO
CHILDHOOD INFLUENCES

Though the children were cared for by various nannies, Samuel had very definite ideas about bringing them up. He, like other Quakers, thought children were perfect beings and that they should not be cluttered by earthly things, to keep their unpolluted minds ready receptacles for the will of God. The Botham children were not given a Bible although Samuel gave both Old and New Testament readings. They were given no religious education or taught the Lord's Prayer (not all Friends were this strict and Anna and Mary did learn the Lord's Prayer and read the Bible when they went away to school). Their father did get them to learn by heart Robert Barclay's Catechism and the Confessions of Faith, texts relating to Quaker doctrines. What interpretation young children would put on such writings is uncertain, particularly as Anna and Mary did not have the texts explained. Mary, not surprisingly, misunderstood the readings.

Mary remembers when she was about five years old that the family were visiting friends for tea when Thomas Bishop, their handyman, came to fetch them home immediately because the Clerk to Lichfield Quarterly Meeting had arrived at Balance Street and had brought with with him two Ministering Friends from America. Tea had just been served but was ended abruptly as the Botham family departed, Polly, as Mary was known as a child, was carried by Thomas Bishop and fell asleep before they reached Uttoxeter, where both girls were put straight to bed. Mary believes one of the visitors was David Sands, well known in his day.

Samuel was often away from home, and Mary describes the transformation that took place in her mother at these times. She became bright, happier and cheerful and spent more time with her children who were normally left with the servants. In 1804/5 Samuel was employed by the Corporation of Leicester to enclose the town fields, lay out their 'race-ground', now Victoria Park, and plan and lay out the new Public Walk. Mary said it was,

> *a great improvement to the town, from its fine trees and shrubberies full of flowering undergrowth. The maps were very handsome, and, to our admiration, bound with blue ribbon, the colour of the Corporation. This commission, with surveying in the Forest and for numerous noblemen and gentlemen, often necessitated his absence for days and weeks at a time. My mother, being thus disengaged, would require us to sew or knit for hours together at her side, whilst she busily plied her needle or her [spinning] wheel in the parlour or the garden porch. I particularly remember her spinning in the porch below opening into the basement storey, the wheel gave a hollow, louder sound, which caused us to bring our low seats close to her knee, that we might catch every word of her utterance. Never ceasing our employment - for, to use her phrase, 'we must not nurse our work' - we listened with breathless attention to exciting tales of her ancestry and of her unmarried life.*

She taught them poems she had learnt from her father, and others, both *"grave and gay"*, no doubt nurturing Mary and Anna's love of poetry and language. Mary was very close to her elder sister; she describes them as being like twins, even dressing the same. This was fortunate as they rarely had other children to play with. Mary and Anna spent so much time together they developed their own words and their own language, very like the Brontë sisters. At four years old Anna was unable to talk, perhaps through lack of adult stimulation and it was decided to take her to a cheerful old woman each day to help with this.

Home
In 1805, the house in Balance Street had new windows put in and the floors levelled. Samuel bought panelling from Uttoxeter Old Hall when it was demolished and had this fitted in their

Howitt Place. The Bothams' house in Balance Street as it is today.

Uttoxeter Old Church, before 1828 when it was rebuilt. Painted by Francis Redfern.

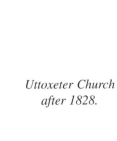

Uttoxeter Church after 1828.

Balance Street house. Mary talks of the cellars as

> dark and dismal places, at least so they seemed to us children, and in them were found little yellowish lizards, called by Nanny .... 'askers,' and toads and frogs. We had been threatened with confinement in these cellars if we ever should be very naughty; and in the earlier years of my childhood, a story being told of a cruel father who had kept his unhappy child for years in a cellar, this and the threat together made the cellars awful places, into which we only now and then ventured to peep under the heavy wooden shutter, which excluded the light, by raising it an inch or two, which was all that the chain which secured it inside would admit of.

Mary's love of her home shows in the detailed descriptions of the house and garden in Balance Street in her writings. The garden sloped to the south and was separated by a low wall and iron palisade from a meadow through which ran the stream, the Muckle Brook. A small wooden bridge led to hilly fields, the Bank Closes. She describes three poplars which grew too big and were felled in her childhood as they had become a nuisance. In the back garden there was a large sundial. Samuel, who always seeking to improve things, bought the house next door, the now-demolished Mayfield House, and incorporated its garden within his own. When fields near his house were offered for sale he bought them as well, so that eventually all the land they could see from their house, all of what is now Westlands Road, and up to Cullamore Lane, belonged to him. He wanted to own the fields to the side of his house also towards the road, adjoining the Hockley. He was fearful that someone would buy the land to build houses.

The Napoleonic War

The alterations to the house took place during the Napoleonic War, a war that lasted for twenty-three years. The children watched the men at work, and they used the scraps of wood to make play-things, thoroughly enjoying a new experience of seeing and talking to workmen. One of the men, *"James Dumerlo, the half-silly painter,"* who hated children and therefore enjoyed frightening them, *"in the wantonness of a mischievous spirit"* told them *"they have burnt Lichfield down to the ground, and have killed all the women and children, and will be here tonight or to-morrow morning at farthest!"* He kept sending the children down the garden to see if Napoleon's army was crossing the Hockley Brook!

The population as a whole was afraid that there would be a repeat of the French Revolution in this country. Radical politicians were suspected of stirring up the people, especially C.J. Fox, who was a radical and a Member of Parliament with Admiral Gardner of Uttoxeter. Anyone who was not a known member of the established church was regarded with suspicion, by both middle and working classes, but in Uttoxeter non-conformists were tolerated to some extent although the opening of the Independent Chapel in 1792 was greeted with rowdy and malicious behaviour, as was the opening of the Wesleyan Chapel in 1812. Samuel Botham appears to have been regarded with much respect despite being a Quaker.

There was a woman in Uttoxeter who looked after Ann Botham during an illness, and whose husband was a soldier. He was taken prisoner in France, and she occasionally received a letter from him when it could be smuggled out of the country. Although much out of date, these letters brought great excitement for the girls. Also when they accompanied their parents on summer evening drives the conversation would be of battles, rising food prices, the distress of the poor, the increase of the army, and of the jails being filled with young male Quakers who refused to enlist in the army because of their religious beliefs.

Later when Mary and Anna corresponded with their friend and former teacher, Mrs Parker, they received a letter from her which referred to a *"small volume"* entitled *A Visit to Flanders by a Scotch Gentleman*. It describes a visit to the site of the Battle of Waterloo soon after the battle which affected the witness considerably:

to think of two hundred thousand men collected for the express business of slaughter. The field, at a little distance appeared as if covered with crows, so thickly strewed lay the caps and hats of the dead. From the appearance of the soil, it had been literally flooded with blood. The tremendous roar of cannon lasted from morning till night, and was heard in Brussels, the distance of nine miles, like a continued peal of thunder for eight hours. Whole ranks lay dead, with horses innumerable, and the roads were filled with the wounded creeping and dropping as they moved, while others were trampled to death by the horses and baggage wagons. At Brussels and Antwerp several large buildings were made to serve as hospitals, and here some anecdotes are related of a shocking nature, particularly that the wounded French lay mimicking the convulsive contortions of their comrades dying in adjoining beds. The author mentions an officer's lady who had just heard that her husband's head was shot off. They saw the poor creature running wildly about the market-place, while her little boy followed her, crying and screaming also. 'He is not dead.' cried she. 'My husband's head is not cut off - he is coming.'

Contemplating these horrid features of human crime and misery, the pious mind is excited to fresh ardour in the support of those public institutions which have for their object the dissemination of the glorious gospel of peace. In this order the Bible Society appears divinely illustrious.

The Bible Society was new to Mary as it was not until about 1815 that the British and Foreign Bible Society opened in Uttoxeter for which Mary and Anna attended the inaugural meeting held at the Red Lion Inn, one of Uttoxeter's coaching Inns.

In *The Two Apprentices*, one of Mary's stories, she tells of soldiers arriving in Balance Street with wagons loaded with goods together with their wives and children. They were lodged in the town and the households were expected to feed them.

Most newspapers at the time were weekly and carried national and international news but very few local stories. Samuel Botham restricted himself to one weekly newspaper. He never told the children what was in it but Mary says that from her infancy they were always aware of the terrible war which became year by year more awful and menacing. News of bloody battles ending in glorious victories would set the church bells ringing, and the feeling of joy then penetrated even their house. Periodically fast days were proclaimed which of course the Bothams did not observe. To the children the fasts became associated with Stephen Chesters who kept them whilst the Bothams did not. He was the minister of the Independent Chapel at Bear Hill, an area of Uttoxeter Market Place, and a very stern man who the Bothams thought mistreated his wife and adopted nieces. Anna and Mary were terrified of him when he lived next door in Mayfield House in Balance Street.

Mary describes the hatred - almost beyond description - that they felt for the French:

We were frightened out of our wits at the prospect of an invasion; but I remember consoling myself with the thought, when driving through Lord Vernon's park at Sudbury, that at all events those frog-eating French would marvel at such magnificent trees, because they could have nothing like them in their miserable France.

In the evenings they would go out for a ride with her parents, on a *"little turn-down seat in the gig, upon which we were seated between their knees."* These were happy occasions with their parents, and all the talk was about the Napoleonic Wars. Every morning Samuel read the newspapers, and as he would not allow his wife to read them, he would relay the news to her during the evening drive - news about the wars, the possible invasions, the lost battles and the victories. All this was heard, though perhaps not wholly understood by such young girls, but it was sufficient to frighten them and make them feel very anti-Napoleon.

The cost of imported goods increased, exported goods lost their market (and men's jobs) and with the combination of war and severe winters the price of food rose, leaving the poor even poorer. Men had been taken from the land, leaving fewer agricultural workers and the 19th century began with a severe agricultural depression. In January 1801 a 6d loaf of bread had risen in price to 17d. There was no social security. The *Staffordshire Advertiser* for the week 9th March 1799 reported that Uttoxeter had collected by subscription £30, which was to be distributed as bread and coal to poor labouring families who had been deprived of work by the severity of the winter. Such philanthropic acts must have taken place throughout the country. Mary's mother organised and handed out financial and food relief to many people, including maimed and wounded Irish soldiers. It would appear that Anglo-Irish relations were not good at the time and the soldiers' pay was not reaching their relatives in Ireland.

Mary and Anna met people who visited and stayed with the Bothams in Balance Street, mainly Friends. Most Friends travelled greatly, which widened the children's knowledge of the world, although not their knowledge of life itself. The idea of the frog-eating French may well have been from a conversation she overheard. In *My Own Story*, Mary describes the post boy who in 1805 used to come every day on a pony from Lichfield with letters and papers. When just below the bottom of the Bothams' garden, coming up the Hockley, he would blow his horn. If he was bringing news of a victory, he wore blue ribbons in his hat and blew tiralee on his horn, which would start the bells ringing and the whole town would be out to greet him. Mary especially remembers the Saturday when he brought the news of the victory of the Battle of Trafalgar and the news that Nelson, the country's hero, was dead:

> *The bells rang out a merry peel and then were stopped and after a pause the muffled notes of a tolling bell were heard over the hushed streets of Uttoxeter. The people were grave and sad, on a dull drizzling October day in keeping with the peoples' feelings.*

Uttoxeter

Mary writes in *My Own Story* about Timber Lane, part of which is now the Staffordshire Way, at the top of which Samuel had a flax field:

> *We were never tired of going with our father to see the growth of his fields. The walk thither was the most charming in the world; we either went through the loveliest old pasture fields, all the way going from our own garden across the meadow, and up our own hilly fields or else a little way round by an old woodland lane, the most picturesque of its kind. In wet seasons, or in winter, this lane was almost impassable, for it lay deep below its banks, and a little gurgling stream, that ran first on one side of it and then on the other, crossing it here and there in the most wanton sort of way, at such times overflowed it! but now it was confined within its own little stony bed, and trailing plants, which love watery situations, hung fantastically over its banks, dipping their lovely green sprays down into the water as if to drink, or to show how beautifully transparent the water was. There was the golden saxifrage, with its exquisite flowers, like the setting of a jewel; there was the evergreen periwinkle, with its blue and white blossoms, and its myrtle-like foliage. Starwort, and pink campions, and ragged robins, and blue robin-run-in-the-hedge, on the dryer [sic] banks; old mossy crab trees bent in crooked ruggedness half across the lane; and a succession of oak-trees, venerable and gnarled timber-trees, of the most picturesque forms and woodland character, cast a green and pleasant shade over the whole way.*

She wrote about a common flower, the cowslip:

> *Again, again on dewy plain,*
> *I trust to see you rise*
> *When spring renews the wild wood strain*
> *And bluer gleam the skies.*

The Traveller on the Hill-top

> *Again, again, when many springs*
> *Upon my grave shall shine,*
> *Here shall you speak of vanished things*
> *To living hearts of mine*

and of the Uttoxeter Fair of which there were several in a year, horse fairs, cheese fairs, damson fairs, hiring fairs (gay boy fair), etc:

> *There is a town in Staffordshire*
> *That I was born and bred in,*
> *And sweet May Fair can make it gayer*
> *Than even a royal wedding.*

Mary obviously considered herself 'Uttoxeter born'. In *Wood Leighton* there is another description of this old lane; those who know the area would still recognise the lane.

A description of a walk to Bramshall Wood from Uttoxeter (Wood Leighton):

"At one time we bent our way to Bramshall Wood. This lay about a mile and a quarter from the town. A little side street led you at once to the outskirts of the place. Here you passed the rope maker's yard - a pleasant little paddock, surrounded with high hedges and trees where you could see, through the gate the man going backward and forward on his level walk, while his boy sat under his shed at the end turning his wheel.

On the other hand was the sieve-maker's shop with its door thrown open, and a confused heap of shavings and ashen-hoops and sieves of all sorts and sizes, seen within. Anon you came to gardens, with their little, sunny, old fashioned cottages in them; then to the crofts, where the towns-people kept each his horse or cow. Then you passed the lawyer's pleasant villa amongst its trees, with its goodly gate, and well-rolled gravel walk leading up to it; and then the retired tradesman's more capacious mansion, close to the road side, as if its inmates were not desirous in their retirement to shut out all knowledge of passers-by, and yet showing over its garden walls the tops of the trees and shrubs that spoke of a pleasant place within their limits. Then you were out amongst the fields, with nothing but the toll-bar and turnstile between you and the wood; and then you were in it. It was not a large area but sufficiently large so that one could not see from one end to the other. A beautiful clear stream came running all through it, with its bright gravelly bottom....

This is a description of Stone Road, Uttoxeter coming from Carter Street. The ropemakers and sievemakers have long gone, but the old Shakespeare cottages and the toll house have only disappeared within living memory. Bramshall Wood has also gone and only the tradesman's mansion, The Mount, remains.

Through Mary's descriptions written over a hundred years ago, we can envisage what Uttoxeter was like at the beginning of the 19th century. She records that her father had ideas of how to improve the appearance of the town:

The town was wretchedly paved, and the streets were full of the most awkward projections and irregularities; there were no lamps, there was a pinfold in the town-streets, and the inhabitants were indifferently supplied with water, whilst the finest of streams ran idly by the town. All these things suggested to his mind the design of improving and benefiting the place. He formed plans and made suggestions; he talked with all his friends....

Samuel was asked to undertake these alterations and the town declared it would raise the money. In the event, due to a malicious relative, Samuel was actually out of pocket when he had completed the alterations.

The work went on rapidly under our father's eye; unsightly objects were done away with; regular pavements were laid down; lamps hung here and there; old deformities and obstacles removed, and corners, which hitherto had been nothing but nuisances, were given up to the adjoining inhabitant to add to his garden or his court. In the prevailing spirit of the time, people built up new walls or put down new palisades. The aspect of everything improved daily. People looked on

Shakespeare Cottages in Stone Road which Mary passed on the road to Bramshall Wood which she describes in Wood Leighton. Photograph taken in 1925.

Interior of the Friend's Meeting House, Uttoxeter, as it is today.

Hockley Lane, the road to Stafford, leading to the Muckle Brook in the distance.

Carter Street, Uttoxeter, near to Balance Street where Mary lived.

with surprise; they called our father the public benefactor - the most public-spirited man of the place. To him it was a labour of love, and his best reward was now to see the approbation which his work was winning was not water now freely given for the use and accommodation of the poorest of the inhabitants; and through him there was now no danger of breaking one's ribs by running them against a projecting post or rail, or breaking one's shins over a step or a scraper.

From various books we also know that Samuel was responsible for erecting bollards along the town streets so that the horse and carts did not run people over. He tried to tidy up ownership of land to make for easier maintenance. The people had agreed to the proposals but they did not want to pay for the alterations; they withheld payment until Samuel withdrew his services. After a while the townspeople made financial amends, and asked Samuel to continue with the improvements, but due to his wife's illness he declined.

Anna, who took a keen interest in the weather from an early age, could remember that in February 1805, when she was about seven, there had been snow on the ground for many weeks followed by heavy floods which submerged the meadows and turned the streams into torrents. The thaw began during the night before Wednesday market when people came on horseback and by carts from as far away as Birmingham and Newcastle-under-Lyme. Carriers brought letters, parcels and other small goods. By midday there was a flood which led people to leave the market early. Only a few lingering drinkers remained. Anna remembers that at about five or six o'clock they looked out of the parlour window and saw the meadow in the grey light below their garden nearly covered by the Muckle Brook running rapidly like a river. The Hockley road, the main road to Lichfield and Birmingham, crossed the brook by a ford and a footbridge . The water was dashing over the bridge and Anna saw something dark being tossed about. Soon after she heard that one of the Birmingham carriers had tried to cross the flooded ford and had been washed away and lost. He had been drinking in the Talbot Inn.

In November 1806, Mary's younger sister Emma was born. She was very weak, and her mother very ill, so she was sent out to a nurse. Many times they thought she had died. She was petite and supposed to be the liveliest of the three girls, but her eye sight was to cause a lot of problems after her marriage. She wore glasses but in those days they were extremely heavy and worn only when essential. Her lack of education caused her sisters much anxiety. Charles, the only and much wanted son, was born in July 1808 and brought great joy to his family. Once again their mother was very ill after his delivery.

The Horse Fair, Balance Street, Uttoxeter about 1920. This fair was held two or three times a year and was well known to Mary.

The Damson Fair, Balance Street, in the early 20th century. The fair dates back before Mary's time. Mary tells of the arrival of soldiers here during the Napoleonic Wars (The Two Apprentices).

CHAPTER THREE
FURTHER INFLUENCES AND INSPIRATIONS

Mary was a plump, dark-haired, hazel-eyed child, lively and quick with her answers. Friends Meetings were a trial; she had to sit still and silent like the rest of the congregation. Mary remembered the very moment she realized she was a personality with a mind of her own: *"It seemed to me that before I passed the pinfold I could only say and think Bunkum - such was the expression in my mind - but after passing it I had the full use of all intelligent speech."*

Anna was slimmer, with golden brown curly hair and blue eyes. They had no toys, and other personal things were marked with their name. When Anna was about six she had scarlet fever, a serious contagious disease. Mary was sent out of the way to The Heath in the care of her Grandfather's housekeeper, Jenny Troughton *"or Trutton as they call it in Staffordshire"*. Ann Botham nursed Anna herself, and Anna remembered her love and tenderness. The only treatment was bleeding and blistering, which left the patient weak and convalescence was therefore slow. One day Anna fainted while running upstairs, Ann picked her up and Anna remembers her cuddling her and crying, saying, *"My precious I thought I had lost thee"*.

> *Our mother in the winter spun a great deal. It was not the custom for gentlewomen to spin in those midland parts of England at that time; spinning was a fashion which had gone out for a quarter of a century at least, but she was from South Wales, a woman of strong energetic character, who adhering to good usage rather than fashion, had brought the wheel with her, and used it for some years after her marriage. She spun, therefore, every winter, many pounds of flax into beautifully fine yarn, which used to hang in hanks, as they were finished at the top of the kitchen, among hams, salted beef, and dried herbs. I now have table-linen of her spinning and most probably shall leave some of it to my own children.*

In the summer of 1806 Ann Botham represented Staffordshire at the Yearly Meeting in London. This was the annual general meeting for Quakers, and representatives from all over the country attended. It cost about £5 to go and it was several days before anyone in Uttoxeter knew whether or not she had arrived safely at the Swan with Two Necks where she was to stay. Her sister Dorothy met her there and the two sisters returned to Uttoxeter together. Aunt Sylvester was a very fashionable lady, tall, dark and handsome, dressed in blue. This was the first time Anna and Mary had met her. When she came downstairs on the Sunday dressed in a white gown trimmed with blue ribbon, a blue mantle and a blue-trimmed straw bonnet, the children worried about what their father would say, but she laughed and went off to church.

John Botham, Mary's grandfather, left the house in Balance Street after having accidentally wounded Anna with a large pair of scissors in a moment of "excitement" in 1801. He went to live with some people *"on the now enclosed land, which had formerly been Heath. Here he taught local neglected and poor boys to read"*. This was before the days of the National Schools or Sunday Schools. His rooms at Balance Street were left empty, and this room faced the street adjoined the girls' playroom. From here they eagerly watched the world go by. They could see the town boys playing at soldiers, and the young recruits being exercised. Mary describes the feeling of the time: *"the very air was full of soldiery, military excitement and terror."*

Grandfather was happy at the Heath and the children went to see him each week, occasions when they could walk numerous ways through the town but not through the undesirable area - although they did sometimes. They remembered his sunny sitting-room smelling of herbs, the chafing dishes, and the curious glasses and retorts that lay around Gerard's Herbal. It was in this setting that he held his school. He was responsible one day for the introduction of wild plants to the girls, who had reluctantly gone on a walk with him. He told them so much that they did not want the walk to end.

> *The old gentleman gave us almonds and raisins when we came, and sometimes a new book. The books which we had then were very different to those which children have now-a-days. They were externally mostly square, and bound, many of them, in beautiful paper, stamped and printed in green and gold, and red and lilac. I wonder one never sees such paper now; - beautiful books they were to look at on the outside; but alas! - I grieve to say it - They were very dry within. At that time the Taylor's charming Original Poems, and more charming Nursery Rhymes, were not written - nor had any of Maria Edgeworth's earlier ones penetrated into our out-of-the-world region. Our books bore such titles as The Castle of Instruction, The Hill of Learning, The Rational Dame and so on; and seemed written on purpose to deter children from reading; however, we were thankful to our grandfather for whatever he gave us.*

A Victorian herbal. Herbalists were an important part of medicine at this time. May Howitt's grandfather was a successful herbalist and Mary and her husband William would have a pharmacy and herbalist shop in Nottingham later.

No wonder Mary wanted to change the style of children's writing! Mary describes her grandfather thus:

> *His features were good, but his countenance severe; over his very grey hair he wore a grey worsted wig with three stiff rows of curls behind and was attired in a dark brown collarless suit of an old-fashioned cut, wearing out-of-doors a cocked hat also of an old Quaker type, a short great-coat or spencer and in winter, grey ribbed worsted leggings drawn to the middle of the thigh. Although a stickler for old customs he was one of the very first in the Midland counties to use an umbrella. A substantial concern covered with oilcloth with a large ring at the top by which it was hung.*

In the spring of 1807 John Botham died.

Like other professional men, Samuel employed resident nannies to look after his children. They were all local girls as Samuel felt these would not taint his girls, but he was wrong. The nannies, who could have been as young as fourteen, were told they could not take the children into the town, and the Market Place, regarded by Samuel as a place of vice, was strictly out of bounds. The first nanny, Hannah Finney a *"low spirited and dull"* girl, went to Coleford with the family, where she fell in love with a worthless carpenter whom she married to her cost. Anna remembers Hannah was not kind to her and felt that the experience had a lasting effect, marring her peace and holding her in "bondage" throughout her life.

In 1804-5 the girls had a nanny of about thirty years old who was not the sort of person the Bothams thought her to be. She was dismissed when they found out but not before the children had learnt quite a few things from her. Another early nanny was Betty Pedley, the daughter of the Bothams' weaver, who wove Ann's homespun flax and wool, and who lived between 'Wills-Lock' (Willslock) and Loxley. *"She was a childish sort of girl"* and Mary and Anna were not particularly fond of her. Betty brought home snippets of red material and she made a regiment of soldiers dressed in red for the Town children who played at drill outside the Bothams' house, something a Quaker child would not have been allowed to play with.

The Traveller on the Hill-top

The children's nannies were a vital element in their upbringing. Rhoda, who lived in the Market Place, told them about the things she knew or had seen on the town; she gave them a detailed description of bull baiting, held annually in the Market Place.

...it was the annual bull-baiting - a practice which our father combated for many years, and at last succeeded in entirely putting an end to. This bull-baiting occurred in the autumn. At the fair at that season a handsome bull was bought, and a day or two before the baiting was led round the town decorated with ribands, and attended by a rude rabble of men and boys. The patrons of the sport on this occasion gave money, some more and some less; at our house, of course, nothing was ever given. We watched with a kind of horror the passing of this procession from our nursery window, and Nanny, who seemed not to have by any means the abhorrence of the thing which we had been taught to feel, took the liveliest interest in it, and even once, to the great scandal of the whole household, threw out a riband for the bull's horns. On the morning of the bull-baiting, towards four or five o'clock, the inhabitants of the town were awake in their beds by the bull's chain being struct violently against the walls of their houses and on the pavement before them. In the early, chill grey of the morning it came - a sort of yell and a banging of this heavy iron chain, and a rattling, and a grinding, another yell, and then they went on.

Again the bull, decorated with garlands and ribands, was led round the town, accompanied by all the rabble of the neighbourhood, hallooing and shouting like so many savages. We always watched the procession go by, and always felt a kind of curdling horror. At ten o'clock the bull was fixed to the stake in the market-place, and such of the higher class of the inhabitants as patronised the sport occupied the upper windows of the houses, and the market-place itself was thronged with people, leaving a space in the mdidle for the poor creature and his tormentors.

Whilst we were playing in the garden on the three days that this lasted we heard the barking and the yelling of the dogs, and the roar of the bull, and the shouts of the people. Sometimes, too, the creature broke his chain, and ran furiously through the streets, driving everything before him, and often doing much damage. If the bull came as far as our house, we never failed to see it, for to us, of course, this was a very fearful, but interesting spectacle, and furnished enough to talk of for a week.

After the third day's sport the bull was shot. This seemed to me like a sort of murder, and I remember very innocently saying what I really felt, that I wondered that old William Woolley, who shot the bull, was not afraid of being haunted by his ghost. I said this gravely, meaning what I said, before grown-up people, and I could not conceive why everybody burst into a fit of laughter.

In *My Own Story* Mary describes Rhoda as young, smart and active, and of a good family. She took them to see Uttoxeter Hall, opposite the present Alleynes School, where they swung on the big gates. King Charles and Prince Rupert had stayed there during the Civil War. The Hall, which was supposed to be haunted, had found it difficult to keep its tenants or owners and by this time was dilapidated and in disrepair. She was dismissed when Mary's parents found out how she was influencing the children. They appointed Nanny Woodings, who was older and whose father was a wagoner from Hill Ridware near Rugeley. But there is some discrepancy as to when Rhoda and Nanny Woodings were employed. In *My Own Story* Mary implies that Rhoda and Nanny Woodings were employed together, Rhoda to look after baby Charles and Nanny Woodings in charge of the girls, whilst in *In Their Several Generations* Amice Lee implies that Nanny Woodings had been the girls' nanny and was given a new position on the appointment of Rhoda. In any case, there was much friction and jealousy between the nannies, though this is not reflected in Mary's autobiography.

Nanny Woodings was a grave-looking women of twenty-five with a strong dialect, a very abrupt and determined person, very plain, with big hands and feet. Her dress was equally plain. She was a clever woman working her way into the family's affection slowly. She also

must have had remarkable powers of observation, a retentive memory, a turn for all that was picturesque and traditional, considerable superstition, and a remarkable faculty for relating

Timber Lane, in Uttoxeter, now part of the Staffordshire Way, which was described several times in Mary's books.

Carter Street, Uttoxeter, painted by Francis Redfern, the 19th century antiquarian and historian of Uttoxeter (The History and Antiquities of Uttoxeter 1865).

anything clearly and effectively. She cast, as it were, a spell over us; we sat and listened for hours to her histories, which seemed never to come to an end; and there was something so appropriate - so racy and picturesque, in the old dialectic language which she used, that I never liked any story told in modern polite English half as well as hers; they seemed to me to want richness and picturesqueness. From this cause I trace, even now, my great love of dialect, and the singularly pleasing effect which it always produces on me when spoken.

Nanny was a good tactician too; she did not launch out into all her broad singularities of character at once - they stole upon us by degree; and, indeed, had it not been so, our parents must have been startled, and assuredly would have dismissed her. Many of her peculiarities in fact they never did know...

Nothing in the world could be more charming than walks into the town with her. We knew the exterior of things before she came; but who, like her, could pull down with a touch, as it were, the front of every house, and give us a peep into the interior, however secret or strange? Who, like her, was full of anecdote about all the people we met, from the grandee of the town down to the buyer of hare-skins in smithy-lane?...

There, in the gloomy house, lived the great army-contractor A, whose slaughter of cattle for the army was every week so immense, and who made purchases all over the country. Did we know that in any upper room of that house, the window of which, small and grated with iron, opened on the leads, had been kept for years, chained down to her bedstead, his unhappy wife...

This was just one of several gossipy stories mentioned in *My Own Story*. What better apprenticeship could there be for a future writer?

There was another house, too, which interested us greatly. It was a sort of old, low, red-brick mansion; and stood, half buried in trees and ivy, within an ancient wall, over and about which the ivy grew in heavy masses. There, as our father had often told us, the Duke of Cumberland had been entertained by the Gardiner family, to which it still belongs [and did still into the middle of the twentieth century] *when he spent a night in the town in his pursuit of the Scotch rebels, in 1745, and in fact on his way to Culloden; and where he received an entertainment so much to his mind that he conferred upon the town an exemption for ever from soldiers being quartered there...*

There is a plaque to Admiral Gardiner outside this building at the top end of the High Street.

Mary said that there was *"something wild and picturesque"* about Nanny Woodings's appearance. James Britton, in his obituary of Mary, mentions this nanny as being a *"singularly gifted woman if not a woman of genius, she knew by heart every song that ever swung in the wind on a ballad monger's stall."* He credits her with good powers of observation, a retentive memory, and a gift to appreciate all that was picturesque and traditional, a very advantageous habit for a would-be writer to copy. She was considerably superstitious and she had a *"remarkable faculty for relating anything clearly and effectively."* She had lived at Hill Ridware adjacent to woods and she told tales of fairies, whispering spirits, of ghosts and murders, some of them in the woods between Uttoxeter and Abbots Bromley.

She also had stories of haunted madhouses, of white ladies that appeared by the side of lonesome waters, of headless women who sat spinning besides stiles and of black dogs that haunted bridges. She knew the very farm kitchen where the household work had been performed by an indefatigable brownie or hobthrush who, however, had been driven away by the proffered reward of a hempen shirt. She knew that wagoner whose team of five strong horses was unable to move the wagon which a malicious fairy had tied by the wheel with a rush; and beyond all the rest she herself had seen ghosts.

All her stories were told in dialect, country language as the contemporaries called it, and Mary's love of dialect stemmed from those days. James Britton said how easy it was to trace in Mary's works the results of her early training, to which she attributed her *'flights of fancy'*. Nanny Woodings also took them on walks, and it takes very little to imagine why these walks were so exciting. Mary's interest in fairy stories was to be long lasting; in fact she and

Elizabeth Gaskell, the novelist, enjoyed exchanging ghost and fairy stories in later life.

Nanny Woodings ran the household, often ordering around those who were supposed to give her the orders. She often caused friction amongst the other servants, yet despite this the Bothams felt they could trust and rely on her. One thing Samuel admired about her was the way she saved her wages - he gave her a substantial interest on it. She eventually took to wearing Quaker dress, attended Meetings, and used the Quaker form of speech. She appeared to have a dual personality; she had a temper which she did not display to her employers but to the children was fearful. Her eyes became glazed and her gaze fixed and vacant. She made a curious vibrating and tremulous sound from her throat, which they called Nanny's purring. The children were aware that it was no good talking to her at these times.

She could also be a liability. On one occasion when the Bothams had gone to a Quarterly Meeting and were away from home for several days, Nanny on her own initiative refurbished the Bothams' bedroom using her own money. Surprisingly, although taken aback, Ann was pleased with the result. Nanny was not reprimanded! Nanny was also able to distinguish all the ingredients in a pickle or other edible gift, which when mixed to her instructions would give the same result as that of the gift. She was clearly a special woman. Ann was very ill after the birth of Charles, and the usual monthly nurse stayed on for three months. Nanny took on the duties of her mistress.

Ann had also been ill after Emma's birth in 1806 and she and Emma were nursed by Sarah Gee, the wife of Uncle Summerland's groom in The Hockley. When Aunt Sylvester had visited, she had given a fashionably dressed doll to each child. Samuel was away, and the nurse and Nanny cruelly tried to get the girls to give away their dolls. The nurse said her dear little niece had no dolls, Nanny said her Sister Hannah was a poor thing and had no doll. Mary and Anna did not know what to do, they had no parent available, so they gave their highly treasured dolls away. The girls were very lonely and began to miss their dolls more and more, especially as they had both gone to strangers.

Nanny however had a great secret which was found out many years later: she was having an affair with one of Samuel's trusted clerks. After fifteen years with the Bothams, she left to have a child, who died. She then became ill and after eighteen months she herself died. Her savings were used to give her a "respectable" funeral.

In later life when Mary thought of her upbringing she referred to *"our childhood with its isolation and peculiarities"* [L&R] to her sister Anna, and they must have wondered what they had missed in their early years. They both felt they had spent too much of their life in servants' company, and been made to do wrong things like the time Mary had been made to write a love letter containing things no nine year old should know about and leave it in a book for her father to find. When Samuel found it he was not pleased but did not reprimand Mary.

It is difficult not to be struck by the dark, brooding nature of Mary's childhood, overseen by a stern, repressed father who abhorred emotion and creativity, a lonely and depressed mother and an intelligent but at times irrational nanny. Deep feelings and passions seem always to be simmering under the surface. The effect on her personality of the great importance placed on discipline and self-control cannot be doubted.

Mary wrote about Uttoxeter as she had known it as a child, especially in *My Own Story*, the story of her life up to the age of nine, in which she gives numerous descriptions of the townspeople and of the town itself. She recorded bullbaiting and the lapidary works which employed many people. Both Francis Redfern (the nineteenth century Uttoxeter antiquarian) and William Torrance (the twentieth century Uxonian historian) quote from Mary's writings when they refer to some of the historical aspects of Uttoxeter. Indeed, Mary is the primary source for the history of the lapidary business in Uttoxeter.

The father of Miss Grace [Copestake] had been a speculative man, and had introduced the lapidary business on rather a great scale, into the town. He built extensive wooden shops all round the large court of his house, Uttoxeter Hall, which was enclosed with a high, dreary looking wall.

Uttoxeter jewellry belonging to the Copestake family, lapidarists, who lived in Uttoxeter Hall.

Mary describes the interior of the Hall and a riding event which took place in the front of the Hall. Her books contain further descriptions of the Hall and its people:

One spot of surpassing interest to us children was 'The Hall' at Uttoxeter. It was a large, irregular brick mansion, standing by the roadside outside the town, and though much dilapidated, must originally have been a place of importance. Here Mr Thomas Copestake, the great jeweller and lapidary, had dwelt and carried on an important and extensive trade, which in the last century brought much wealth to Uttoxeter. The articles usually made were tiaras, silver buckles, and all kinds of jewellry. Small white pebbles could be abundantly picked up in the neighbourhood, which were purchased by Mr Copestake, if without fault, at a penny apiece, but after they had been polished and cut, they had the appearance of stones of the first water. He was also entrusted by the Government with orders for the "Star of Honour". It took about three weeks to make one of these decorations, which when finished was worth about £100. Mr Copestake, when at the height of his prosperity, employed a hundred and forty men, without reckoning apprentices. On the town side of the old hall was a large court, enclosed from the road by an ancient red-brick wall. Round the three inner sides of this court were erected workshops two storeys high, the upper storey having long casemented windows for the greater admission of light, and here in old times Copestake's jewellers and lapidaries had worked. He had unfortunately damaged his great trade and his reputation by mixing an alloy with gold in the manufacture of gold lace. Birmingham, Derby, and even London began to compete with imitations and cheap inferior articles, and carried off the demand from Uttoxeter. In our childhood, therefore, the workshops had fallen into decay, the court was overgrown with grass, and the whole had a strange air of desolation about it. Now and then, however, the courtyard was turned to account, as on an occasion which remains indelibly stamped on my memory. Here came an equestrian troop, and no doubt a better place for the exhibition of their feats could hardly have been chosen; the old deserted shops, with their flights of steps outside and their large windows within, afforded tiers of boxes as in a theatre. We, the children of Friends, brought up with Puritanical rigidity, to whom the very mention of a play, a dance, or a horse-rider's exhibition was forbidden, were nevertheless conducted surreptitiously to the show by two young women Friends who had been permitted to take us a walk. It was a summer evening, and passing through the weather-beaten door in the old red wall, we came into a crowd and could only get standing-places. I could not see much, only people laughing. There was a great deal of shouting and merriment, and a great crushing where we stood. Nevertheless it was to us little girls very exciting, and it was quite dusk when we got home, where we never spoke of the adventure.

Mary describes the desolate, weed-grown court and the decaying workshops as they then stood, and how when it ceased to be the fashion for gentlemen to wear buckles set with stones Copestake's business fell off, and he was a ruined man. He died and Miss Grace undertook the settling of his affairs:

she sold all she could to pay his debts, and then was left with the bare walls of the desolate old house, for she was compelled to sell all the furniture excepting what was needed for the few rooms which she inhabited, and there she lived with an ancient man and his wife, her sole domestics. Poor Miss Grace became a little wrong in her head, either with care or sorrow; and it was enough to make her crazed to see the things which she saw night after night in that doleful old house. What, then, was the house haunted? - of a certainty; what old place like that was not haunted! There was the spectral lady who stole down the private staircase now and then, at uncertain periods, in stiff silks which rustled at every step. Mysterious hands there were, which held a bloody bowl above a certain closet door, and which not only Miss Grace had seen, but a most excellent lady - a Mrs Parker, who with her daughter had at one time taken a part of the house for a school; and in a consequence of which and other such eerie visions had been obliged to leave. And not only she and Miss Grace had seen them, but several of 'the lace girls' also. These 'lace girls', as they were called, were young women employed by Miss Grace in working lace, which she received from the manufacturers in Nottingham, and employed girls to sprig and work in frames."

The Friends' Meeting House in Carter Street is set back from the road behind the house which belonged to the Friends. Two neighbouring cottages, owned by Samuel Botham, formed a group of buildings around the meeting house. Mary described her visits to the Meeting House:

We children went to meeting twice on First-day walking demurely hand-in-hand behind our parents; and once on Fifth-day (Thursday) with our mother alone, if our father was absent in the Forest or elsewhere surveying. These meetings were far from profitable to me. The nearest approach to good which I remember in these seasons of silent worship was the circumstances that the side-windows were reflected at times, probably owing to the sun's position, in a large window placed high above the gallery, looking down the Meeting House and opposite to my seat. These windows of light, seen through the large one, in the sky as it were, represented to me the windows of Heaven. It was these or similar ones, I imagined, which were open in Heaven when the rain poured down for forty days in the time of Noah. The sight of these beautiful windows was a privilege, I believed, granted to me when good. This, I am sorry to confess, was the nearest approach to Heaven which those silent meetings afforded me. The blotches of damp on the Meeting House walls presented to me, however, wonderful battles from the Old Testament; the knots in the backs of the old wooden seats merely secular subjects, odd and grotesque heads and faces of human beings and of animals. How grieved would my parents have been at this want of mental discipline!

Mary tells us that her uncle John Summerland and his wife lived in the house attached to the Meeting House and that there was a garden dividing the two. It seemed strange for them to be able to visit the Meeting House on their own:

I remember the strange eerie effect of lifting the heavy iron handle that raised the ponderous latch and sounded through the empty building with a solemn response. It was most exciting to us on these occasions to be at liberty to sit even in the gallery, where the preachers, when they came, sat, then to go over to the men's side and try how it was in our father's seat or in John Shipley's, and then to go up into the chamber where the 'Women's Meetings of Business' were held.

Mary explains how little William Burgess was the only child they were allowed to associate with for fear of contamination, and how he accompanied them on the escapades. They explored the graveyard, *"a pleasant green field into which the side-windows of the Meeting-house looked and where in the springtime, a sheep, with her lamb or lambs would be put there to graze."* The sheep must have been an added distraction when the children attended Meeting.

On 3rd July, 1808 the Bothams were summoned to the Red House in Carter Street to see the dying Joseph Summerland, Samuel's half brother. The girls were impressed by his kind expression. He had a feeble husky voice and was obviously in pain, and he died two days later. There was a better relationship with the Summerlands after his death.

Education

Next door to the Bothams' house there was a Dame School run by a Mrs Parker (who lodged there). The episode of the love letter had led Samuel to consult another person and he had gone to Mrs Parker for her opinion. She persuaded the Bothams that it would do Anna and Mary good to go to school. Samuel liked her and relented. He allowed Anna and Mary to go to her school on condition that they did not sit with the other children, so they sat together and apart from the others. Mrs Parker left Uttoxeter a year later, but she wrote to them for many years.

Later when Anna felt that school produced questions and problems that she did not understand Mrs Parker discussed literature with them in her letters. Following the publication of Walter Scott's popular poem on the Battle of Waterloo, which she felt fell short of public expectation, she went as far as to say, *"It has been said by some that Mr Scott himself fell at Waterloo."* Mary did not give her own opinion.

When Mrs Parker left, Ann and Samuel decided after much deliberation to send the girls away to a school in Croydon, Surrey, run by Sarah Bevan and Anna Woolley, on the recommendation of a Friend, Ann Alexander, who had just retired from a Friends' School in York. Anna and Mary had to undertake a 150 mile journey. On 14th October 1809 they set off for London with their mother in a chaise hired from the White Hart Inn in Uttoxeter as Samuel did not feel inclined to let his family travel by coach. There had been many accidents, and he preferred them to 'post'. Nanny had packed so much food for the journey they did not need it all and gave it away to some of the poor they saw by the roadside. They travelled via Ashby-de-la-Zouch and spent the first night with their cousins at Groby Lodge near Leicester. Their route was then to Leicester, Northampton, Newport Pagnall and Dunstable, where they slept, then St Albans and on through London over Westminster Bridge to Croydon.

The day after they started out was George III's Jubilee. They had to miss the celebrations in Uttoxeter - not that it would have made any difference to the Botham household, as Quakers would not have joined the festivities, and they saw more than they would have at home. As they passed through the various towns, the flags were flying, the bells ringing, the bands of the militia men, school children and clubs leading processions to Churches and Chapels. There were ox and sheep roasting in the streets, and big barrels of ale tapped at many of the places they passed through. There was laughter, singing and clattering, and long tables in the streets with the Squire looking on and the *"Clergy in good humour laughing"*. The children and Ann joined a stagecoach at Leicester and spent their second night halt at Dunstable. All the way there was revelling and drunkenness, and lights illuminating 'GR'. At the Inn there was a dinner and a grand ball. Ann let her daughters look down from upstairs to see the guests arriving in their finery, something that would never have been allowed by their father. Mary felt her mother enjoyed being able to re-live some of her past experiences, if only remotely. This must have been quite an experience to the two young country Quaker children, and something they never forgot.

After Ann had taken the children to Croydon, she returned to London to stay with friends. The school adjoined the grounds of Addiscombe College. Anna recalled that in 1809 Croydon was a quiet little town of one long street out of which branched the road to Carshalton and Beddington, which passed the ruins of the old Episcopal Palace. She liked the houses on St George's Street, the old buildings of Archbishop Tenison's School and the knotted roots of an elm tree which she liked to sit on. At the School, Anna and Mary wore very plain clothes, while the other girls wore more interesting dresses.

Our little brown cloth pelisses, cut plain and straight, without plait or fold in them, hooked and eyed down the front so as to avoid buttons, which were regarded by our parents as trimmings, yet fastened at the waist with a cord. Little drab beaver bonnets furnished us by the Friend hatter of Stafford, James Nixon, who had blocks made purposely for our ultra-plain bonnets. They were without a scrap of ribbon or cord, except the strings, which were a necessity, and these were fastened inside. Our frocks were, as usual, of the plainest and most homely fabric and make, while the others wore silk.

The resentment in this statement, made when she was an old lady, is very apparent and her comments on the needlework by her and her sister compared to that done by the other girls at the school are also bitter:

Each girl had her fancy-work. We had none, but were expected by our mother to make in our leisure moments half-a-dozen linen shirts for our father, with all their back-stitching and button-holes complete.

Anna and Mary had no skill in decorative handicrafts, but they could do other things the rest of the children were incapable of, more practical things that they had done around the house in Uttoxeter. The comments show the difference between the 'plain' Quakers and the 'wet' Quakers. Mary enjoyed mastering these new skills in handicraft, splitting straws and various types of coloured paper work, and she enjoyed the school garden.

The other children were nearly all from London and had never heard other accents or dialect. They teased the Botham girls - they thought the very word 'Uttoxeter' uncouth. Mary and Anna once again felt different and went around with their arms wrapped around each other. The Bothams had never celebrated Christmas, so when the holidays arrived only two months after their arrival, they remained behind while the other children went home. The separation from their parents for so long must have been traumatic. One other girl stayed and her parents sent her a parcel of goodies but Mary and Anna's parcel consisted of six cut out shirts for them to make up for their father and some candied peel. They were mortified. The following term two of their cousins joined the school, Mary Ann and Maria Marriage of Essex. Their mother, James Botham's widow Rebecca, who had remarried, invited Mary and Anna to spend the midsummer holidays with them, but they were unable to accept this invitation. They were recalled home before that time because of their mother's illness.

Ann Botham developed a severe cold during her stay with friends in London that autumn. The weather had been horrible, with dense fog. When she returned to Uttoxeter she was confined to bed with an extremely bad cough - there were no antibiotics in those days to treat infections. Early in the following summer she was again so ill that it was arranged for a Friend from Leek to escort the girls back from Croydon after the Friends' Yearly Meeting, around Easter time. The girls were shocked to find how ill their mother was; they were not allowed to see her for several weeks. Various physicians came, some of whom travelled considerable distances, and they gave more and different medicines. Mary said they were pleased when the bottles were replaced by pills, implying that Ann had been too ill to swallow pills. During this time Mrs Parker started to take the children on their regular evening walks, as Samuel had no desire to do so while Ann was so ill. Ann Botham spent several weeks in Buxton taking the waters following the illness.

In August 1810 Anna was sent to a Friends' school in Sheffield on the recommendation of Mrs Fairbanks. The school was run by three Quaker women, one of whom was the widow of Alexander Kilham, of Kilhamite Connexion fame, a form of Methodism. Anna and her father and mother went to Sheffield via Ashbourne, where they lunched at the Green Man, still there today. The next night was spent at a Friend's house in Grantley. They also stayed with Mrs Fairbanks on their way. Anna tells us she was frightened at the thought of highwaymen as they travelled across the moors.

Mary remained in Uttoxeter, but it was not long before Anna was back home. In the middle of that winter there was a fever scare in Sheffield and most of the children were sent home. Anna, who had been at this school for three months, did not return there and in the spring of 1811 Mary went in her place. Mrs Kilham was active in the movement for the abolition of child chimney sweeps and she would go out at night, visiting properties. She took Mary with her one night and left her standing alone in a desolate area. While she was standing there she saw the 1811 comet, which left an impression on her of Divine omnipotence, something no school or fellow being could have given her.

Amongst the friends Mary made at school was Hannah West of Uttoxeter. She was a member of a large family who were all brought up as Quakers. Her father Joseph was a grocer and tallow chandler in the Market Place, and she was later to marry the journey-man butcher, Anthony Godbehere, who worked for Joseph Shipley, the Quaker next door. Mary and Hannah were not been allowed to talk to one another at Meeting before or even after their friendship in Sheffield. Adherents such as the Wests sat below the gallery and to one side in the Meeting House and Mary, who would have sat with the women, would have been brought up not to talk to the non-members of the Society. Hannah found the strict Quaker principles of the Sheffield school difficult to adjust to and she brought to Mary an awareness of a different home background with less Quaker discipline.

In 1812 Samuel took Mary away from the school, dissatisfied with the quality of the teaching and of spelling in particular. The school closed soon after. Hannah Kilham went to Sierra Leone as a missionary, where she soon became ill and died.

Anna missed her sister very much while she was at Sheffield, but she had more contact with her mother and came to understand the reason for the quarrel with the Summerlands and the problems of her mother's youth. She learnt to understand her father better and to admire him - of all his children she knew him best. Meanwhile Mary was still unhappy about clothes:

It was at Sheffield that I grew painfully conscious of my unsightly attire. The girls had, for fine summer Sundays, white frocks and petticoat, a small Friends' bonnet and a little shawl. On week-days, when they wore their printed frocks, I could bear it; but First-days (Sundays) were bitter days to me. There was no religion to me in that cross; and I rejoiced that the trying, humiliating day only came once a week, when I had to appear in the school-train, marching down to Meeting, the one scarecrow, as it appeared to me, of the little party.

Anna was now a young woman and wore a dress cut low on the bust and a muslin kerchief which was not shaped and required much pinning and folding. It was difficult to arrange properly. Samuel would not allow the fashionable Friend's cap which was light and balloon-like, but insisted on the close fitting shapes which the girls considered to be like night caps. Both of them were quite capable of making any garment they saw, but were not permitted to make the pretty clothes they would like.

Late in the summer of 1813, Ann took Anna, her eldest daughter, on a visit to their Wood relatives in South Wales. They travelled from Birmingham to Bristol by stagecoach (Mary does not tell us how they got to Birmingham in her description). They travelled with Ann's old friends, Evan Rees, Thomas and Sarah Robinson, all Quakers, and one other person, all packed together like sardines. They arrived at Bristol at midnight after a long day's travel. The plan for the Bothams had been to take a packet (passenger boat) immediately for South Wales, but because of *"contrary winds"* it was three days before they could sail. These days were spent, together with Evan Rees, with a family by the name of Gilpins, whose small son Charles, then running around in a white frock, was to become a famous MP. A Bristol Friend took it upon himself to take visiting Friends on a tour of his town, so in this way Anna was introduced to the sights of Bristol.

The journey across the Bristol Channel should have taken twenty-four hours, but because the winds were still not favourable they tossed about for three whole days and nights. Despite their discomfort, *"Anna enjoyed the rising and setting of the sun at sea, the gulls and other marine birds, the moonlit nights, the phosphoric light on the vessel's track."*

For Anna the visit to Swansea was her *"coming out"*, what Mary describes as her *"life of liberty"*. They stayed with their Sylvester relations where there was no restraint in conversation and laughter. Their uncle was full of fun, their aunt was friendly and the sort of person who puts everyone at ease. She was always well-dressed and Anna must have admired and envied the clothes her aunt was able to wear. Ann's eighteen-year-old nephew Charles and her young niece Mercy were also at home and they were *"most cordial"*. Anna was in an hilarious household with lots of laughter, so foreign to her, and music around her every evening. As to her mother, it was the first time she had been home for eighteen years. No wonder there was so much pleasure in the household.

Many of Ann's former friends and acquaintances visited them and, as was polite in those days, these 'calls' were 'returned'. Happy memories remained after the visit to Ann's friend Anna Price, who previously had lived at Falmouth, but now lived at Neath Abbey with her six adult children. Ann encountered intellectual conversation combined with cheerful company, *"a polished circle, a freedom of intercourse which was cheerful, even mirthful"*. These Price cousins all enjoyed literature and were conversant with contemporary works. They were admirers of Dante, Petrarch and Spenser, of whose works neither Anna nor Mary had any knowledge. The eldest girl, Deborah, was editor of *The Cambrian*, which dealt with subjects like Welsh poetry and legends. She was engaged to Elijah Waring, a Quaker of much learning - they would be the parents of Anna Letitia Waring, the writer of the well known hymns - "Father, I know that all my life is portioned out for me," and "In heavenly love abiding, no change my hear shall fear" - hymns of joy, hope and peace.

Ann and Anna also visited their uncle William Wood in Cardiff. He introduced them to the legend of King Arthur and when he learned how interested Mary was in the subject, he sent her an article, possibly from an Archaeological Society, amounting to 50 quarto pages.

Roger Lyndon came over from Merthyr to see his half-sister and niece and he *"gave a bias to Anna's mind which she never lost."* He was well versed in family history, his ancestors and their activities, and he gave Ann some of the famous 'Irish Patentee's' half-pennies. He lent her a copy of Lavater's *Physiognomic Fragments*. As a result Mary and Anna sought out Lavater's works in Uttoxeter. Mary says they adopted his system, and *"afterwards judged rightly or wrongly of every one's mind and temper by their external form."*

The Bothams visited Landaff and the ruined cathedral where a service was in progress in the chancel; they saw the cloisters and the graveyard, which was fragrant with herbs. Anna was thirsty for what this holiday was giving her - an introduction to local society life, the sights, as well as books and ideas. It must have had a dramatic effect on a socially and culturally deprived girl. The memorable holiday finally ended, and they returned by another route. They went to Newport by Tintern, where Anna was impressed by the scenery of the Wye valley. Between Monmouth and Gloucester they had a Church of England clergyman in the coach with them. Ann conversed easily with him and when the topic of religion was discussed he was very surprised at Ann's replies and wondered how she knew so much, particularly as she was a Quaker (her dress would have given this away). Ann replied: *"By conviction and observation"*, and after a pause he said apologetically, *"I thought the Society of Friends was too secluded and taciturn a people to interest themselves in worldly matters."* Mary comments that the conversation resembled that of a religious novelette of the day about a coach journey of a widow and her daughter.

On their return, Mr Botham engaged Thomas Goodall, a master at Thomas Alleyne's 'Free Grammar School for Boys' in Bridge Street, Uttoxeter, to teach the girls Latin, spelling, the globes, and anything else he

The Wye Valley.

could. Unfortunately Mr Goodall died prematurely and another teacher was hired to teach the girls. He was already teaching other Friends' children and was very good at mathematics. Anna and Mary were not happy with the sort of 'attentions' this teacher showed them but they did not dare tell their parents, so they concocted an excuse, which Mary does not explain, to have him dismissed.

Both girls wrote poetry and prose, and they also felt the desire to express themselves in an artistic form, so they copied the new Wedgwood style in papier-maché. Their house had no pictures and both girls loved to paint. Anna painted nature - blue larkspur, anemone and wallflower. Their father was very upset to see the paintings which were well done; colour was a very dangerous thing he said - *"better not to indulge in colour"*. He destroyed Anna's paintings. Although she respected her father and did no more colour paintings she cried and cried when alone. Much as Samuel loved art and music, he feared it because of what it might make him do which he considered unholy. His wife Ann had no feeling for music or singing, but both the girls had inherited their father's talents and enjoyed music and rhythm, consequently they liked poetry. Quaker schools at that time prohibited all music, including hymns. To his credit, Samuel Botham obviously wanted his children to have a good education at a time when it was considered unnecessary to educate girls. He had even considered sending the girls to Ackworth, in Yorkshire, which William Howitt, Mary's future husband, and his brothers attended.

Thomas Howitt of Heanor, William Howitt's father.

Thomas Howitt of Heanor, father of William Howitt

The former family home at Heanor Wood.

The home of William's family at Heanor.

CHAPTER FOUR
GROWING UP, COURTSHIP & MARRIAGE

In the autumn of 1815 or 1816, Ann and Samuel went to North Wales for a holiday. The teenage Mary and Anna enjoyed themselves in their parents' absence and Mary remembers running around the garden in windy weather with her hair flying and a wonderful feeling of freedom. A young relative Susanna Frith, also a Quaker and of independent means, came to Uttoxeter to stay with Uncle Joseph Summerland's widow and paid several visits to the Botham girls while their parents were away. They had much in common, especially poetry.

The girls felt deprived of fashion but they managed to enjoy it vicariously by making stylish gowns for their friend Martha Astle who was poor in Mary's eyes and had no gift for sewing. They also drew pretty patterns and embroidered them on collars for her. Once she went to a subscription ball at the White Hart Inn attired in a white muslin and green satin bodice made in Balance Street; Mary and Anna considered her the height of elegance. Mary found these balls very trying. She could hear the post chaise going round the town picking ladies up, going out to enjoy themselves, and she was not allowed to go.

At other times, Mary and Anna took Martha on rambles so that they could study botany. Martha did not like botany but she enjoyed their company. Martha's father, Captain Astle, had trained for the Anglican ministry and was at the time the incumbent of Bromshall (now known as Bramshall, two miles out of Uttoxeter). As a young man, he had entered the army and during the Battle of Bunkers Hill in the American Civil War he had hidden in a pig-sty. Afterwards, whenever he was out in the town the 'street-boys' would shout at him *"Bunker's Hill, Bunker's Hill; run, the cannon-balls are coming"*. He was one of Uttoxeter's characters, a very clever man who knew Dr Samuel Johnson and who was the lexicographer in Hazlitt's edition of Boswell's *Life of Johnson*. To Samuel Botham's Quaker mind he did not demonstrate acceptable demeanour and attitudes!

Martha's mother prided herself on being a lady, coming from an ancient family and having titled relatives. *"She always sat by the fireplace, on a table by her side a big book and her fan."* She did no needlework and Ann Botham thought her a *"feckless"* woman. Mary and Anna were sometimes sent with a gift of game or fruit for her, and told to ask after her health. She puzzled the girls with the reply, *"Indifferent, thank you"* and they did not know what to say, or whether to be glad or sorry. Martha's parents were separated. Captain Astle lived with his son Edmund elsewhere in the town.

Samuel and his wife had become acquainted with the Uttoxeter Vicar Rev. Stubbs when he joined in Samuel's efforts to put a stop to bull-baiting in the town, one of the highlights of the Wakes. When the Vicar was thrown out of his gig and killed around 1811, Ann visited his widow and her only child, little Jonathan, with her daughters. Mrs Stubbs and Ann became firm friends. This was of great help to Mary, the would-be authoress, as Mrs Stubbs retained her husband's library of classic works, history and topography, and religious material both English and foreign.

I can never sufficiently return thanks for the unrestricted range of that scholar's library, which not only provided me with the best books to read, but made us aware of the beauty of choice editions - Tonson's Faerie Queen and other important works, handsomely bound in quarto and embellished with fine plates, at which we were never tired of gazing, some of the landscapes remaining in my memory still. Nor have I ever forgotten Piranesi's magnificent engravings of Rome, brought from that city by the Evanses of Derby, and lent by them to their friend, Mrs Stubbs.

Mr Pipe, who lived in the big house next door to the Bothams, had an extensive library and

46   The Traveller on the Hill-top

Mary and Anna were able to borrow books from him also.

When Rhoda left, the maturing Anna and Mary undertook the care and education of Emma and Charles. Mary cared for Emma, and Charles was never happier than when he was with his "dear Nan". They set up a schoolroom in the stable loft. Mary found a passage which she copied out from Young's *Night Thoughts*, *"'Tis impious in a good man to be sad"*. She says she had always *"warred"* in her mind against the enforced gloom of their home, and the passage *"spoke the very spirit of the religion"*, and thinking it a great fact which ought to be trumpeted abroad, she copied it down. Her father saw it and was very upset at such a *"sentiment"* and extremely angry with Mary for spreading such words.

About 1815-16, Mary's cousin, Martha Shipley, married another cousin, John Ellis of Beaumont Leys near Leicester. Samuel Botham's mother and John Ellis's grandmother were sisters. In 1817 Anna and Mary went to stay with another cousin, Rebecca Burgess, at Groby Lodge in Leicestershire. Rebecca was the daughter of John Summerland of Uttoxeter and therefore half niece to Samuel Botham. Following this they went to stay with John Ellis at Beaumont Leys. John's mother and sister Anne were keeping house for him and caring for his ten month old son, because his wife had died in childbirth. This was a convivial house where many Friends were entertained. At this period many Quaker families throughout the Midlands knew each other, through marriage or their various meetings.

On this occasion there was a young man staying there by the name of Daniel Harrison, a Yorkshireman. He was a close friend of William Howitt, who was known to the two young Bothams because of his writing and also because grandfather Botham visited his mother and supplied her with herbs. When Mary later visited William's family in Heanor she was overawed by the vegetable medicines his mother made, and she realized why her grandfather had enjoyed visiting them. William's writings were well known by that time, and Mary was very excited at meeting his friend. Anna and Mary were now introduced to controversial religious and academic discussion and they formed a great admiration for Daniel, who was such a contrast to the people they were used to. They were surprised and thrilled by his singing of songs like "Blue Bonnets of the Border" to them as they walked in Bradgate Park.

On 6th November that year Princess Charlotte died in childbirth. The news upset the party at Beaumont Leys, as it rekindled the events and grief of ten months previously. The country was distressed by Princess Charlotte's death; she was the only child of George IV, which meant that her death and that of her child left the line of succession to the throne in doubt. It was just after the end of the Napoleonic War, and revolutionary feelings at the time indicated that the monarchy was far from secure.

In 1818 William Howitt came to Uttoxeter for a holiday and stayed with his cousin Susanna Frith, also kinswoman of Mary and Anna Botham. Anna and Mary met him and they spent much time with him. William was rather short and stocky with a square face and bright humorous eyes, a great talker willing to discuss and argue on any subject. Like most Quakers, he usually carried a stick. He described his first meeting with the sisters to his cousin Susanna:

     .....in came a very comely and bright young lady Friend to whom I was introduced. She was Anna Botham. I was greatly pleased with her grace and intelligence. Very soon, came in another sister whose lively and clever appearance charmed me. I had heard much of the Botham family, though the only member I had ever known was the old Friend John Botham, these young ladies' grandfather. I accompanied them home to call on their parents who received me most cordially.

They were all interested in nature - William was nicknamed the *"Botanist"*. Their tastes in authors and poets were similar. He introduced them to the new Romantic poets, Crabbe, Wordsworth, Coleridge and Shelley, and also the engravings of Thomas Bewick, Scott's *Waverley Novels* and the *Edinburgh Review*, for which they were later to write. They were all fond of walking and some of the places they walked at were Alton Towers, well known to the Botham sisters, Chartley Moss, an ancient glacial pool where trees grow on a raft of moss, and Sudbury, Derbyshire, part of the estate of Lord Vernon.

Mary was surprised when her father was agreeable to accepting William as a suitor. William's liberal mindedness was so different from how Samuel expected Quakers to behave.

William and the Howitt family

The Howitt family was connected with the families Tantum, Middleton, and Botham, histories of which are now deposited at Derbyshire Record Office, Matlock. There is a "Common Place Book" written by Thomas Howitt which is still in existence and is the history of the family. Thomas was described as *"a large, important man who would sit for hours at a high desk pouring over copies of wills and deeds connected with old county families."* [SG] William himself was to write his autobiography, but his instructions were that it was never to be published and it is with a member of the family still.

William was one of six sons and used to argument and discussion. The environment in which he grew up was very different to that of the submissive wife and daughters of the Botham household, where religion was never discussed. William's father Thomas was a colliery manager whose childhood had been plagued by financial problems and estrangement from his maternal grandparents. He was received into the Society of Friends at the age of twenty in 1785 and the following year he married Phoebe Tantum, whose family were direct followers of George Fox. She was the daughter of Francis Tantum and Elizabeth neé Redfern. Elizabeth was a hard vixen of a woman with a harsh tongue and an interest in medicine. She was taught by a famous doctor, Dr John Taylor of Whitworth, who had treated George III's invalid daughter Princes Amelia with cephalic snuff made from the leaves of assarabacca - the same snuff that John Botham made in Balance Street. Dr Taylor's treatments were very painful and Elizabeth ruled her family with an iron hand. William described her as a *"woman of steel"*.

Thomas and Phoebe lived for many years at Heanor Wood and later at Heanor. They had many children, of whom only six sons survived to adulthood: Thomas, Emmanuel, Francis, William, Richard and Godfrey. William's mother, had acquired her mother's medical knowledge and was well known in Heanor and around. She was always willing to help minister to the sick without payment and she had a wide knowledge of herbs, which she grew herself, including the famous assarabacca. People came from far and wide to see her with their ailments and she was often sent for in the middle of the night.

All the boys had fiery tempers and it was not unusual to find two or three of them not speaking to one another. Richard fell in love with Anna and when she refused to marry him, he accused her of trifling with his affections. True to the Howitt temperament, he was very angry with her and threatened to take the matter to the Quaker Meeting. Fortunately *"not all the family supported him and the matter was dropped, though a long and sad resentment followed."* Almost all of the Howitt brothers had enquiring minds and adventurous spirits. Thomas emigrated to New York. Emmanuel visited America in 1819 and published an account of his visit. William was to become known throughout the English speaking world as a writer. Richard was a well-respected writer and poet, and in fact was considered the most poetic spirit of the family. A sensitive man, full of fun, he was to become a favourite uncle and his life as a bachelor intertwines with that of William and Mary. Godfrey, the youngest, became an accomplished naturalist and physician and emigrated to Australia. Only Francis remained in Derbyshire, where he farmed.

Like his brothers, William went to Ackworth School between the ages of ten and fourteen (1801-1804) and he wrote his first book while he was there in 1802. It describes his arrival at the school and is called *The Boy's Country Book*. He also wrote a poem when he was thirteen years old, an account of *"my youthful life"*. The children did not usually go back to Heanor for holidays but William had a six month spell at home when there was an outbreak of scarlet fever. The school did not teach geography, history or natural history as that would be worshiping nature. Samuel, who was extremely interested and knowledgeable about nature, decided not to send his daughters there because of the lack of those subjects. It is possible, too, that he turned down this school for their girls because it was coeducational and he did not want them to have any contact with boys. There was no mathematics, only arithmetic, and no French or Latin, though this was to change not long after William had left the school.

The *Boys Country Book* contained descriptions of nature and of his life at the school, including accounts of the severe discipline. William said the school had a good library and he read much poetry, amongst other books. He was also able to discuss a lot of natural and moral philosophy. The school disapproved of the book, but described William as a healthy, energetic boy fond of books and country pursuits. Twenty years later John Bright called it a *"harsh, if not barbarous school"*.

After William left Ackworth, he remained at home farming for a while. Then he went to a Friends' Private Seminary in Tamworth, where he had the chance to learn French, an opportunity he did not use and much regretted later in life. He learned subjects relating to medicine and law. His eyes became inflamed through extensive reading so he decided to study chemistry, but his eyes were still a problem. He developed little white specks which felt like grains of sand, making studying very painful, so at the age of fifteen he decided to give up his education. For the next two years he enjoyed the farm and other country pursuits, including shooting. But his father believed everyone should learn a trade, and William was sent to Mansfield to be an architect. He had no interest in this and on completion of his apprenticeship he tore up his indenture. Before he was twenty-one years old he had worked for a builder, a carpenter and a cabinetmaker. While he was apprenticed to Richard Hallam, a Quaker, he spent his spare time exploring the countryside around Mansfield. He was only five miles from Byron's home at Newstead Abbey and he visited an employee there, which gave him a lasting affinity with the poet. His poetry excited him.

William felt he would like to be a doctor, but he was, by then, too old to train for that profession, however he persuaded his father to allow his brother Godfrey to study medicine in Edinburgh, which was not only the best medical school in the United Kingdom, but the only one open to non-conformists. William decided that the dispensing of medicines would give himself a living and he studied chemistry again, although his ambition by was to be an author,

Marriage

Mary and William were engaged for two years and on the 16th April 1821 they were married at the Friends' Meeting House in Carter Street, Uttoxeter. Despite Samuel's dislike of silk dresses Mary wore a silk gown of dove grey with a bonnet of the same material and a soft white silk shawl. She walked the short distance to the Meeting House for the ceremony, quite unlike a wedding in any other Christian Church with statements made by the couple in front of the assembled worshippers. Fifty years later Mary reminisced:

It had been a fine April morning fifty years earlier when William and I, with our nearest relatives, walked to Meeting, all the little town of Uttoxeter looking on. I wonder I did not feel very nervous. We had some of the Friends to dinner - a better one than usual; if I remember rightly, a cook was

> *engaged for the occasion from the White Hart. Then William and I and all the young people strolled in the garden, and up to the Bank Closes, a nice little home walk. After our return rain fell. We had more Friends to tea; all those who had not been invited to dinner. Afterwards the sun came out, and we left in quite a splendid sunset. I remember so well how bright the evening was after the rain, and have often thought it was like our life - marked by April showers with a lovely, calm sunset.*

The Bank Closes could be reached by going through a gate and over a small bridge at the bottom of their garden, over the fields, returning by the road, making *"a nice circular walk."* Mary says on another occasion her mother had quite upset her staff by hiring a cook from the White Hart, the most prestigious hotel in town, to prepare this important meal.

After tea, Mary and William left Balance Street for Hanley in the Potteries, where earlier in the year William had bought a chemist's shop. There was no Quaker Meeting House in the Potteries, the nearest being in Leek, some nine miles from Hanley. Surprisingly, the first Sunday after her marriage Mary attended a Catholic chapel. There appeared little opportunity for discussion until William made friends with some other dissenters, mainly Unitarians. This gave him his opportunity for argument which was not welcomed by them. It was whilst they were in Hanley that they met Thomas Mulock, the father of Elizabeth, another important writer whom they would meet again as Elizabeth Craik when they lived in London.

William felt Hanley was restrictive. He had ambitions which could not be fulfilled in this pottery town and he received a good offer for his business, so seven months later, in about December 1821, they were packing up and preparing to leave Hanley. Mary wrote to Anna on 5th Day, 12 Mo., 13th, 1821:

> *We are preparing for a decampment. I am sitting in a perfect chaos of books, papers, valuables, and rubbish. I suppose we shall be ready to depart from here on Second-day so you may, if you please, send the gig for us; and I shall thank thee to see that I have a cap made up to wear at home.*

They visited Uttoxeter and then went to Heanor to live with William's parents until they could establish themselves in Nottingham. Whilst there, they went on a tour, the first of many. They left Heanor at 5am and rode saddle and pillion to Derby. The next day they boarded a coach bound for Liverpool from where they got the Steam Packet to Dumbarton. They visited Gretna Green where, at that period, the number of marriages was increasing. The price for an English marriage service varied from a glass of whisky to £100 and the custom had already been established that the ceremonies took place in the blacksmith's. The post boys from Carlisle had a share in the profits of these runaway marriages and they organised a system of hindrances to all those who were chasing the young couples.

For Mary and William this was a tour in the footsteps of the famous writers and poets. Scotland had just been 'discovered'. Walter Scott has been described as the first tourist advertiser through his writings; he loved and wrote about the Highlands. Byron had written poems about Scotland, Wordsworth and Keats had visited it. George IV had made a State Visit to Scotland, the first by a reigning monarch since 1603 and perhaps the beginning of the Royal Family's love of Scotland. James Boswell had accompanied Dr Samuel Johnson there fifty years before. In 1813 George Stevenson had visited the Isles, and his poems reflected his visit. Travel was for literary empathy; people wanted to see and feel what these poets had felt, and for Mary and William, the 'would be' writers, the tour would have been a necessity. They wandered around Edinburgh, and walked backwards and forwards in front of Sir Walter Scott's house to see if he was at home. They saw Lady Scott and her daughter walking in their plantations in the spring sunshine. However, they had to wait until they spent a night at Melrose before they actually saw the 'great man'. At breakfast the waiter called them to the window where they saw him walk by.

During their holiday William and Mary walked from one place to another, stopping at any house willing to take them in for the night. This was normal in the days before hotels. They took with them one small valise and wore clothes that *"defied all changes of weather"*. They did get very wet on more than one occasion and for four weeks they faced wind, rain, snow and sunshine. One day they climbed Ben Lomond, *"wading through heather, skirting the black and trembling bogs; not a sound seemed to live there but the twitter of a small bird always found in the heather; the casual call of the raven, the less frequent and plaintive call of the plover or the bleat of the solitary sheep wandering on a far-off slope or coming to look down gravely with its grey face from some rock above."* When they were near the top a storm overtook them and they descended,

......through whistling wind and darkness so great that we could not see one another at more than an arm's length - holding each other's hand in this manner we endeavoured to retrace our steps till we could get below the cloud. After several hours, sometimes stopped by precipices, sometimes by torrents and sometimes fearful of being engulfed in tottering bogs and all the time sinking in the wet spongy moss, the rain pouring down plentifully we escaped in safety to a farm-house at the foot. Women, children and clamorous dogs had long noticed us descending and were assembled at the door gaping in amazement at our temerity, but as we approached all withdrew into the house and when we reached the door everything was so still, there might have been no soul in it.

They gained access to the highland farmhouse, built of stones and thatched with bracken, to find it inhabited by thirteen people and two goats. They stayed a while there to rest and talk to the inhabitants, and then were off again across the stepping stones to Glen Dhu.

The tour covered Edinburgh, where they were joined by the newly-qualified Dr Godfrey Howitt, William's youngest brother. They walked into the town of St Andrews at 10 o'clock at night in moonlight and walked the next day along the city's *"grass-grown streets"*. From there they walked to Melrose, along the border and back to Gretna Green. In her autobiography Mary gives an interesting insight to Scottish life; how when she and William wanted a ferry boat at twilight, various people who were doing another job kept telling them *"to wait a wee"*. After they had found lodgings, the landlady wanted them to *"wait for a fool"*

A Victorian engraving of Glencoe, Scotland.

but they went to bed with *"a supper of their oat-cakes* [not the Staffordshire kind] *their whole stock of eggs, three in number, procured a glass of whisky toddy, none of the best, and added a supplement out of our own budget."* She gives a lovely description of the kitchen at these lodgings,feeling they made a writer want to get out her pencil to describe it.

> *Around the ample fireplace hung several pairs of tartan hose, wet with traversing the spongy moors. On the floor, among sticks, dust, half-roasted and half-crushed potatoes, crowded the whole tribe of dirty half-naked children and several large shepherd dogs. Overhead were guns and a variety of household implements. About one-fourth of the room was occupied by a press-bed with sliding panels, which from its aspect appeared to be the nest of the chief part of the family. In our bedroom the sheets were so thoroughly saturated with peat-smoke that we did not lose the odour of it for days.*

They went with Godfrey to Lanark by coach to see Robert Owen's theories in action. Owen was a philanthropist and social reformer, who had built a model factory and village for his workers. Other Quaker and non-conformist factory owners built similar enterprises; they realized that good housing, education, adequate food, and opportunity for relaxation made for healthy, happy workers. They felt all children should have the opportunity for education, so they built schools and churches or meeting houses. This is the belief of Quakers, that all men are equal in the sight of God and should be treated so. Bournville is such a settlement to this day. The Howitts were very impressed with Lanark.

William and Mary returned to Heanor via the Lake District which they explored. On their return they wrote an enlarged narrative of this pedestrian journey, with original descriptive verses, under their pseudonyms, Wilfred and Wilfrida Wender. It appeared in the *Mercury*, a Staffordshire paper, in the spring of 1822, under the heading "A Scottish Ramble".

Throughout his life William seems to have put people's backs up, but to Mary he must have come as a breath of fresh air, with his willingness to embrace whatever the world threw up, and his spirit of adventure. His family was much more natural and free than hers had been, and he appears to have had a happy, outdoor childhood He was accustomed to very strong, unconventional female figures and he encouraged Mary to travel, to meet people, and to write.

In July 1822 Mary and William spent five weeks in Uttoxeter prior to moving into a small house in Lower Parliament Street, on the corner with Newcastle Street, in Nottingham. The building was demolished about 1900. In the summer of 1823 William's brother Richard came to work for William and stayed with them. There were many arguments between the brothers. When Mary and William moved to a larger house in the Market Place opposite Long Row, facing the lower corner of the Exchange, Richard took over the tenancy of the Parliament Street house and shop. William gave up the business to spend all his time as a writer. Mary describes the new accommodation as *"part of a fine old mansion built by a French architect for himself. It has tall doors, much carved over the great mantelpieces, handsome ceilings and several wainscotted rooms."*

During these early years, Mary and William made contact with many local writers, one of whom was Letitia Elizabeth Landon - 'L.E.L.' Mary took over the editing of *The Drawing Room Scrap Book* from L.E.L following Letitia's marriage to Mr Maclean in 1838, but was not happy with this work. She had undertaken to write poems to accompany engravings chosen by the publisher and sometimes used her translations of German poetry. At this time she was able to write a poem in a day and the work was worth £100 per annum. She encouraged Anna to write. Anna sent Mary some poems which pleased Mary but they disagreed on how to publish them. Mary wanted them to be included amongst hers but Anna wanted a work of her own published. Neither was done and Anna later found she had no inspiration to compose poetry.

They probably knew Elizabeth Fry, as her brother Joseph John Gurney was the Quaker minister in Nottingham. They held discussions in their own home and later, when William's brother Richard had the house to himself, an even larger group of people gathered to discuss anything from religion and current affairs to the social state of the nation.

Whilst Mary was in Nottingham she began her writing of poetry and prose, drawing upon her observation of the scenes around her, and her love of nature derived from her childhood in Uttoxeter, as can be seen in her poem 'Wild Crocus in Nottingham Meadows':

Ah, though it is an English flower,
It only groweth here and there;
Through merry England you might ride, -
Through all i s length from side to side, -
Through fifty counties, nor have spied
This flower so passing fair.

But in these meadows it is growing.
And now it is the early spring;
And see! from out the kindly earth
How thousand thousands issue forth!
As if it gloried to give birth
To such a lovely thing.

Like lilac-flame its colour glows,
Tender, and yet so clearly bright,
That all for miles and miles about
The splendid meadow shineth out;
And far-off village children shout
To see the welcome sight.

I love the odorous hawthorn-flower;
I love the wilding's bloom to see;
I love the light anemones,
That tremble to the faintest breeze;
And hyacinth-like orchises
Are very dear to me!

The star-wort is a fairy flower;
The violet is a thing to prize;
The wild pink on the craggy ledge,
The waving sword-like water-sedge,
And e'en the Robin-run-in-th'-hedge,
Are precious in mine eyes.

Yes, yes, I love them all, bright things!
But then, such glorious flowers as these
Are dearer still. I'll tell you why:
There's joy in many and many an eye
When first goes forth the welcome cry
Of - "Lo, the Crocuses!"

Then little toiling children leave
Their care, and here by thousands throng,
And through the shining meadow run,
And gather them; not one by one,
But by grasped handfuls, where are none
To say that they do wrong.

They run, they leap, they shout for joy;
They bring their infant brethren here;
They fill each little pinafore;
They bear their baskets brimming o'er,
Within their very hearts they store
This first joy of the year.

Yes, joy in these abundant meadows
Pours out like to the earth's o'erflowing;
And, less that they are beautiful
Than that they are so plentiful,
So free for every child to pull,
I love to see them growing.

And here, in our own fields they grow -
An English flower, but very rare;
Through all the kingdom you may ride, -
O'er marshy flat, on mountain side, -
Nor ever see, outstretching wide,
Such flowery meadows fair!

The Nottingham meadows were noted for their magnificent blue colour, but unfortunately the crocuses disappeared during the twentieth century. Nottinghamshire Council have now started to replant the meadows with the wild blue crocus.

Mary returned to Uttoxeter late in the autumn of 1823 for Anna's wedding to Daniel Harrison. He had set himself up in business as a merchant in Liverpool before he came to Uttoxeter to seek Anna's hand in marriage. On 9th October they married and to please her father she wore a dress of a plain grey woollen material. Her mother was most upset as it was considered essential even for a Quaker to have a silk dress for her wedding. She felt it necessary to explain to Daniel about it, but he replied that his wife could have as many silk dresses as she wanted and a few weeks later he gave her a parcel containing a length of the finest lavender silk.

After the wedding Daniel and Anna left for the ancestral home in Wensleydale en route for Liverpool. This was the last time all the family were gathered together. It was the custom at that time for the bridesmaids to accompany the bride to her new home, so Mary went with Anna and Daniel to their new house in Everton, Liverpool. After the formalities of the reception amongst the Liverpool Friends, the newly-married couple attended their first Meeting and next day by noon, the 'Bride's Visiting' began. Anna found this an ordeal and was relieved when Daniel stayed at home to introduce the visitors and hand out the cake and wine. After a second appearance at Meeting on First day came invitations for tea-drinkings and supper parties, and it was many months before the round was completed.

Liverpool Friends at that time prided themselves on two excellent Book Societies, whose members were acquainted with *"the shining lights of Liverpool, the Roscoes, Yateses, Sandbatches, Henry Chorley and Mrs Hemans."* Over the years Anna was to discuss much of what she read with Mary through her letters.

Mary returned to her own home in Nottingham via Uttoxeter in the November. She had left all the family feeling well so she was very surprised to hear of her father's illness a few weeks later. He died on 19th December and was buried at Carter Street burial ground. The *Staffordshire Advertiser* for 27th December 1823 carried the following obituary:

"At Uttoxeter, on Tuesday last, Mr Samuel Botham, a Member of the Society of Friends. He was sincerely and deservedly respected by numerous friends and acquaintances."

Anna and Mary returned to Uttoxeter for the funeral, after which Anna accompanied Mary back to Nottingham to be with her for the birth of Mary's first baby, Anna Mary, who was born on 15th January 1824. This was Mary's fourth pregnancy; she had lost three babies previously. (She had written to Anna during one of her pregnancies that she was *"in good health"*, and that Godfrey had bled her as a farewell token.) She was dangerously ill for several months following the birth and was actually unconscious for part of the time. William wrote to his father on 7th April 1824 that Mary was delirious, and that nothing could be done: *"My delightful dream of earthly happiness is all over! I am the most miserable man living."* The doctor gave little hope of her recovery and Anna and William watched by her day and night. The baby was frail but Mary knew nothing about this as she remained delirious. One day when Anna was sitting on the bed, Mary raised herself and flopped her head on Anna's knee, and instantly her restlessness calmed. The doctor had just entered the room and he told Anna she was not to move until Mary woke up naturally and of her own accord. He tried to make Anna comfortable with cushions, but she was pregnant and felt very faint at times. Still, she managed to remain in this position until Mary awoke eight hours later, when it was declared that she would recover.

Mary suffered from deep depression following the baby's birth, and Anna tried hard to cheer her up by her letters. William and Mary were to have many children but like so many nineteenth century parents, they saw many of their children die at birth or shortly afterwards. Those to survive were Anna Mary (known as Annie) (1824-1881), Charles Botham (1826-1828), Alfred William (1830-1908), Claude Middleton (1833-1844), Herbert Charlton (known as Charlton) (1838-1863), and Margaret Anastasia (known as Meggie) (1839-1930). Only Alfred and Meggie were to survive Mary. Mary often admitted that she had neglected her children as they had taken second place to her literary work, their bread and butter.

After Samuel's death and Anna's marriage, the Bothams moved. Their mother, Ann, let the family home in Balance Street to Dr Kennedy and went to live next door in a slightly smaller house with fewer outbuildings which was part of her husband's estate. William and Mary maintained close contact and Ann kept her daughters informed of the activities of their sister and brother, who were still with her. There was a relaxation in the severity of the life-style which Samuel had enforced and which had so marred the children's childhood. Emma decided she would dress as she wanted to, although modestly, and do her hair differently.

A few years later, when Mary was on a visit to Uttoxeter, she went to Caverswall Castle. She had visited the Castle about thirty years earlier as a child with Anna and her father. In *My Own Story*, Mary describes the castle as *"a handsome old mansion, with its corner towers, its moat, and its drawbridge......the vastness and singularity of the building, the lovely garden, the paved court, the drawbridge and the moat - they all stirred that incipient poetry within us, and that love of the picturesque, which was already beginning to be a passion as well as a feeling."* Samuel had referred to the owners, the Tidesmores, not as papists but as refugee Catholics. The Bothams had been very warmly greeted by Mrs Tidesmore, and the young Mary had spent the day playing with the large family of children, some of whom were of her age. They were interested to know if Mary and Anna had a brother, to which they replied, "One." The Botham girls were shown around the house, visiting the small rooms in the tower, and went to the graveyard to see the grave of the Tidesmore girls' brother, who had fallen into the moat and drowned when he was three or four years old. The inscription read:

> "Weep not for me, my parents dear,
> I am not dead, but sleeping here,
> A living flower, that shall expand
> Its beauty in the heavenly land."

Quakers do not normally have tombstones and this stone, together with the sisters' conversation about him, seemed so natural that it made a deep impression on Mary. The little Quaker girls were taken into the church, they sat in the pews, climbed the pulpit steps and finally pulled the bells, thoroughly enjoying themselves. This visit made Mary realise that Roman Catholics were just ordinary people, friendly and loving, and not what she had heard of the dreaded papists.

Like most children who have enjoyed such a visit they promised to return, but children do not anticipate changed circumstances. The Tidemores left their home and the Castle was sold for a nunnery. Many years later Mary bought a nun-doll and a crucifix there for Anna's daughter. Anna was horrified when she received them and thought they were idolatrous, but to Mary they were beautiful. Even at this period, she was evidently drawn to the Catholic faith.

Charles

The brother of Mary and Anna, who had aroused the curiosity of the Tidesmore children at Caverswall Castle, was to become the cause of much concern especially as his future career now had to be decided in the absence of a father. His future was discussed with Ann's daughters and sons-in-law.

He was a lovable individual with a good sense of humour, and was able to get away with things other members of the family dared not do; for example he would laugh out loud and although his mother gave him a look of disapproval, his father said nothing. Anna had given him his early education and later he had gone to Thomas Goodall's school where he learnt Latin and arithmetic. He was not interested in education except geography and calculations, the two subjects which would help him when he grew up. He, like his sisters, was observant and at an early age he wrote a journal. He gives an account of a walk he undertook to Alton with his father who was visiting the estate when he was received by the steward on the 20th November, (no year is given):

It was very cold but fine till we got near the turnpike on the road to Alton then it began to snow fast when we got to tithe-barn [Tithe-Barn is a hamlet] *at a little village about 2 miles from Alton we saw a publick-house which was the sign of the swan but instead of the swan being white it was orange which I thought very curious. ...we saw the greatest dog I ever saw. Anthony Todd when he came to us, - asked my father wether he would take a little cold meet but my father declined but said he would take a cup of tea. My father asked if they would lend him a map of the estate. We stopped there about an hour then we went to dinner. About past 3 o'clock we set off for Uttoxeter. It blew very cold all the way home when we were come to the brook house it began to be quite dusk and when we were got to the cotton mill it was quite dark so when we were got to the place I had used to call the dove in shade lane* [possibly Slade Lane] *when I was a very little boy I had like to have walked into it and we reached home about a quarter past 6 o'clock.*

Samuel believed his children should be able to do things that were useful regardless of their sex, and equipped a carpentry workshop for them. Charles made model ships with meticulous attention to detail. Where he obtained the patterns or blue-prints is unknown but the named replicas were accurate. In 1817 Anna went to a cousin's wedding in Hull. She was very impressed by the docks, the flags of Sweden, Denmark and Holland, and the wonderful sight of the open sea. She sent home sheets and sheets of descriptions of the port, its ships and the flags she had seen. With her artistic skill she was able to send detailed drawings of the ships and riggings, and the sheepskin coats worn by the sailors who went into arctic waters.

At the age of fifteen, Charles rode his horse to his Burgess cousins at Groby Lodge. It was harvest time and he spent several weeks helping there. He and Lucy, the youngest daughter of the family, became great friends and her father offered to teach Charles farming.

On his return he wrote to Anna that he found life in Uttoxeter dull, nothing ever happened in the town. He also told her he had plans which he was not going to divulge, even to her. Many years later, as a widow in Rome, Mary wrote *Reminiscences of My Later Life* for the magazine *Good Words*, in which she describes more fully than in her autobiography the death of her brother. She has a romanticised view in her old age of her brother, but this could be attributed to the guilt the family felt about his death:

The handsome, manly, generous-hearted boy, although but fifteen, having no occupation at home, was as anxious to fix on a profession as any of us. Father had thought of the law for him. There seemed some uncertainty however, whether as a Friend he could conscientiously fulfil all the duties, and enjoy all the privileges, of an attorney. Richard Phillips was a lawyer, but he had a partner not belonging to our Society to attend to business done in the law courts; and were Charles, as in his case, reduced to mere conveyancing, he would find little employment in Uttoxeter.[GW]

The family was aware of Charles's passion for the sea and shipping (he had studied the *Life of Anson of Shugborough)* and "dreaded" the consequences, so they eventually obtained an articleship to Mr Rowland Roscoe, a merchant in Liverpool. Though Emma was not happy about the arrangement and had a premonition of impending disaster, Charles consented and left for Liverpool in October, 1824. It had been arranged that he should lodge with an elderly Quaker couple, Joseph and Mary Nicholson, and spend his spare time with Anna and Daniel, who were expecting their first baby.

Alas! how little attention do parents and guardians pay to the innate tastes and abilities of the young. Had Charles, who displayed great skill with his lathe, been placed with a shipbuilder, instead of with a merchant, his sad fate and our misery might have been averted.

The pride and hope of his family, and the admiration of all beholders, Charles had hitherto led a most guarded and secluded life; his mind had been carefully trained in moral and religious principles by his indulgent but anxious father; and his attractive exterior and manners subjected to the peculiarities of Friends. Now placed in a more exposed situation, in a large seaport, the natural bias speedily asserted itself. His dress, language, conversation, the tone of his voice assumed so completely the character of a sailor that a stranger would have supposed him born and bred at sea

How carefully and accurately he had studied the building of a ship is proved by a three-masted schooner, about a foot in height, of exquisite workmanship, pronounced by connoisseurs to be perfect in all its parts, which he constructed in his spare hours, and calling it the Anna Mary sent as a present to his first little niece, my daughter. [GW]

Charles became acquainted with seafaring youths, who found out he was the only son of a widow, so they persuaded him it would help his mother financially if he earned his own money by going to sea. He was also encouraged by an ex-soldier who shared lodgings with him who told wonderful stories of his exploits at the bombardment of Copenhagen and at Waterloo, and of the fame and fortune others had gained across the seas. Charles succumbed. He began to believe Mr Roscoe was not satisfied with his work. - he was in fact very satisfied - and in August 1825 Charles suddenly disappeared:

He left his lodgings one First-day morning, attired in his best suit, which awoke no suspicion in the minds of Joseph and Mary Nicholson, until the next day came, and he had not returned. Moreover, the sailor's jacket and trousers, which he wore sometimes when employed about the shipping, and his worsted stockings, were found to be missing. A letter, addressed to his sister Anna, and brought to land by a pilot, informed his distracted relatives that, "but for his mother he should earlier have carried out his resolution to go to sea. He hoped, however, that as she would henceforth be burdened with no expenses on his account, she would allow herself greater comforts. He expected to be out for three months, and would write again from Quebec, where he should be in about four weeks." [GW]

On August 24th Anna wrote to Mary telling her Charles had left her house the previous Sunday very happily, shouting *"farewell, farewell."* Anna, who was six months pregnant had shown her brother the room she had prepared for him once the baby had arrived. The following Sunday he failed to turn up so Daniel visited his lodgings, only to find he had disappeared. The following Wednesday, Anna received Charles's note. It said he was tired of the monotonous life in the office and he did not think Mr Roscoe was satisfied with his work.

Anna took all his belongings and installed them in his room in her house, with a work bench with all his tools in the hope that he would take up residence on his return. But she had a premonition that all was not well when his half-finished model fell off the shelf and broke in half. The family made enquiries and discovered he had 'engaged' himself with a Captain Bell, part owner of the trade ship Lady Gordon. Captain Bell had been detained on land with a broken leg and Captain Clementson had stood in for him. He received Charles along with the other apprentices and sailors who were to work the Lady Gordon on her journey to Quebec. Charles had obtained indentures, but because of the hurry to set sail they did not get signed. The family hoped he would be released from the indenture on his return and Mr Roscoe offered to take him back, giving him a more responsible position. *"Nothing more was to be ascertained, and though the thought was bitter of our idolized son and brother having thus severed himself from us, we believed he had acted from good but mistaken motives, and would ultimately do well where ever placed."* [GWJ

The Lady Gordon sailed down the Mersey but once out to sea she encountered head winds and heavy seas, *"which made her toil on her northern way for seven weeks."* A month after she left Liverpool Charles was ordered aloft for some change of sail. He fell to the deck, breaking his leg badly. There was no surgeon on board so the captain ordered that everything that could be done should be done by the sailors. Mary wrote in hindsight that *"rough, hearty Cumberland men waited on him as, with pale and altered face, his body racked with pain, his mind with regret, self-banished from home and country, he lay studying the Bible as his only resource, and finding in its sacred pages consolation and encouragement."* [GWJ

When they arrived at Quebec Charles was taken to *"the great hospital and convent"* the Hotel Dieu where he was cared for. He had blood poisoning, and at the end of November his leg was amputated. From then on he declined, and was so ill that a Friend who tried to visit

A Victorian engraving of Liverpool.

him was not permitted to do so. Charles died a few days later. The family were unaware of any of this ill fortune so when the shipping intelligence mentioned the Lady Gordon lying off in Quebec in the second week in November they expected to receive the promised letter from him. No letter arrived and they concluded they would have to wait for Charles himself to arrive in Liverpool. Still, neither letter nor Charles arrived, but *"a last sad letter, and the statements of the crew, especially of the ship's carpenter, told the terrible tale."* [GW]

A Quaker sea captain, William Boodle, visited Anna later and told her how when he was in a provision shop in Quebec a French physician came in and after noticing his style of dress and hearing his type of speech, told him a young man, a stranger from England and one of the Society, was lying ill at the hospital. He requested that Captain Boodle pay Charles a visit. This he did, and Charles confided in him the details of his ill-fated adventure. Many complimentary things were said about Charles's courage in the face of great pain, and his faith. Captain Boodle came away *"much affected by the interview"* and hoping to return again. The next thing he learned was that Charles had had his leg amputated and that he was allowed no visitors. The next time Captain Boodle visited, Charles had died. Dr Holmes, the physician, wrote to Ann Botham letting her know that she was in Charles's thoughts at the end.

> *And that mother, bowing her head in submission, felt Divine love had found her poor boy and borne him to the haven of peace, where the wicked cease from troubling and all temptation to sin is at an end. Yet for long weeks and months it seemed to her a terrible dream, from which she must wake to find her bright, buoyant Charles at her side, until she held in her hand an indubitable document, signed by the Earl of Dalhousie, Governor of Canada, certifying that - "Charles Botham, a mariner, aged seventeen years, died on the 3rd November in the Hotel Dieu, and was buried on the 4th of November 1825, in the burial ground of the parish church of the Protestant parish of Quebec."* [GW]

It was Emma who had to console her mother all the time Charles was at sea and both were in close contact with the Harrisons, Ann the ever-anxious mother, Emma feeling guilty because she had not revealed her early fears, and Anna thinking of the brother she had had charge of, the brother she had educated, ever after blaming herself for encouraging his ambitions by sending him the information she had innocently obtained in Hull.

When Mary heard of the death of her brother she had just given birth to a son on 21st February whom she named Charles Botham Howitt (Charles was the name not only of her brother but also of her seafaring uncle, Charles Wood). The child died young, yet another heartache for Mary and William.

After Samuel's Death

Prior to Samuel Botham's death around 1821, he had unwisely gone into partnership with James Blair and William Warner, both solicitors. He did not want this partnership and had intended to decline, but James and William persuaded him to sign. Ann had written a note which was delivered to Samuel at the bank, begging him not to sign the agreement. Unfortunately Samuel, being under pressure, put the note in his pocket without reading it. Afterwards, he told his wife that if he had read the note, there was no way he would have signed. The enterprise entailed connecting lime kilns and a colliery by a tramway at Cheadle (Staffordshire) linking up to a nearby canal. The capital was mainly to be supplied by James Blair and William Warner, and Samuel was to be responsible for the surveying and engineering. This enterprise succeeded no better than the Coleford one, and Samuel lost all the money he had saved (which had been earning good interest) from his ten years' work enclosing the Needwood Forest.

After his death Ann discovered that Samuel's last occupation seemed to have been to secure the house property and land for himself. He had been buying and selling some property through James Blair, in order to buy the Timber Lane Fields. He disliked crowds and auctions so he had asked James to make the purchases on his behalf. However, James had bought the property himself and resold it to Samuel at an inflated price! Once again, Samuel, always trusting others, had relied on James Blair's honesty, and once again he had been deceived. The deception upset him bitterly and the family felt it contributed to his death. Ann found herself very short of money, and her main economy was to move to a smaller house.

Emma considered getting herself some work in order to help her mother. Emma and her mother managed well together until Aunt Dorothy Sylvester and her youngest daughter Mercy visited during 1829 and 1830. Aunt Sylvester's previous visit had been before Emma's birth and Ann and Anna had not seen her since the South Wales visit many years before. Aunt Dolly was well entertained by her sister, and on her departure several months later, Aunt gave a big thank-you party. But Ann was impoverished by her sister and niece's visit, her expenses having increased by £100.

What happened on that visit to alter the relationship between mother and daughter cannot be explained, but Mary was aware that there had been a deterioration and was concerned. Emma had enjoyed her aunt and cousin's visit immensely. She was popular and had many suitors, but she would not take them any of them seriously, and Mary realized her mother was worried about Emma's future. By around 1831 all the Botham property in Uttoxeter had been let and Ann and Emma went to live near Anna in Lancashire. They had a small house or lodging in Preston. Emma was most upset at leaving Uttoxeter.

Market Place, Uttoxeter.

William and Mary's house in Nottingham.

View of Parliament Street in Nottingham showing the junction with Newcastle Street, the site of the Howitt's herbalist and pharmacy shop. These buildings were demolished in 1898.

CHAPTER FIVE
LIFE IN NOTTINGHAM

Death of Byron

Another grief affected the Howitts in 1824, when William's hero Lord Byron died in Greece. Mary described the scenes in Nottingham following his death in the early summer of 1824 when she wrote to her sister Anna:

7th Mo., 18.1824.

> Poor Byron! I was grieved exceedingly at the tidings of his death; but when his remains arrived here, it seemed to make it almost family sorrow. I wept then, for my heart was full of grief to think that fine eccentric genius, that handsome man, the brave asserter of the rights of the Greeks, and the first poet of our time, he whose name will be mentioned with reverence and whose glory will be uneclipsed when our children shall have passed to dust to think that he lay a corpse in an inn in this very town. Oh! Anna, I could not refrain from tears.
>
> Byron's faithful, generous, undeviating friend, Hob-house, who stood by him to the last, his friend through good and evil, - he only, excepting Byron's servants and the undertakers, came down to see the last rites paid. Hobhouse's countenance was pale, and strongly marked by mental suffering.
>
> But to particulars. On Fifth-day afternoon the hearse and mourning coaches came into Nottingham. In the evening the coffin lay in state. The crowd was immense. We went among the rest. I shall never forget it. The room was hung with black, with the escutcheons of the Byron family on the walls; it was lighted by six immense wax-candles, placed round the coffin in the middle of the room. The coffin was covered with crimson velvet, richly ornamented with brass nails; on the top was a plate engraved with the arms and titles of Lord Byron. At the head of the coffin was placed a small chest containing an urn, which enclosed the heart and brains. Four pages stood, two on each side. Visitors were admitted by twelves, and were to walk round only; but we laid our hands on the coffin. It was a moment of enthusiastic feeling to me. It seemed to me impossible that that wonderful man lay actually within that coffin. It was more like a dream than a reality.
>
> The next morning all the friends and admirers of Byron were invited to meet in the market-place, to form a procession to accompany him out of town. Thou must have read in the papers the funeral train that came from London. In addition to this were five gentlemen's carriages, and perhaps thirty riders on horseback, besides Lord Rancliffe's tenantry, who made about thirty more, and headed the procession, and were by far the most respectable; for never, surely, did such a shabby company ride in the train of mountebanks or players. There was not one gentleman who would honour our immortal bard by riding two miles in his funeral train. The equestrians, instead of following two and two, as the paper says they did, most remarkably illustrated riding all sixes and sevens.
>
> William, Charles, Thomas Kott, and that odd Smith (thou rememberest him) went to Hucknall to see the interment. It, like the rest,

Byron

was the most disgraceful scene of confusion that can well be imaged, for from the absence of all persons of influence, or almost of respectability, the rude crowd of country clowns and Nottingham Goths paid no regard to the occasion, and no respect or decency was to be seen. William says it was almost enough to make Byron rise from the dead to see the scene of indecorum, and the poor, miserable place in which he lies, though it is the family burial vault .

Is it not strange that such an unusual silence is maintained by the poets on the subject of his death.

The family life of William and Mary Howitt continued to be edged in tragedy. Another son, born between Charles Botham and Alfred, had survived for only a few hours. Mary wrote to her sister,

Alas Anna, is it not sorrowful to see child after child depart! I dread these times always, looking for sorrow. I wish even that children were like apples one gathers from trees or nuts (I would not mind if the shells were ever so hard to crack) so one could gather one, or a handful as one listed."

Later, she confided in Mrs Oliphant, the one authoress with whom she had a personal friendship. They had met when Margaret Oliphant was a young woman struggling to raise her children while writing to support them and her invalid husband. Mary empathised with her, and with the guilt she felt at the deaths of her infant children, a loss brought about, she felt, by her own mental strain. Mrs Oliphant wrote,

She told me of the many babies she had lost through some defective valve of the heart connected with over much mental work on the part of the mother - a foolish thing I should think, but yet the same thing occurred twice to myself. It alarmed and saddened me terribly, but I like her greatly. Not so her husband, who did not please me at all."

On another occasion Mary remarked of William, *"Men are such idiots."* Presumably Mary felt that William did not understand her feelings.

In 1830 Mary appeared to be suffering from depression and she became superstitious, possibly because of her interest in spiritualism. Particular days and months inspired a dread of misfortune. She sought solace in the company of her sister Anna, whom she visited at Everton at this time. They would have had much to talk about and the delight of seeing her nephews and nieces should have done much to lighten Mary's spirits. However, the visit must have shown Mary that she was moving away from the strict Quaker codes of her upbringing, and that Anna was questioning these as well. It was the accepted Quaker mode of dress, the public identification of a Friend in the community, which appears to have occupied the two sisters' concern. In a letter dated June 14th 1830 Mary wrote about the Society of Friends' attire,

Why, dear Anna, if thou feels the disadvantage and absurdity of Friends' peculiarities, dost thou not abandon them? William has done so, and really I am glad. He is a good Christian, and the change has made no difference in him, except for the better, as regards looks. I am amazed now how I could advocate the ungraceful cut of a Friend's coat; and if we could do the same, we should find ourselves religiously no worse, whatever Friends might think. I never wish to be representative to any meeting, or to hold the office of clerk or sub-clerk. All other privileges of the Society we should enjoy the same. But I am nervous on the subject. I should not like to wear a straw bonnet without ribbons; it looks so Methodistical; and with ribbons, again say, I should be nervous. Besides, notwithstanding all his own changes, William likes a Friend's bonnet. In all other particulars of dress, mine is just in make the same as everybody else's. Anna Mary I shall never bring up in the payment of the tithe of mint and cummin [sic]; and I fancy Friends are some-what scandalised at the unorthodox appearance of the little maiden. As to language, I could easily adopt that of our countrymen, but think with a Friend's bonnet it does not accord; and I like consistency. I quite look for the interference of some of our exact brothers or sisters on account of my writings, at least if they read the annuals next year, for I have a set of the most un-Friendly ballads in them. What does Daniel say about these things? I hope he does not grow rigid as he grows older........

The letter reveals Mary's wavering adherence to the Quaker way of life, fired by William's adoption of more liberal views. She was caught between the wishes of her husband and the undeniably strong influence of her upbringing, dominated as it had been by her father. William's influence eventually prevailed. The letter to Anna is the last time Mary writes about the dress issue, except when later in life she was to discuss her childhood in her literary works.

William was in fact a tremendous influence on Mary throughout his life, and not only in matters of dress. He encouraged her to write as a means of working through the depression which followed the deaths of her infants. Both of them were building a reputation and making contacts in the literary world.

Slavery

The 1820s and early 1830s was a time of reform in England, fueled by the economic depression which followed the Napoleonic Wars. The rapid growth of towns during the Industrial Revolution and the growing desire for democracy and the fair representation of the people (the ideals behind the American War of Independence and the French Revolution) added to the political instability of the time. The concept that "all men are created equal but are everywhere in chains", propounded by the French philosopher Descartes, inspired a critical assessment of the unchanging state throughout the civilized world, and highlighted the need to reform the 'status quo' or else suffer the consequences of a popular revolution which, as in France, would destroy the established system.

These ideas would naturally appeal to people like Mary and William Howitt, brought up according to Quaker ideals. It is therefore not surprising that they should campaign for the reforming issues of the day, including anti-slavery. Mary would have heard detailed accounts from her family since her grandmother Jemima Wood's first husband, Capt. Lyndon, was captain of a slave ship which took slaves across the Atlantic. Jemima and the Lyndon side of the family had lived in Jamaica, and could see nothing wrong with the system of slavery.

Mary and William discussed anti-slavery in correspondence with other Quaker friends and placed articles wherever they could in their effort to get their views across. They were in contact with Henry Ward Beecher (1813-1887), an American preacher who spoke out against slavery and for women's suffrage, amongst other causes. In 1850 Harriet Beecher Stowe's book *Uncle Tom's Cabin* was published and took the world by storm.

William Wilberforce (1759-1833), Mary's aunt's suitor, had entered Parliament in 1780 as MP for Hull and he kept the anti-slavery campaign active. In 1826, whilst still in Nottingham, William and Mary wrote letters on the subject. It is interesting that at this time they are still using the Quaker type of speech; the letters are dated by the numerical month, the letters using "thou", "thine", and "mayest" amongst other quaint wordings. The letters are held at the John Rylands Library, Manchester (Eng M.S. 414/22 & 25).

Nottingham 4th mo.4th 1826:

Esteemed Friend,

We had heard of thy proposed volume thro' our friend J.H. Wiffin and been invited to advocate the noble cause of Negro emancipation before I had the pleasure of receiving thy letter. Both William and myself have been very happy to furnish something tho' perhaps but little, towards thy excellent undertaking and can assure thee that [although] thou mayest have abler thou hast no warmer advocates nor sincere friends towards the redemption of the oppressed African from a bondage which disgraces the nineteenth century.

We are obliged by the explanation of the two Sheffield works for their subject, we had seen I. Roberts advertisement in the Iris and had supposed it to be the same with mine.

We were much pleased to see so respectable a number of contributions as those been mentioned and sincerely hope so much talent will not write without producing a strong impression in favour of Negro freedom.

The Traveller on the Hill-top

The piece entitled the English Peasant is what William has written purposely for thy volume the other on West Indian Harry is one which Dr Davidson wished him to send. It appeared two or three years ago in several papers; he has however made some alterations and additions to render it more fit to appear before the public in an elegant volume and in company of high names and excellent contributions.

Wishing thee an entire fulfilment of all thy hopes and expectations

I am very truly Thy friend
Mary Howitt

The following day William wrote,

Respected Friend,

Herewith are enclosed our contributions to the "Negro's Album" or, whatever the work is to be entitled, which after perusal, we shall thank thee to seal up and forward to M.A. Read. Besides the short piece which I have written purposely, I have also made some alteration and addition to the one originally requested, which, after all, I leave to the judgement of the fair editor.

I remain, very respectfully thine etc   *Wm. Howitt*
Timberhill
5th mo. 4th 1826

At the end of a letter to Mrs Rawson, one of Mary's friends, dated June 14, 1833, Mary writes in terrible handwriting the following regarding slavery:

An English gentleman in Kingstone craved
The price of a young tawny of fifteen,
Who stands for sale among a crowd of Slaves,
A sight, thank God, these eyes have never seen!
The sum is named, but the shrewd buyer waves
Awhile the bargain, and with careless mein
Says "had the lad been but a right jet black, he
Would suit my taste much better as a lacky!"

"A black!" retorts the seller "if you knew
What blacks are, you would take a wiser tone.
Why sir, for [?] and spirit, nay for hue
He's a cut diamond to a Negro drone
And hark-ee - look at me sir - and then view
What he will make - for the young dog's my own!"
"Your own! - your son! - and sell him? God on high!
That I should go on Devil's treatment to bring!"

After Mary's sister Emma emigrated to Ohio, a state in America where liberated and escaped slaves tended to settle, Mary had additional reason to work for the anti-slavery movement. The ex-slaves told Emma stories which she repeated in her letters to Mary. But Mary had Quaker relatives and friends in America even before Emma and her family emigrated. Anna's daughter Agnes went there between 1860 and 1868 to visit her married sister, Mrs Ellis Yarnell, and sent weekly letters to her mother. All of these contacts supplied Mary with information regarding life and politics in America, including the uneasy relationship with Britain during the Civil War.

Round about the time of her visit to her sister Anna, Mary was stirred out of her lethargy by the unexpected visit, to her home in Nottingham, of the wife and sister of the poet William Wordsworth. This must have renewed memories of the Howitts' pleasant Lake District sojourn a few years earlier. Dora Wordsworth, in a letter to her friend Miss Boules (who was later to marry the poet Robert Southey), dated July 1831, gives some insight into the life and works of the Howitts at this time.

William Howitt, according to Mrs Wordsworth, *"had reform fever and forward put the cloven foot of Quakerism."* William had found Dora to be a good listener and when they were alone together he would put forth his reform ideas. The disestablishment of the Church of England was a major issue at the forthcoming election. William advocated its downfall and stated that the clergy of the Establishment must be either fools or hypocrites. He criticized absentee vicars who lived away from their parishes, taking the stipend without doing any work and paying poor salaries to the curates they employed to carry out duties on their behalf. Other vicars, often younger sons of landed gentry, did live in their parishes but were more interested in country sports than in their work; some wore their hunting habits under their cassocks whilst others did not even turn up to take the services. His comments, whilst no doubt genuinely felt, reveal William's tactless and abrasive personality - Dora Wordsworth was both niece and sister to Anglican clergymen. Mrs Wordsworth remarks in her letter that she liked Mary, *"but could have liked William better if it were not for his religious evangelism."* Despite these comments the Wordsworths and the Howitts remained friends and visited each other at intervals. It was during this visit that William's brother, Dr Godfrey Howitt, saved the life of Mrs Wordsworth. She had been taken seriously ill whilst in Nottingham, and this incident may well have cemented the friendship.

William's best friend at this time was Benjamin Boothby, a lawyer, a political reformer, and another disestablishmentarian. The friendship began when baby Maria, who was later to marry into the Howitt family, was gravely ill and William's advice helped her recovery. In 1853 he went to Australia as Governor of the Supreme Court.

Nottingham Riots

William Howitt's reform fever often made him unpopular. He wrote articles to put his ideas forward and published them wherever he could. In 1831 the most immediate political issue was the movement to extend the electoral franchise in order to rid the country of "Rotten Boroughs' and give full representation to the emerging manufacturing towns of Lancashire, Yorkshire and the West Midlands, which provided the wealth but had no Parliamentary voice.

The Howitts, who believed in the sanctity of private property and hated violence, were residing in Nottingham when they witnessed and recorded the riots and local agitations which preceded the passage of the 1832 Reform Bill. For a few years the 'lowest class' had become 'a perfect nuisance to society'. There was a general rejection of authority and Nottingham had become a dangerous place. Continental trade disturbances with French and Dutch markets meant many people who were on Parish Relief were working sixteen to seventeen hours a day for 6d. Three days after the Reform Bill of October 7th, 1831 was rejected by the House of Lords, the people rioted. Nottingham Castle was burned, watched by mobs who later scaled the walls and danced amongst the flames and within the castle rooms. The large crowd which filled the Market Square moved en masse towards the Castle shrieking and yelling. The Howitts witnessed the burning of the castle and could see the silhouetted shapes of the drunken rioters inside. Some found themselves cut off in the upper rooms when the staircase collapsed and many perished. William's account of this event is considered the best first-hand report there is of the burning of the Castle. He described the scene as seen from the roof of their house, which was flat and leaded, thus:

First in the dusk of the evening, the vast market place of six acres filled with one dense throng of people, their black heads looking like a sea of ink, for the whole living mass was swaying and heaving in the commotion of fury seeking a vent. Suddenly there was a cry of "To the castle! to the castle!" to which a fierce roar of applause was the ominous echo, and at once this heaving, raging ocean of agitated life became an impetuous, headlong torrent, struggling away towards Friar Lane, leading directly to the castle.

Anon arose a din of deafening yells and hurrahs from the wide castle-court. The mob had scaled the walls. They surrounded the vast building as a stormy tide surges tumultuously round an ocean rock. Anon and a red light gleamed through the different rooms in view, followed by the hoarse roar of the whole place with a deep fiery glow, mingled with clouds of smoke that burst from the windows and streamed roofwards, tipped with tongues of flame, hungry for the destruction of the whole fabric. Through all this, even when fire seemed raging through the whole building, there were seen figures as of black demons dancing, as it were, in the very midst of the flames in the upper rooms whilst cries as dread and demoniac were yelled forth from below. In fact, numbers of these incendiaries, made drunk with their success, were still dancing in the rooms in delight over their revel of destruction. When all access by the staircase was cut off, and only when driven by the aggressive flames, did they issue from the windows and descend by the projection of the stonework, which, luckily for them, was of that style in which every stone stands prominent, leaving a sunken band between it and its fellow.

Soon the riotous, voracious flames burst through the roof, sending down torrents of melted lead, and to heaven legions of glittering sparks and smoke as from a volcano. The scene was magnificent, though saddened by regret for the destruction of a building which though not antiquely picturesque like its predecessors, was invested with many historical memories, and by its size, symmetry, and its position on the bold and lofty rock, formed a fine feature in the landscape. It was a steadily rainy night, yet the wet seemed to possess no power over the raging mass of fire. Frequently parts of the roof or beams within fell with a louder thunder, and sent up fresh volumes of smoke, dust, and coruscating sparks. The rioters had torn down the wainscotings of cedar, piled them up in the different rooms and fired them, and the whole air was consequently filled with a peculiar aroma from the old cedar thus burning. In the morning the great fabric stood a skeleton of hollow doorways and windows, blackened walls, and heaps of still smouldering and smoking materials within. [autobiography]

William and Mary enjoyed political discussion from the time they first met and it should come as no surprise that they used their literary skills to try to change people's attitudes.

In the spring of 1833 Emma married, much to her mother Ann's relief. Harrison Alderson, a few years her senior, was a cousin of Daniel Harrison. She had met him after her move to Preston a year or two earlier. The Harrisons and the Aldersons were ancient yeoman farming families in Dentdale, North Yorkshire, both early converts of George Fox. Harrison took his faith seriously and had a subduing effect on his rebellious wife, not that Emma minded in any way - surprisingly, she was the only one of the Botham sisters to die a Quaker. He and William Howitt did not see their faith in the same light; while William wanted to question and argue about matters of doctrine, to Harrison it was strictly laid down by George Fox. He had a good ear for music and like his father-in-law, Samuel Botham, he suppressed this urge. He had been complimented on his playing but worried that such praise would feed his vanity, so he went into a field one day, played all the tunes he knew, and threw away his pipes. This musical gift was to be handed down through the generations.

Emma's education, or lack of it, also caused Mary much concern. She had been Emma's teacher and knew what her education lacked, yet she thought writing might be a good career for her. Though Emma did not take up writing as a career, she kept a journal like her sisters. She also helped Mary by writing about her life after she emigrated to America in a way that Mary could use for her own works.

Mary was pregnant again and unable to attend her sister's wedding. In the late autumn of 1833 Claude Middleton Howitt was born in Nottingham.

Early Writings

The Howitts were soon to make a name for themselves, and this is demonstrated in *Blackwood's Magazine*'s of April 1831 with a narrative between two people, Christopher North and Ettrick Shepherd, a representation of the real poet James Hogg:

> *Shepherd: Is Nottingham far intil England, sir? For I would really like to ay the Hooitts a visit this simmer. Thae Quakers are, what ane micht scarcely opine frae first principles, a maist poetical Christian seek, ... and feenally, the Hooitts, the three Hooitts, - na, there may be mair o' them for aught I ken, but i'se answer for William and Mary, husband and wife, and oh! but they're weel met; and eke for Richard, (can he be their brither?) and wha's this was telling me about anither brither o' Wullie's, a Dr. Godfrey Hooitt, ane o' the best botanist in a' England, and a desperae beetle-hunter?*
>
> *North: Entomologist, James, A man of science.*
>
> *Shepherd: The twa married Hooitts I love just excessively, sir. What they write canna fail o' being' poetry, even the maist middling o't, for it's aye with' them the ebullition o' their ain feeling, and their ain fancy, and when ever the's the case, a bonny word or twa will drap itself intil ilka stazy, and a sweet stanzy or twa intil ilka pome, and sae they touch and sae they sune win a body's heart; and frae readin their byuckies personal characters are revealed in their volumms, and methingks I see Wully and Mary-*

One of William and Mary's joint efforts was a small book entitled *The Forest Minstrel, a book of poems*. The preface shows their attitude to their faith: *"latitude of phrase and of sentiment which as members of the Society of Friends we have allowed ourselves."*

Whilst in Nottingham William wrote his *History of Priest Craft* which gives an indication of the interest in Roman Catholicism in the country at the time. Roman Catholics were not liked and there were still anti-popery feelings. *A Popular History of Priestcraft in All Ages & Nations*, which he published in 1833, criticizes the clergy as in part being overpaid and inactive, and in part ill-paid and over-worked, working on a paltry pittance for lazy and absent clergy. Some were lukewarm in their duties and cold in their relationship to their parishioners, yet adhered to the most absurd and impolitic institutions or rites and dogmas.

The next article William wrote on the subject was published under a nom-de-plume, possibly to prevent him receiving the criticism he must have received with his *History of Priest Craft*. Like his wife, however, he wrote about topical issues and in general his temper and position, as the extremest of Dissenters, freed him from the need to achieve respectability. In 1833, his beliefs were still based on the ideas with which he had been brought up, namely the Inner Light and the undesirability of unnecessary religious ceremony. William and Mary were still using the simple manners and the antiquated form of speech. They disliked flattery and oaths (because they believed everyone should be as good as their word), titles given to men (since all people were equal), and even believed in the equality of the sexes as there was no sex in souls and everyone was one in Christ Jesus (this at a time when a woman was her husband's chattel). They believed in civil and religious freedom. It is not surprising that they should continue their articles about slavery or write against oath-taking, against the subjugation of women, against war, poor rates, tithes, and religious establishments. Indeed, in the year 1824/5 William received a summons for non-payment of the church rates which he had refused to pay on principle. He presumably paid later as he was not imprisoned.

It was during their time in Nottingham that Mary wrote one of her novels for adults, *A Year in the Country, or The Chronicle of Wood Leighton*, originally as three books - a fashion of the times. First published as a single volume in 1836, it is still only a small book. Wood Leighton is Uttoxeter, as Mary says in the preface of the revised three-volume edition in January 1835:

From the foregoing statement I hope it will be clearly understood that though I have a pleasure and pride in acknowledging that the description of Wood Leighton and the country about is in its main features the description of a real town and neighbourhood, which will be easily recognised by the inhabitants, those inhabitants are not to look for any living portraiture of themselves among the characters, which was totally beside my intentions.

The book does, however, contain the name of Daniel Neale, whom she mentions in her autobiography as a real person, and Uncle Nabob is based on one of her mother's uncles. A nabob was an eighteenth and nineteenth century name for a man who had made his fortune in India; a woman would have been known as nabobess. In *The Chronicle of Wood Leighton* Mary describes the town - Uttoxeter;

Of Wood Leighton itself I shall say nothing more, than that it consists of three or four considerable streets of low, old fashioned houses; some of antiquated wood-framing, the intervals filled up with regular and uniform brickwork; others, of building of various materials, positions and dates; and others, of lath and plaster, neatly whitewashed, or greenish with age, and marked and dotted in manifold figures of men, women, and four-footed creatures, or with quaint arabesque patterns, according to the taste of some artist whose head, as an old sibyl of Wood Leighton expressed it, does not ache now. Here and there the regularity of the street is broken by a garden with its old hedge, well barricaded at the bottom with dead sticks and tub-staves, to exclude all the variety of small depredators; here and there, by a wall of old brickwork, entered by a door, and over which hang the dark, thick branches of venerable yews, beyond which may be seen the tall, solid chimneys, or gabled front of some ancient and more important house, the abode of one of the magnates of the place; and beside it, perhaps, stands a crazy wooden barn, or an isolated cottage, at the door of which sits an old man looking with an air of apathy on all that passes; or some little shop, in whose lofty and small bow-window may be seen divers of the multifarious wares in which, as it set forth over the door, Dorothy Smith is a licensed dealer; - or by an old public-house, The Cross Keys, or the Travellers' Rest, furnished with its wooden horse-block, on the steps of which may be seen two or three idle townsmen smoking their long pipes, and listening to the knot they always assemble round them who, with folded arms, talk over the affairs of the town or of the nation, and are thence called such-a-one's parliament.

At the pump, which is found in every street, and is in one or two instances an extremely picturesque little edifice of old stone or yet more ancient looking wood, may be found a similar group of female gossips; some old and grotesque, both in figure and costume, standing with arms a-kimbo beside their brown nondescript vessels; and others, young, strong, and graceful, standing firmly yet lightly, balancing with one hand the pitcher on their heads, and with the other perhaps holding by the hand a rosy, impatient child; frequently forming groups of great interest and beauty.

These streets all meet in a shapeless sort of market-place, where may be found the smarter shops, and here and there a more modern red brick edifice, square and formal, with a door in the centre, four sash windows, with outside shutters painted yellow oak colour, making a most unpleasant contrast to their ancient and respectable neighbours, the houses of lath and plaster. The ornament and grace of the market-place is its ancient cross and well, both once united; the cross worn away and crumbling with time, but yet upon which may still be discovered traces of the rich carved work that once adorned it; its steps, too, worn to the very base with the feet of many generations, but its bountiful well, pure and clear, and fresh as ever, pouring out in the dryest summers its free sparkling waters, like a never-stinted blessing. I love these old holy wells and crosses; though they may belong to an age of ignorance and superstition, it was a truly Christian act to place them by the wayside, and in the market-place, for the use and blessing of all ....

Uttoxeter did once have a market cross which, according to the local antiquarian Francis Redfern, disappeared around the end of the eighteenth century, the time of Mary's birth and childhood. Unfortunately, the 19th century gentleman James Britten, in his long obituary to Mary, said, *"Wood Leighton's scene was laid in the neighbourhood of Nottingham, the unprejudiced treatment of Catholic matters, and the sympathetic sketch of the 'poor but pious'*

An artist's impression of the 18th century Market Cross, Uttoxeter.

Father Cradock, must have been noticed at a time when the new Oxford school was directing attention towards Rome." To people who know the market town of Uttoxeter, there can be no doubt that this is the location of the book. The description of Wood Leighton, both from within the town itself and when viewed from a height on a road going out from it, is as Uttoxeter, although enlarged, looks today. Descriptions of a walk to Bramshall wood along a road known as Stone Road are as it was within living memory. Mary continues with a passage relating to the Uttoxeter Parish Church:

There is an extremely beautiful effigy of alabaster, singularly perfect from having been walled in, and only discovered of late years, of an abbess who, as the tradition says, travelled on foot, perhaps in penance, attended by a lay sister. Night came on as they were approaching Wood Leighton and they lost their way, for many hours wandering about in a wood below the town - a marshy, desolate wood in those days - and had given themselves up for lost, when they heard the cheering sound of a curfew-bell; their spirits revived, and the sound directed them which way to advance. They reached Wood Leighton, and the abbess, a delicate, feeble woman, took to her bed and died on the third day, leaving a sum of money to be paid yearly to the ringer of the curfew-bell; and to this day the bell is tolled an unusual length of time.

The effigy is wonderfully beautiful; and if the abbess in figure was but half as graceful as she is here represented, she must indeed have been a splendid woman, and the habit of her order admirably suited to set off the symmetry of her figure. Nothing can be more graceful than the contour of her bust."

This circumstance is authenticated by the town records - singular but most interesting documents, preserved from the year 1252, when Wood Leighton was made a borough town:

1417 November: The abbess came. Paid for doctor and attendants, seven shillings and fourpence. The abbess gave the rent of the Spicer's Field which she had purchased, for the nightly ringing of the curfew-bell, by the space of one quarter of an hour; after the hour of eight at night.
Paid to him that fetched the notary, threepence.
Paid to the three women that laid out the body, sixpence.
Paid for making the vault, and the cost of burial, five pounds ten shillings and threepence.
Paid to the man who rode with the sister Maud to Derby, one shilling.
1419: Paid to the mason and his men who put up the monument and stone figure, seventeen shillings and fivepence.

Mary has taken selected entries from Uttoxeter Overseers accounts and used them in her story of Wood Leighton. This legend about the abbess is also recorded in Francis Redfern's *History and Antiquities of Uttoxeter*, although he may have taken the incident from Mary's book as he used her works extensively when writing his History of Uttoxeter.

About the same time Mary wrote a book for children called *Mary Howitt's 'Illustrated Library for the Young'*, which has different chapters on Shells, the Chinese, Pets, Cats and Parrots and lastly one on Bears. All of the chapters are illustrated in colour and with lithographs. It was designed to be educational, although the information she presents would no longer be accepted. The writing style is also very different from today's children's books.

In December 1835 William found he had been elected by the Council as an alderman of the Borough of Nottingham - against his wishes. Today a person who had previously been banned from taking public office because of his beliefs (religious or political) would jump at the opportunity to put his ideas into practice and to discuss them openly. William evidently chose not to and it was because of his election as an officer on the Town Council, for which he had no time, that the Bothams left Nottingham and went to Surrey. He was aware that in the capacity of a councillor he would have been able to influence social conditions in the city, but he felt he had not got the time to carry out these duties and at the same time make his living as a writer.

Uttoxeter Market Place and High Street.

CHAPTER SIX
WIDENING THE EXPERIENCES OF LIFE

Esher

In 1837 Mary and William went on a three-month tour of the North, during which they stayed with William and Dorothy Wordsworth. The Howitts and the Wordsworths had many things in common. All were lovers of nature, all four were poets and Dorothy was a diarist (Although there is no known diary belonging to Mary, she must have kept one to be able to assemble her autobiography). This visit to the Wordsworth family was the foundation of a long friendship. William and Mary went on to visit Edinburgh, the Western Isles, Staffa, Iona, Culloden and Kilmorack, all of which were to be used in William's *Visits to Remarkable Places,* which were very descriptive books, full of insight. They still offer, today, very good accounts of the places and people at the time the Howitts visited them, and invaluable to local historians. Many of the novels that Mary and William wrote were set in places they had visited, and in such books it is possible to recognize the area in the story.

When they had finished travelling, Mary and William moved to Esher. They took over the lease of a house which had an orchard, a well-stocked and productive garden and a paddock. They kept a cow, a pig, poultry and a pony for their chaise. There was a river nearby on which they could boat and they had seven miles of fishing rights. This was more like the surroundings in which they had both grown up and a welcome change from Nottingham Market Place. They had moved south to be near London, where most of the literary circle of the time lived. Esher was in the country, which they liked, and it was cheaper than living in the capital. West End Cottage was on the Portsmouth road opposite where the Duchess of Kent and her daughter, Princess Victoria, (later Queen Victoria) lived. There were other writers living in the area with whom they had previously only been able to correspond, and who might help them in their writing careers.

From 'The Drawing Room Scrapbook' 1832 edited by L.E.L, and by Mary after 1838. See page 51.

In Esher Mary found the Friends old-fashioned, even worse than those in the Midlands and in the North. They had no newspapers or books, no bible, and they would have nothing to do with politics. Their clothes were *"plain beyond reason"*, and the Friends who visited the Howitts, after they had presented their certificate from the Nottingham Meeting, were very cold and unfriendly. Nottingham was one of the first areas to accept open-mindedness.

Financial Problems

The 1830s were lean times for the Howitts. William was trying to publish a large book called *Visits to Remarkable Places*, and until that work was finished and published there was no money. Anna Mary had to leave school and the cow, pony and pigs were all sold. Life in

WIDENING THE EXPERIENCES OF LIFE
Victorian engravings of Windermere in the Lake District, of Fingals Cave, Staffa, in the Western Isles and a Rheinland town near Heidelberg.

England and particularly in Esher was too expensive. Mary's brother-in-law, Daniel, sent money, clothes and toys for the children when he learned of their plight from the numerous letters Mary wrote to his wife, Anna. Other gifts were to follow, and the only thing Mary could send in return would be books - once they were published. The handsomely leather-bound books, freely ornamented with gold, were expensive: *Colonisation and Christianity* cost 10/6d and *The Boy's Country Book* cost 8/-.

In 1836 William wrote to Mr Bakewell to advise him about getting Mrs. Bakewell's work published. He describes at length the pitfalls of publication and bemoans the fact that for one of his early works, *The Seasons,* he was paid £100 whereas others got £500. Because there was no copyright laws and other people republished his books through different publishers (our current copyright law dates back only to the Berne International Copyright Convention of 1886), William lost a lot of money. Also, on many occasions it would appear that the Howitts, whose Quaker upbringing taught them to trust people, were let down by those people to whom they turned for help and advice with regard to their writings.

There is a letter in Nottinghamshire Archives Department which relates to the cost of postage. It was not until 1840 that a postage stamp system was introduced by Sir Rowland Hill; until that date the recipient paid the postage. The equivalent of the 1d. postage of 1840 would today be 80p. Mary had been travelling around the country and at the time of her letter was staying in South Wales. Her publisher had returned a manuscript to her but instead of posting it to her current address, as she had requested, he had sent it to the place she had been staying at previously. It had then had to be sent on and Mary had had to pay the postage for both journeys. It is obvious this was not the first time she had had to pay more than one lot of postage on a manuscript which was costly to post, and she complains that she is losing money because of all the postage she is having to pay.

William had an economic plan which was to serve most of their lives. They would submit prose, tales and verse for journals, such as the *Edinburgh Journal* and *Monthly Repository*. Mary wrote the ballads and William wrote the descriptive and controversial political verse. They were to publish topographical, biographical, and 'nature' notes on incredible places. For the rest of William's life he was to write regularly for a couple of newspapers, and he also reviewed books. He and Mary arranged their writings in such a way that books and articles could be recycled. Mary would publish a poem in a magazine, and then include it in a small volume which included a few previously unpublished verses.

William often spent a whole day collecting material for his work, walking or travelling by train. He estimated twelve to sixteen hours of travel were required before he worked in his study. Mary stayed at home where she could oversee the growing family and the running of the home while she continued to earn royalties, and she continued with her writing on the dining room table. She envied other women who had their own studies, as William had (and she would have her own study in future houses).

Gentleman's Magazine of May 1838, quoting from *Bird & Flowers and other Country Things*, describes the *"good sense, correct taste and elegant fancy"* of *"this most favourite poetess of the age"*. The reviewers for *Gentleman's Magazine* were under the impression that Mary was William's helpless sister and called her *"a poor little warbling linnet amid a pack of ravens and butcher birds"*. After the reviewers discovered that *"she had assumed the name Howitt voluntarily"* they wrote, *"Mary Howitt in mercy send us no more of your books."* [VS] This appears an odd reaction to Mary's writings, but William continued to upset people with his political activities and he upset his wife's reviewers at the same time. He was very positive in everything he said and did, so that others often found him an obstinate and difficult man.

Between 1836 and 1840 Mary and William were writing for Taits and Chambers' *Edinburgh Journal*. In April 1836 Lady Byron had William's article outlining the fundamentals of Christianity from *Appeal to Society of Friends* reprinted at her own expense.

At this time Mary borrowed her second £25 from Anna. These would appear not to be the only sums of money she received from her sister, for in another letter she declines the offer of money, saying she had already had too much money from her.

Joseph Hume, a Liberal MP, established a daily paper called *The Constitutional,* to advocate reforms. He wanted an article or two each week from the Howitts; as the paper was published daily, the articles had to be despatched by 10pm. Major Carmichael-Smyth, the manager of the paper, had a nephew who was working in Paris as a newspaper correspondent. He sent for him to take over the editorship of *The Constitutional* and one day in 1838 or 1839, as William Howitt was going into the Fleet Street office, he met a thin young man in a long dark blue cloak, whose nose seemed to have had a blow that had flattened the bridge. He turned out to be William Makepeace Thackeray, the Major's nephew.

Unfortunately the paper was already in crisis and William talked to Thackeray, wondering how he was going to take over and run a daily paper without any funds and already in debt. Thackeray had no more idea than William, who felt very sorry for the young man, who had left a well-paid post at his uncle's request. William thought little of Major Carmichael-Smyth in the circumstances. For her part, Mary never liked Joseph Hume and called him evil. When the paper went bankrupt, William was left to pay unhonoured bills out of the money he had received from *Rural Life,* which took most of his profit.

Mary and William also knew John Ruskin, who through a cruel letter to their daughter Annie finished her artistic career.

Mary's book *The Birds and Flowers* was published in 1838 for a Christmas Library, and in 1839 she followed it with *Hymns and Fireside Verses*. At least one of Queen Victoria's ministers, George Henry Byng, received a copy from the Queen herself.

A Christmas Carol

Awake arise good Christians
Let nothing you dismay:
Remember Christ our Saviour
Was born upon this day.

The self same moon was shining
That now is in the sky
When a holy band of angels
Came down from God on high.

Came down on clouds of glory,
Arrayed in shining light,
Unto the shepherd - people,
Who watched their flocks by night.

And through the midnight silence
The heavenly host began
"Glory to God the highest,
On earth goodwill to man!"

"Fear not, we bring good tidings
For, on this happy morn,
The promised one, the Saviour
In Bethlehem was born!"

Up rise the joyful shepherds
From the ground whereon they lay,
As ye should rise, good Christians,
To hail this blessed clay.

Up rose the simple shepherds,
All with a joyful mind,
"And let us go with speed!" said they
"This holy child to find!"

Not to a kingly palace
The son of God they found
But a lowly manger
Where oxen fed around.

The glorious King of Heaven;
The Lord of all the earth,
In mercy condescended
To be of humble birth.

There worshipped him the wise men,
As prophets had foretold
And laid their gifts before Him,
Frankincense, myrrh and gold.

Long looked the simple shepherds,
We wander far and near,
And bid ye wake, good Christians,
The joyful news to hear.

Awake, arise, good Christians,
Let nothing you dismay,
Remember Christ the Saviour
Was born upon this day!

The verses must sound familiar to the reader. The first and last verses are a modified version of *God Rest Ye Merry, Gentlemen*, and also other familiar phrases from other carols appear within these verses. It is difficult to decide what makes a hymn survive. None of Mary's hymns seem to have survived to be printed in modern Hymnaries. When one thinks of a hymn or a song, it is often the music that brings the words to mind, and maybe Mary's hymns were not accompanied by catchy tunes or by any tunes at all. William and Mary's knowledge of music would have been rudimentary at this stage of life, even if Mary's knowledge of it improved later on, because of the Quakers' attitude to it during their childhood.

During 1839 finances improved for the Howitts. Mary met the Cheapside publisher, Mr Tegg, who was a wealthy, self-made Scotsman and who had ideas about educating the masses, an idea with which the Howitts had sympathy. He had read Mary's short story for an Annual, *A Night Scene in a Poor Man's House*, and asked her to write a series of short stories to illustrate what he called '*household virtues*'. He wanted '*a baker's dozen*', thirteen stories for which she was to be paid £1,000. Mary thought it would take her nearly two years to produce the thirteen books. Mr Tegg annoyed her considerably, and he created difficulties, but Mary found him an honourable man.

1839 also saw the culmination of many plans and discussions. There had been growing unrest in the country due to the increasing population, the overcrowding and the lack of work. Many professional people felt they could give their children a better life by emigrating to the 'new' countries. William's brothers Richard and Dr Godfrey Howitt, with his wife and children and two brothers-in-law, were emigrating to Australia. They were due to sail during the summer but there were delays. Mary tells how 'The Lord Godrich' could not leave as scheduled because the sailors refused to sail on a Friday. Then the wind changed so that the ship spent ten days tacking between London and the Downs. Adverse winds continued after they had entered the Channel, causing a slight collision with another emigrant ship and they had to dock in Portsmouth for repairs. The ship was found to be unseaworthy and to have insufficient crew and provisions. The ship was well insured and the owners were not bothered whether or not it sank! Some of the family travelled to Portsmouth to say their good-byes once again. The ship was revictualled and the voyage recommenced in October when there were still fierce storms and they narrowly escaped another collision. When all was calm, the sailors had an explanation for their misfortunes; a passenger had thrown a black kitten overboard; if the sailors had known who it was, there would have been trouble.

Heidelberg

In June 1840, William and Mary, with their children Annie, Alfred, Claude, Charlton and Meggie, together with two servants, books and household belongings, left London to sail to Rotterdam. From there they went to Mannheim and then by coach to the university town of Heidelberg, where they remained for two years.

The Howitts were attracted to the idea of living in Germany because they thought they could see several advantages in education there. They were also under the impression that the cost of living was lower than in England, having been told they could live well on £200 a year. Mary was trying to live on £400 a year and found that her expenses were higher than that. They later discovered that the Rhineland, particularly the university town of Heidelberg, where they had gone, was one of the most expensive areas in Germany but because wages were lower than they were in England servants cost less, and schooling was cheap.

When they arrived they looked around for a place to rent and found the first floor of a house. They found life was simpler and the habits of the people less formal than in England. Here the family could appreciate nature, music and social enjoyment, which suited seventeen year-old Annie (Anna Mary). She was allowed to go to impromptu dances where there was waltzing, which was not allowed by the English Quakers.

Heidelberg was in the habit of having town parties. The second year there, Mary decided to contribute to the activities, which consisted of Christmas trees, decorations, parties and dancing. Mary and an attendant squire led the train of seven sleighs; she had four horses to pull hers and her out-riders were dressed in blue. Afterwards they went galloping through the town cracking whips. Mary says her party was pronounced the best of the year but she also exclaimed at the cost! This was the year that a German tradition was introduced in Manchester - a German family decorated their house with a Christmas tree. Queen Victoria was impressed with the idea and did likewise. Mary enjoyed this custom while in Heidelberg, particularly as she was so fond of the trees which grew in Needwood Forest.

Translating

The period in Heidelberg in many ways was a period of enlightenment and development for both Mary and William. They made many friends, amongst whom was a Swedish lady named Frederika Bremer. Mary learnt Swedish from her which she found easier to learn than German. The knowledge of Swedish made it comparatively easy for her to learn Danish, which meant she was then able to translate from that language as well as from Swedish and German. She translated *Sojourn in the East* by Miss Bremer following her visit to America.

Frederika had strong religious and social views, particularly regarding the *"dark and narrow sphere allotted to woman in that country"* [GW]. She had two sisters whom she felt she wanted to liberate. She wrote about Swedish family life and after her travels, which included Switzerland, Greece, and Palestine, she used her knowledge of these subjects for fiction as well.

Miss Eliza Acton, who wrote books on cookery and household management and from whose works Mrs Beaton drew extensively when writing her famous book, was to become a lifelong friend of Mary's. Eliza had read of some Swedish dishes in Frederika's books *The Home* and *The Neighbours* and wanted to know how to make the *"far-famed citron-souffle"* for the second edition of her *Modern Cookery*. She was well aware that in many of the 'lower classes' of English society, mainly in the industrial towns, people were completely incapable of cooking a potato properly and unable to make bread, their staple diet.

The Howitts were so taken with the *"originality, freshness, and delicate humour"* of Danish works that they were determined to translate them into English and they did, publishing the books themselves and accepting all the financial risks.

> *The Danish literature we found richer than the Swedish, both in quantity and variety. The pristine lore of Iceland and Norway was especially collected and translated into Danish. We were enchanted with the fable or saga literature and found again almost all our ancient nursery tales: the little old woman whose petticoats were cut shorter, Jack the Giant-killer, the pig that would not go over the brig, and the rest.* [GV]

William was translating German literature into English, for example Gustav Shab's poems *Student Life*. Johan Ludwig Uhland, a folk poet, was also known to the Howitts. Mary translated all the Icelandic sagas and Hans Christian Andersen's *Improvisatore*, originally from German but later directly from the Danish, into English. Hans Christian Andersen had written the book whilst in Italy and Mary stated that it was the poetical character of life in that beautiful country which had inspired him.

She continued to translate articles and books, amongst which were several more of Hans Christian Andersen's stories, including the fairy tales that remain with us today - *O.T., or Life in Denmark*, Only a Fiddler, *The Constant Tin Soldier and other Wonderful Stories*, his *Picture Book without Pictures*, and *A True Story of My Life*. First published in 1846 in book form, these were the first English translations of Andersen's work. He was thrilled, as he wanted to be known in England, but unfortunately his relationship with Mary was later to become strained to say the least.

Claude

Although schooling had proved to be cheaper in Germany than in England, the cost of living in Heidelberg was not. In April 1843, William and Mary and their younger children, Charlton and Meggie, left Heidelberg for England. Their eldest daughter Anna Mary, now nineteen years of age, was to stay behind with friends to study art. Alfred and Claude were to continue their schooling as boarders in Germany.

Alfred was the quieter of the two and considered handsome, but Claude too was fortunate. He captivated people with his boyish behaviour and the Germans liked him. One day before his parents left Germany, Claude was playing with some friends when one of them, for a joke, picked him up by the collar and put him over a fairly low balustrade. Claude wriggled out of the grasp, fell, and landed on his feet. His knee hurt following the incident but he thought he had merely strained it so he said nothing. His parents noticed he was limping and he explained what had happened but the family continued to pack for their return to England and Claude's knee was forgotten. On 12th March 1843, Mary celebrated her birthday at Heidelberg with *"a pedestrian excursion into the remnants of the ancient Hardt Forest"*

The Traveller on the Hill-top

with friends and family, including the injured Claude.

On their return to London the Howitts took the lease of a house, The Grange, in Upper Clapton north east London, for a year. They would have liked to have been in Chelsea amongst their friends and the famous writers who lived there, people such as Charles Dickens, the Carlyles, and the promiscuous William Thackeray and his 'mad' wife.

William was about to depart on a tour for a book to be called *Homes and Haunts of the British Poets,* commencing with a visit to the Wordsworths in Rydal, when he received a letter from Anna Mary which filled them with alarm. Claude was desperately ill, his *"knee had suddenly developed the most alarming features of disease,"* and the English physician at Mannheim who had seen him, desired that *"his parents might be immediately apprised and be taken home, with scarcely the delay of an hour."* William left for Heidelberg instead of Rydal and brought Claude home.

Claude was taken to all the well-known doctors of the day and they all advised amputation, for they feared for his life. First to be consulted was Mr Liston, an eminent physician in London. Then Mr Pease of Darlington (the Quaker banker who financed the creation of the ironworks at Middlesbrough and the Stockton to Darlington Railway and William's special friend) suggested that Claude saw Dr Bevan, who said that he would do it if it were his child. Mary and William did not want their son to have his leg off, so they consulted physicians, surgeons and homoeopathic doctors. Eventually they found someone who would comply with their wishes, although he was not happy about doing so.

Sir Aston Key, who was recommended by Dr Bevan, a Friend, *"saw danger on every side",* immobilised Claude's leg and sent him home with his parents. He told them that:

> the knee had been jarred by the sudden dropping of the boy's entire weight from a second flight of stairs to the pavement. His naturally strong constitution had been weakened by the excessive amount of study peculiar to German schools, and which he had pursued with his whole being, by the innutritious food, and his having slept in a chamber under a hot metal roof. No means had been immediately taken to counteract the effects of the accident, which had likewise been aggravated by the pedestrian excursion into the Hardt Forest. Thus white swelling had set in, and by that told us this with the utmost gentleness and consideration gained such entire power over the system, that even amputation could not arrest it. Sir Aston Keytion, then declining a fee, left us to our sorrow." [GW]

Mary said she had never cried so much as to see the happy boy helpless, pale and *"wasted with fever".* They made a little cart for him which his six-year-old brother towed around the garden. Claude's thirst for knowledge was insatiable. Mr Thomas Tegg became a good friend to him, bringing him books and spending time talking to him while he reclined in his cart. Later in the year Claude had the pleasure of his sister and brother's company. The Howitts had decided that they wanted all their children to be with them, so Anna Mary and Alfred returned to Clapton from Germany, escorted by Herr Muller, a favourite usher in Claude's former school who had been engaged by William and Mary as a tutor.

Claude did not respond to any treatment and he died on 12th March, 1844, Mary's birthday. He had been a very brave boy. Mary never got over his death. She blamed herself for it and remembered it annually for the whole of her long life. In *Reminiscences of My Later Life* Mary wrote about his death:

> Winter came and went. By that time he was too feeble to go out of doors. Then it pleased Almighty God, in the springtime of his life, to call him to a better home. A wild, stormy night ushered in March 12th 1844, the anniversary of that unfortunate birthday picnic. The wind roared round the house the rain beat against the windows and I, sitting up with our sick child, felt my being filled with a strange terror of woe. Morning came, the storm subsided, the chamber was dim with a heavy cloud. Then the sun broke through, a bright ray illumined the bed from head to foot, the room was full of light, and the dear spirit had departed.

In the spring of 1844 Mary was relieved to hear that Anna, who had been ill for several months, had been safely delivered of her twelfth child. Anna and Mary both gave up counting the number of pregnancies they had had. Of the many children Anna bore, only two are mentioned by name in Mary's autobiography.

That summer the Howitts left the cramped quarters of the Grange for a house in Lower Clapton, The Elms. Here Mary had a writing room of her own with another room adjacent where she could make herself presentable at a moment's notice if visitors should arrive. William also had his library [L&R]. At Clapton there was more opportunity for discussion, particularly of the religious kind. The Howitts mixed with theologians and independents, and the Professor of Theology at Upsala in Sweden was a particular friend. He later went to Tasmania as the first Catholic Bishop. They became reacquainted with Mrs Todhunter, an old friend from Nottingham; her son, Joe, was to be a life-long friend of Alfred. They had Hans Christian Andersen to stay and Mrs Gaskell visited as well. Tennyson became a neighbour in 1846, and remained a friend.

Hans Christian Andersen

After Mary and her family returned to England, Hans Christian Andersen came to stay with them. He wanted her to undertake to be the sole translator of his works, but at the time she was reluctant to take on any more translation work - she had done so much for Frederika Bremer the pleasure had gone out of it. Moreover, he made many stipulations which she felt unreasonable and, in any case, she had other work to do. She declined his offer, though she regretted it later.

Hans Christian Andersen was the classic poor boy who had made good. His widowed mother had worked very hard to earn money to educate him. At school he was a dreamer but was offered a job in a drama group to train as an actor. Many people soon recognised his talent - at the time of his visit to England he was under the patronage of the Danish Royal Family.

Mary found him the most difficult of guests. She describes how his *"oversensitive and egotistical nature much marred our intercourse."* He was a very self-important person and he was offended by Mary's rejection of his proposal. He was convinced that she was making a fortune out of the stories she had translated and published. In fact, the only work that brought Mary any financial reward was *Improvisatore*; Andersen received the entire profit from the other stories, including the fairy tales. She later wrote,

> No literary labour is more delightful to me than translating the beautiful thoughts and fancies of Hans Christian Andersen. My heart is in the work, and I feel as if my spirit were kindred to his; just as our Saxon English seems to me eminently fitted to give the simple, pure and noble sentiments of the Danish mind." (Excerpt from a preface to Mit Liv's Eventyr)

Andersen was taken to the annual hay-making at Hillside, Highgate, with the idea of *"introducing him to an English home, full of poetry, art, of sincerity and affection"*. It was the home of the Misses Mary and Margaret Gillies, one a writer and the other a painter. Amongst the guests were Dr Southwood Smith, Octavia Hill, the social reformer who became a very close friend of one of Anna's daughters, the American writer Henry Clarke and other well-known literary persons of the day. Andersen was surrounded by the children present, who were acquainted with his fairy stories. They watched him make daisy chains. When Henry Clarke, from Boston, was noticed by the few who knew his book *A Kiss for a Blow*, they turned their attentions to him. *"Soon poor Andersen, perceiving himself forsaken, complained of headache, and insisted on going indoors, where Mary Gillies and I, both most anxious to efface any disagreeable impression, accompanied him; but he remained irritable and out of sorts."* [GW]

The other guests were also unimpressed with Andersen's behaviour. The American author Douglass said of him that he was singular in appearance and equally singular in his silence. He walked in the beautiful garden as one in a dream, and although they were both staying in the same house Douglass never saw him. Hans Christian Andersen left the Howitts with much ill-feeling on both sides. Interestingly, Alison Prince, in her biography of Andersen (*The Fan Dancer,* Allison & Busby, 1998), puts a different light on events. If, as she convincingly suggests, he was not only moody, flambuoyant and over-sensitive but homosexual, one can only marvel at the undercurrents of his meetings with Mary Howitt - a middle-aged, down-to-earth, inevitably puritanical and sexually repressed Quaker.

Reunions and Inspirations

In the summer of that year Mary and her daughter Meggie visited Anna in Liverpool, and then her mother in Uttoxeter, bringing her niece Margaret Ann Harrison with her. While she was in Uttoxeter she decided to write *My Own Story*, an account of her life in Uttoxeter up to the time she went to Croydon to school. Her mother was obviously happy to see Mary, Margaret Ann and Meggie and Mary was pleased to see the old places of her youth, the Hockley and the *"Talbot"* (by this she could mean the Shrewsbury and Talbot, in earlier times the Far Talbot, as she appears to be describing the area where she had lived).

On her return to Clapton Mary wrote *The Two Apprentices*, of which she said she had *"had the scene laid in Uttoxeter, so if it is read there, the little town will wonder at my impudence."* She had been inspired to write *it* while visiting her mother. The idea for the story arose from an occasion many years before when Uttoxeter had earned a special dispensation during the 1745 uprising, after the Duke of Cumberland stayed in the town with his army on his way north to fight Bonnie Prince Charlie. This dispensation prevented the army from billeting soldiers in ordinary people's houses, but instead they had to be put up in inns and for one night only. When Mary lived in Nottingham, she had a *'monthly nurse'* called Alice Cheetham with whom she had become quite friendly. She brought her to Uttoxeter once when she visited Balance Street. It was in this street that the army soldiers were assembled prior to finding them lodgings for the night, something Mary had often seen during her childhood. Alice who had lost all trace of a son to the army many years before, while she was in the Balance Street house saw her long-lost son amongst the soldiers. Both of them enjoyed as much time together as the short stay in the town allowed. Unfortunately, he did not keep in touch with his mother after that either,

"It was a terrible evening for the poor people to arrive on," said Joanna to her sister, who sat knitting on the sofa, upon that rainy evening of May-fair day, as the baggage-wagons were unloaded before their windows, and one weary woman after another, stiff with having sat so many hours up aloft among wet boxes and tired children, was helped down from her elevation, and seemed only to put herself in motion with difficulty. The good Joanna [Kendrick] was full of compassion, and pitied their having to find quarters in the noisy and crowded public-houses, where they would be unwelcome guests both to landlord and landlady. Greatly interested as she was by the whole arrival, her sympathies were presently enlisted on behalf of a woman who took much thought about her. She was wrapped in a large gray cloak; and the hood, which was drawn over her head, partially revealed a face which was pale and dejected. The boy ran hither and thither to various groups of women, who began to move off in various directions, and back again to the sick woman, for whose comfort he seemed very solicitous, for he lugged along a small chest, upon which he made her place her feet, and wrapped her cloak about her with the most affectionate care. All this Joanna described to her sister, and then called her servant, bidding her take her pattens and umbrella, and go across, and ask if the poor woman would come in and shelter. Instead of returning with her as was expected, Joanna saw her servant give her her arm, and sheltering her with her large umbrella, move off along

Balance Street, Uttoxeter, at the turn of the century.

The Market Place in Edwardian Uttoxeter.

the street, whilst the boy trudged after, carrying a large bundle. On the return of the servant, it appeared that the woman, who was delicate, had been taken ill on the road; that she was billeted to the Talbot; and, as there were two public-houses in the town of that name, it was supposed to be the one lying at some distance, whereas it proved to be the one just at hand, and thither the maid had escorted..........[There is a Talbot Inn in the Market Place, and there was another locally known as the Far Talbot at the corner of Balance Street and Carter Street.] ....."Are we alone?"......."We are mother" said the boy, throwing himself on his knees at the bed's foot; "there is only the lady, and you and me." [The landlady was Mrs Tunnicliffe, a very familiar name of the area.] She looked steadily at Miss Kendrick, and then said slowly and with difficulty, "I am Rebecca - your unhappy, outcast sister. God brought me here to die. I knew it was so when I entered the town, when the baggage-train could not enter the market-place, but made halt before the very house where I had been a child - from whence I set out when I took my fate into my own hands!" Joanna petrified with astonishment and compassion seized her hand and gazed into her face. "Yes" said the woman, "I am Rebecca, your sister, though you may not recognize me." "My poor, unhappy sister!" exclaimed Joanna, embracing her with tears. "Thank God that you are found at last! You shall live with us - with Dorothy and me - you shall yet be happy!"

Other writings by William and Mary about Uttoxeter were articles for *Kaleidoscope* in their early days, when they wrote under the noms-de-plume of Wilfred and Wilfreda Wender. Uttoxeter was called Deckerton. Many of these articles are repeated word for word in future books and articles under either of their names. The instalment for October 17th 1822 describes how reaping was done when William was a child and gives an account of a walk of twenty miles through the Dove Valley with descriptions of the cliffs and mentioning a castle (most likely Tutbury) and Deckerton Church and spire ten miles away. The next issue is about his cousins and also his father's uncle, wife and two daughters aged twenty and nineteen. The description of the house could well be that of the Bothams' house in Balance Street and the daughters Kate and Ellen's ages correspond to the ages of Anna and Mary when William visited his cousin Susanna Frith. Various town characters appear in modified form; for example, the person Mary writes about in her autobiography as a very fat woman called the Rev Anne Clowes features in *Kaleidoscope* as Reverend Mrs Malatrot. Other characters are equally thinly disguised. Many of these passages are reused in later stories.

Wood Leighton, written in 1835, contains all the elements of a good book; good descriptions of characters and surroundings and a plot which includes mystery, murder, love and suspense. In many of Mary's books, whether autobiography or fiction, she refers to local people by name, often giving descriptions of what they did and where they lived. The description of Uttoxeter Market Place includes the pump and cross which stood where there is now a kiosk and Samuel Johnson's memorial to his penance in his 70s.

In those days the houses in the town did not have numbers so it is not possible to identify positively the houses people lived in. Characters included Daniel Neale, the Irish Beggar, whose mother lived in Pinfold Street and who was trusted with messages by old Catholic families. He preferred to live out in Needwood Forest and sleep rough rather than live with his mother in a house, although he often visited her. Then there is the eccentric Rev Mrs Anne Clowes, the widow of an Anglican clergyman, of whom Mary writes in her autobiography:

With what excitement did we note any interchange of civility between our mother and Mrs Clowes, the wife of a clergyman, and who styled herself in consequence the Rev. Anne Clowes! After his death she continued to reside in Uttoxeter. She was known by everybody, and was an honoured if not an acceptable guest in the best houses of the neighbourhood; yet she lived without a servant in a narrow alley, and had neither bell nor knocker to her house door, on which her friends were instructed to rap loudly with a stone. She occupied an upper room, confusedly crowded with goods and chattels of every description picked up at auctions, and piles of earthenware and china, having

The Traveller on the Hill-top

A letter written by Mary.

Mrs Clowes, attended by two gentlemen
of the town, returning from
an evening party.

Rev. Anne Clowes who was seen as an unwelcome, if honoured, visitor.

THE REV ANNE CLOWES

The Traveller on the Hill-top

the casements filled with as many pieces of rag, pasteboard, and cobwebs as small panes of glass. She slept in a large salting-trough, with a switch at her side to keep off the rats. This mean and miserable abode she termed, in her grandiloquent language, "the hallowed spot, into which only were introduced the great in mind, in wealth, or in birth"; and on one occasion spoke of a most delightful visit from two of Lady Waterpark's sons, when "the feast of reason and flow of soul" had been so absorbing that one of the Mr Cavendishes, one of her sons in descending the stairs, had set his foot in her mutton-pie, which was ready for the baker's oven.

Each Whitsuntide we saw her marching at the head of the Oddfellows' Club, with a bouquet of lilacs and peonies blazing on her breast up to her chin, holding in one hand a long staff, her usual outdoor companion. She was not insane, only a very original person, running wild amongst a number of other eccentric worthies, all of whom left marked impressions on our [Mary and Anna's] minds."

This a poem by Mary, recollects the garden of her childhood in Balance Street:

> *Our little gardens side by side,*
> *Each bordered round with London Pride,*
> *Some six feet long and three feet wide,*
> *To us a large estate.*
>
> *The apple and the damson trees,*
> *The cottage shelter for the bees,*
> *I see them, and beyond all these*
> *A something dearer still;*
>
> *I see an eye serenely blue,*
> *A cheek of girlhood's freshest hue,*
> *A buoyant heart, a spirit true*
> *Alike in good and ill.*
>
> *Sweet sister, thou wert all to me*
> *And I sufficient friend to thee,*
> *Where was a happier twain than we*
> *Who had no mate beside.*
>
> *Like wayside flowers in merry May*
> *Our pleasures round about us lay;*
> *A joyful morning had our day*
> *What'er our eve betide.*

'Wood Leighton' (Uttoxeter) as viewed from the High Wood, an area on the south of the town, is fundamentally unaltered today from Mary's description:

The situation of Wood Leighton, as seen from this height, unites everything of which I can form an idea in the most beautiful pastoral landscapes. About a mile below us, at the foot of those rural enclosures we passed in our ascent, and of which now only here and there a green slip can be seen through their abundant trees, against whose fresh vernal foliage rises the white smoke of their hidden cottages, Wood Leighton is seen, with its clustered buildings and lofty spire, just where a fine valley opens into one still finer, and, indeed, into one of the most luxuriant and celebrated vales of England, and down which the river [River Dove] I have mentioned before flows from the wild regions of the Peak of Derbyshire. It is just, too, where this noble and prolific valley changes its course, and leaves a flat of the most abounding meadows in the immediate neighbourhood of the town. Thus, to the right, we command a view along this extensive vale in all its beauty, beyond the wood-embosomed mansions of two noble lords, as far down as the lofty ruins of Tutbury Castle; and before us, beyond the town, over another region of wood, from the midst of which are dimly seen villages and old grey halls, to the blue and shadowy softness of wild hills, at twenty miles' distance, which form the north of the county, and run on into the still wilder hills of the Peak. To the right of Wood Leighton, and overlooking the valley, though at another angle, on the bold brow of a hill, stands a noble mansion, and its dependent village church and delightful parsonage, half shrouded in surrounding woods - seeming proudly to survey the animated scene - thus plenteous valley - its thousands of cattle - its river winding through its green expanse, and all around it a vast extent of undulating country in the highest state of cultivation. The situation of Wood Leighton seems to fit it for the capital of a pastoral district, which, in fact, it may be considered. (Wood Leighton).

Mary wrote in the romantic style of the Victorian period. She wrote of nature in a very descriptive style, both in poetry and in prose and many of her stories for children are the moralistic tales so popular at the time. The familiar nursery poem *The Spider and the Fly* is probably her best known work in this vein. Some of the titles illustrate what she was trying to put across to her readers, such as *Which is the Wiser, Little Coin Much Care,* and *Strive and Thrive*. Mary also wrote for the Religious Tract Society, which promoted religion to the masses by printing 'hand-outs' given away in the streets and at railway stations. Later in 1849, William and Mary wrote for a similar outlet, the Bradshaw's Railway Library, which provided story books to all railway stations in the United Kingdom for travellers at 1/- each. She was also a prolific letter writer, corresponding to publishers, sisters and friends.

Hans Christian Andersen by Carl Hartmann as it appeared in the Howitt Journal July 26th 1847.

The Traveller on the Hill-top

One of the illustrations from "Our Cousins in Ohio" which we believe were drawn by Mary's sister Emma.

Jack's deathbed - another illustration, from "Our Cousins in Ohio".

The 'Spider and the Fly' and the 'Fairies of Caldon Lowe' are two well known childrens' poems with a moral by Mary Howitt.
Drawing by Mary Noon, Joy Dunicliff's daughter.

CHAPTER SEVEN
WRITING FOR CHILDREN & OTHERS

Emma

The depression which followed the Napoleonic Wars had long-lasting effects. Many people left their home shores to find a better life for themselves and their families, including Emma Alderson's family. Mary's sister emigrated to America in 1842 with her husband and three children - their eldest child had died before they left. Emma, her husband Harrison, and Charles William (b. 1837), Agnes (b. 1839) and Anna Mary (Nanny'), (b. 1841) set sail for a new life across the Atlantic. They hoped to find more freedom for Harrison, a strict, simple Quaker minister, and a simpler lifestyle for their children. Harrison also felt he had not received the recognition he deserved in Liverpool. He had attended Yearly Meetings in Liverpool and sometimes in London, and he had done much preaching.

Life had not been kind to them. They had started married life in a small house in Blackburn with both money and work short. They wanted to leave the town and return to farming, the work he loved best, but when they eventually did, the farm was not profitable. Emma wished dearly for '*a clear £150*'. Times were hard, work was slack, the harvest of 1837 was poor, there was sickness amongst the cattle and the potato crop failed. The Aldersons' elder child, a daughter, succumbed to a fever; they nursed her night and day for a fortnight before she died. Emma, who loved motherhood and wanted a large family, was devastated.

The family decided to sell up, including Harrison's share in the family's Dentdale property, to raise all the monies they could. Emma's sister and mother gave them provisions and clothes for the journey. Mary had been like a mother to Emma, yet there is no evidence that she was upset at the prospect of them emigrating. Had she not considered it herself at one time? After the birth of her second child Emma had written to Mary because Mary was very depressed at being pregnant yet again. It was a very matronly letter trying to cheer her sister up, a letter she did not want William to see. Emma revelled in motherhood and could not understand why Mary did not. To Ann, their mother, the decision to emigrate was cruel. She was very close to Emma and doted on Charlie and little Agnes (she knitted constantly for them even after they had settled in Ohio).

The Harrisons sailed on the Shenandoah from Liverpool for Philadelphia, the Quaker city, with the intention of moving on and buying land, letting Providence appoint their new home. They were accompanied by Elizabeth Alderson, Harrison's unmarried sister, and Richard, his nephew of fourteen (Emma was to find Elizabeth a trial but Richard took to farming). A very sad Emma stood on the deck with baby in her arms, waving goodbye to her family. Anna said she would never forget the moment when the ship sailed and the distance between them increased, the ship becoming smaller and smaller through her watery eyes.

It took forty-one days to cross the Atlantic to Delaware Bay. Emma wrote to her mother a daily account of the voyage, the forty-seven letters forming a kind of journal. The journey was rough and prolonged, and everyone except Charlie suffered badly from seasickness. Emma wrote that Agnes had said, when everyone was ill, "*If grandmother was here she'd have spare arms for me!*"

Passenger ships of those days did not provide eating facilities for their passengers. The Harrisons travelled 'cabin' and Emma paid a man on board 15/- a week to cook their meals. She was horrified at the behaviour of her fellow travellers, who when not eating shouted, scolded, and roared at each other. "*A ship was a sad place for morals,*" she felt.

Emma's Life in the USA

On their arrival they took a house in Brownsville while Harrison sought his future in Ohio, where other Quakers had gone. The next year the party went by train to Harrisburg; the trip cost $4 each and lasted five days. They then took a boat upriver. Refreshments were lavish and cheap, beefsteaks, eels, chicken, sausages, fish, cheese, tomatoes - all for 50 cents.

The farm Harrison had purchased for $5,740 consisted of an 'L'-shaped, single-storey, eight-roomed house with two verandahs, outbuildings and thirty-three acres of meadow and woodland. They were on the Kentucky side of Ohio near the Licking River and about three miles from Cincinnati. There were settlements all around. An old man remarked to Emma on the influx of people to the New World, marvelling that in 1825 there had only been five houses and that wolves had roamed the land.

Emma found that Mary was already well-known in America, and she was made very welcome in her new country by her father's cousin, Ann Shipley (of Gretna Green fame) who was an 80-year-old widow. The Shipley children and grandchildren came to help Emma with her sewing and they even made a greatcoat for Harrison. Everything had to be stitched by hand as there would have been very few sewing machines, which were a new invention, in people's homes. Maids, too, were very difficult to obtain and many people adopted young girls so they could have some help in the house. Emma was very keen that her daughters should have a good education; maybe she realized how deficient her own had been.

With the Shipleys' friendship, the open countryside, and a husband of whom she was very fond and who was happy in his farming and preaching, Emma settled happily in America. In her letters she compared the rags and starvation of Liverpool with the abundance of food in America - so much that some would be left on the plate. She also told Mary that American women limited the size of their families. Emma herself loved children but she was to lose two in infancy or as a result of a stillbirth. Another child, Alice Ann, who was always delicate and never developed quite normally, was brought to England when she was about ten years old by Harrison's sister Elizabeth. She was put in the charge of a kind Friend in Esher, but after a short illness, she too died.

1847 brought the Irish potato famine. Emma described how the Irish arrived dirty and emaciated, bringing with them diseases such as typhus to America. She wrote that the very smell of their clothes reminded her of the Irish haymakers in Uttoxeter to whom her mother had given food and clothing.

Emma frequently wrote about slavery too. One black servant girl she employed had been a slave; her mother was black and her father had been a rich planter. He sold her into slavery when she was six years of age. When she grew up she tried to buy her freedom, agreed at $400, and took in extra work to raise the enormous sum. When she was short just $60 she found that the money would not buy her son's freedom as well and there were threats made to him. Their master was quite entitled to sell him independently of his mother. She ran away with her son to Ohio, known as the 'Mercy State', where she was fortunate to meet an abolitionist tavern-owner. He cared for the couple and, realizing the son was quite intelligent, he paid for the boy to be apprenticed as a shoemaker to his brother in Columbus.

Then there was the old ex-slave, aged over a hundred years of age, who lived in a log cabin in the wood near the Aldersons. All his children had been taken from him and sold as slaves to various masters. He had bought his freedom for $250 but the master wanted $350 for his wife because she was so much younger, and at that time she was seventy-four!

Emma describes how the Germans hated the blacks, much more than the Americans. On one occasion in 1846 three hundred and ninety-five liberated slaves from North Carolina arrived in Ohio, a state chiefly settled by freed slaves. When their master died, land, houses and provisions had been bought for them in Ohio at a cost of $30,000. But when they arrived at the place where they were to settle, local inhabitants prevented them gaining access to their property. They had to shelter in the woods with no food or money, because the Germans did not want them to settle in their area.

Emma died in 1847. Her death came as a big shock to the family and Ann Botham never recovered from it. A letter dated 12 mo 18 1847 arrived for Ann from Cincinnati around New Year in which Harrison wrote: *"My Beloved on earth my greatest earthly treasure the delight of my eyes, the solace and comfort outwardly of my life, she for whom I seemed to live - perhaps too much so, the mother and guardian of my precious children, has been suddenly taken from me, leaving me desolate, afflicted, almost crushed."*

Harrison continued his letter, describing the circumstances which brought about Emma's death. Ten days earlier she had given birth to a premature son, Samuel. A few days later she was suffering from a fever and having problems with her breathing, but the doctor in attendance saw no cause for alarm. The fever continued and her husband became more worried. *"I had suffered a good deal in the fear how it might terminate some days before, being very sensitive and keenly alive to the most distant danger at these seasons of the trial of her strength,"* continued Harrison.

The river Ohio was in flood but a friend, Joseph Taylor, *"educated for and practised as a physician,"* arrived at the house after a long detour. Joseph was concerned about Emma's condition when he saw her, but there was nothing he could do to save her (with no antibiotics to cure infections there was little doctors could do). Baby Samuel survived only a few more months. The flowery language used in Harrison's letter must have been a characteristic of the family, as it can be found in some of Mary's works; words like *"dear", "sweet"* are used often with regard to *"sweet little child"* especially in *My Cousins in Ohio*.

Nanny married William Wilberforce Wistar of Ohio. Charles also married in America and descendants of the family are still there, though others returned to England. Agnes married Joseph Simpson, a nephew of Daniel Harrison, who went to America but returned to England later. He started a cotton mill with his brothers at Mayfield, two miles from Ashbourne and ten miles from Uttoxeter. Sold by the family in 1934, it became William Tatton's mill and is now called Mayfield Yarns & Mayfield Holdings. The mill buildings and most of the houses built by the Simpsons for their employees are still there today.

Harrison Alderson leaned on Agnes after the death of his wife, and came to visit them after she had been married for about a year. He found the voyage tiring and had not recovered from it when he became ill. Agnes and her husband lived at Sunnyside House, Mayfield and it was here that her father died. He is buried in the Friends' Meeting House burial ground in Uttoxeter where there is a gravestone (not very usual in a Friends' burial ground) which simply states, *"Harrison Alderson of Burlington, New Jersey USA died 7 Month 27th 1871 aged 71 years"*. It lies at the side of Samuel Botham's grave, his father-in-law.

Soon after Emma had settled in America, Mary, ever-hungry for material for her stories, asked her to keep an account of what her family did over the course of one year (1846). Work on the farm and caring for and educating her children, exacerbated by the lack of servants, left Emma little spare time but nevertheless she did keep the diary diligently, working well into the night by dim candlelight. The pages from her diary, together with drawings of birds and other interesting features, were sent to Mary and she used them to write a children's book called *Our Cousins in Ohio, or A Journal of the Children's Life Round the Year*, published after Emma's death.

The Mayfield Mill of the Simpsons.

Agnes Simpson.

Agnes's wedding in America.

The gravestones of Samuel Botham and his son-in-law, Harrison Alderson, which lie side by side in the Friends' burial ground in Uttoxeter.

The book is a sequel to *The Children's Year*, which was about Charlton and Meggie and illustrated by Mary's eldest daughter, Anna Mary. This was a period when many people were emigrating to America, Australia and New Zealand and Mary wanted those at home to know something of the life of those overseas. William and Mary themselves felt there was no future for their children in England and encouraged them to emigrate. *Our Cousins in Ohio* is written in diary form, a chapter per month, and each entry is dated. Mary says in her preface that the book is *"an experiment in children's books"* and that she hopes it will give greater understanding to children like her own who have relatives living in America. She informs her readers that the book covers the last Christmas her sister lived.

In the book Emma's home is a farm called The Cedars, situated on high ground near the River Ohio. The house and outbuildings are set amongst natural woodland. The area has many sugar maples, the sap being collected in February. The family have two horses, three cows and a calf, poultry and guinea fowl, two dogs increasing to three during the year, a yellow long-legged cat and pigs. The outbuildings include a smoke house and a cheese press, built during the year, which produces the only cheese for forty miles around. A vineyard is also productive. Other crops grown are asparagus, rhubarb, salad (presumably lettuce), potatoes, beans, peas, cabbage, spinach, beets, carrots, turnips, parsnips, water musk, citron, cantaloupe melons, squashes or vegetable marrows, purple eggplant, sweetcorn, popcorn, gourds, tomatoes and sweet potatoes. The family also own a few log cabins in which the farmworkers live.

We are told that at Christmas time bears are hung outside butchers' shops, and that they look funny with their muzzles and paws left on. Most of the neighbours are recent immigrants from Germany, only a few of whom speak English. They are Lutherans and have their own church in the same way that the Society of Friends have their Meeting House in a settlement which supports a few houses, a tavern, a shop, a blacksmith and a shoemaker.

The children in the book are Willie (aged nine), Florence (aged seven and a half), Anna or Nanny (aged six) and the baby Cornelia (born in America), known as Nelly. She has her second birthday in the summer of the year recorded. All the children have daily jobs around the farm and lessons given by their mother before they can play. Florence, even at the age of seven, is responsible for remembering and going to collect her shoes for Sunday Meeting. All except Nelly are expected to see that their clothes are ready and respectable. At harvest time all the children are expected to help, but with their responsibilities comes freedom. Willie takes Nelly in the horse and cart to the settlement, he goes on errands for his father, negotiates terms for him and is away from home conducting this business for a whole day.

Willie's new, permanent teeth are not growing where they should and he has to pay a visit to the dentist to have his upper 'eye teeth' removed. This is in the days before anaesthetics, and poor Willie suffers from poor vision for several days afterwards, besides the swelling and the pain.

The mother in the book describes the countryside - the trees, the flowers, the birds and their migrations, the wild crops to be harvested and the weather. She also talks about social life and political issues; the enormous table that can be spread before an unexpected guest, the friction with some of the Germans, problems for the freed slaves, a mention of the Mexican War and much besides. On the children's birthdays one of the parents tells of their childhood after a special tea. When a birthday fell on a Sunday the celebrations were kept until Monday - presents (all made by the giver), cake and all had to wait. The mother's account brings tears to the children's eyes and they vow never to grieve her. Their father's childhood has evidently been happy. *Our Cousins in Ohio* is an extremely interesting book, giving an insight into America which is not even understood by British people today.

The Traveller on the Hill-top

In 1844 spring came early after a mild winter, *"and spring always had a reviving power physically and mentally"* for Mary. She set herself to finish, in three weeks, another tale for Mr Tegg before allowing herself a holiday. *"When do we go to Liverpool?"* asked little Meggie each day; she had all her dolls and their clothes neatly packed for the journey. The Harrisons gave them a warm welcome at their pleasant house at Birkenhead and Daniel made up a party for a trip into Wales. She tells of a *"rough but amusing voyage to the Menai Bridge where there was an excellent inn"* and that *"Telford's marvellous erection spanned the Strait in airy sublimity."*

The Menai and Tubular Bridge.

Mary and Meggie left the Harrisons to travell direct to Uttoxeter where old Mrs Botham was now living in lodgings. There, she had tea *"with cheese cakes, biscuits and good things for eating"* awaiting them, and little presents of her own making for them all; at 7am that morning she had been working to finish a chemise for Meggie's doll. Her mother *"looked much aged"* Mary thought, and her life was lonely now so many old friends were gone. William joined them before they returned to The Elms at Clapton. Mary makes her mother sound a sad old lady; she implies that her various griefs had taken their toll, the unexpected death of her husband, that of her only son - and the departure of Emma:

> One other great sorrow awaited mother, the departure of her beloved, hitherto almost inseparable, youngest daughter, with her husband and little children, to America in 1842. The grief was followed, a few years later, by the tidings of that daughter's death. They came as her summons to the better land.

Clapton

In 1845 Ann moved from Uttoxeter and went to live with William and Mary Howitt and their family at The Grange, Upper Clapton. The house was recommended to them and Mary considered it a good choice as it was within easy reach of Paternoster Row in the City, where there were many publishing houses; moreover, they were in an area of *"vast districts teeming with ignorance and squalor for whose amelioration we were desirous of labouring."*[GW]

Mary Howitt

Anna (Botham) Harrison
From a coloured portrait drawing by Arthur Hughes in 1878. Most of Mary's letters are written to Anna, from Mary's marriage in 1821 to Anna's death in 1882.

The Elms, Lower Clapton

Soon, however, they moved to The Elms, Avenue Road in Lower Clapton. There were many happy memories of the days spent at The Elms, which was next door to Henry Bateman, a merchant and Congregationalist. He was on the committee of the Religious Tract Society and was renowned for his *"active benevolence, promotion of religious freedom, calm, outspoken denunciation of evil, unflinching adherence to duty and faithful trust in God under all circumstances"* [GW]. The Bateman family were to remain life-long friends.

The child of another neighbour played with the younger Howitt children. She was Octavia Hill, later in life to make her mark as a philanthropist, an educationalist and one of the founders of the National Trust. Alfred, Lord Tennyson, the poet, was also a frequent visitor. While they were at The Elms William received his first letter from Elizabeth Gaskell bringing to his attention *"a fine old seat, Clopton Hall, near Stratford-on-Avon. It described in so powerful and graphic a manner the writer's visit as a schoolgirl to the mansion and its inmates."* [GW] William, in his reply, suggested she should write for the benefit of the people, and Elizabeth did just that.

Ann Botham was accepted into the local Meeting of the Society of Friends, although Mary and William, who did sometimes write jointly, had upset the local Meeting by publishing *Johnny Derbyshire, a Country Quaker*, which mentions the 'enlightened' Quakers. Mary's letters to Anna reveal that she was becoming more disillusioned with, and uncertain of, her faith and both were to leave the Society of Friends. In 1848 Mary resigned, leaving Emma the only Botham girl to die a Quaker. In later life Mary said of her mother:

> I am struck with affectionate admiration at the remembrance of her great tact and forbearance under circumstances not readily assimilating with her convictions, and of her keen observation and good sense, which would have preserved us from various pitfalls had we been willing to profit by them. She chiefly employed herself reading or knitting in her own room, and merely saw our intimate friends, who were very favourably impressed by her peaceful exterior and unsectarian utterances. But whilst she highly approved of our literary productions and sentiments, she took exception to our advocacy of the stage, from the persuasion that virtuous persons assuming fictitious characters became ultimately what they simulate. She consequently eschewed some estimable actresses, our familiar associates, terming them "Stage girls" whom she pitied, but whose accomplishments she abhorred. [GW]

Ann was unhappy with the way the world was moving and chose to withdraw from it. She did not visit or *'give charity'* as she would have done had she been living in Uttoxeter with her husband. She grieved over the loss of Emma and outlived her by only a few months. She died on May 5th 1848 and was buried alongside Claude in the Friends' Burying Ground at Stoke Newington, London.

Mr Tegg and the Baker's Dozen

Mary planned to write another story about Uttoxeter for Mr Tegg, this time about her childhood. It was to be called *My Own Story*. She wrote,

> It is a singular thing from whom we could inherit that really romantic picturesque and creative turn of mind which we both had. There were many peculiar circumstances that operated singularly on our imaginations. I remember the sort of horror that many things occasioned us - Dr Smith's wife shooting herself in bed; William Aker's mad wife who was confined for years and years in a garret; Joe Baines's apprentice who killed himself from ill-usage; Miss Gisborne, who lived shut up with Mary Batman and, perhaps more than all - the insanity of the Summerlands - huge, gigantic men with such awful voices! Then poor Miss Goodwin who was so mild and gentle and ladylike like Crabbe's Schoolmistress, and old Nanny with her wild, strange histories and manners - Rhoda, Mary Saville and good Mrs Parker - all of them, in one way or another, excited our imaginations and awoke our minds. [L&R]

The Traveller on the Hill-top

Amice Lee writes

If Mary had brought some of them into her stories they would have been far more exciting; she might have touched a deeper vein of human experience, certainly than she did in Love and Money or No Sense Like Common Sense. In the little town she knew so well there were comedies and indeed tragedies enough. Thanks to old Nanny's information Mary was acquainted with these: what of the bridegroom who mysteriously 'disappeared'; the children about whose parentage folk looked solemn and shook wise heads; the deserted or love-crossed maids, and Lawyer Pipe's wife who ran off with the fiddler? Reserve in early training, timidity, or Puritan inhibition, kept Mary from any subject which had the least implication of sex. Mrs Gaskell might write frankly of illicit love; Mary could not do so, whatever she felt in her own heart of understanding or pity. [L&R]

Mary was a quiet, kindly, gentle person; her Quaker upbringing had taught her to look for the good things in people and not to look for or build on their misfortunes. This meant that even when she was writing with a view to social reform she did not drive home her points as strongly as she might have. It must also be remembered that publisher Tegg, with his thousands of young readers in England and the Colonies, was paying her £1,000 expressly for tales to illustrate household virtues. In the Advertisement at the beginning of the second edition of *My Own Story*, Mary writes,

This volume completes this series of Tales for the People and their Children. It is a work which has grown in interest as it has proceeded, and I now see my task completed almost with regret. The scope which it embraces is a wide one, and the farther I have gone, the more it has opened before me; the lessons of human life and experience are inexhaustible, and hence it is my intention to continue this class of stories at some future time.

It is but justice to say that of the thirteen stories of which this series is composed, two were written by my husband at a time when I was otherwise unavoidably occupied; nor must I take my leave of the work without expressing my deep gratitude to the excellent projector and publisher of it for his handsome and friendly behaviour throughout this, our literary connection, and still more for his kindness and thoughtful consideration at a time of severe domestic affliction.

To the public, both at home and in America, who have received these books with distinguished favour, I now, as far as regards this series, bid adieu. [Clapton, Aug 30th 1844]

The *"unavoidably occupied"* period was due to Mary's worry about Claude's health, when she felt unable to write. William wrote *No Sense like Common Sense* and *My Uncle the Clockmaker*, both published in Mary's name. Their last child, Margaret Anastasia, was born in early August. She was a strong healthy baby, the last of the family, who in later years fulfilled her parents' hopes that she would be a comfort in their old age.

The titles of the thirteen "Baker's Dozen" books were:

Strive and Thrive

Sowing and Reaping or What Will Come of It

Little Coin Much Care - about how poor men lived, and set in Bartram's Court in Nottingham. A prosperous lace hand becomes a drinking partner of his landlord and his employers. The Peoples' Association arranges a strike, and they march on Nottingham Castle:

It was a wild stormy night in October; Ford and his wife as usual had quarrelled, and with a feeling of aversion towards his home, he joined the hundreds who, having awaited the arrival of the mail and received with groans and every sign of abhorence the news that the Bill was thrown out of the House of Lords, were now wending their way to the forest. There was some thing wild and troubled in the very air....Ford was disheartened and yet desperate...with a hundred such men as he, Orator Timmis might have burnt all Nottingham.

This is interesting when put into the context of what William wrote about the fire at Nottingham Castle and with Mary's account of why it had happened. Mary was often inspired by her social conscience; indeed, the work of the Victorian novelists did much to bring about change in Britain. *Little Coin Much Care* prompted Elizabeth Gaskell to write *Mary Barton*.

Hope on Hope Ever or The Boyhood of Felix Law

Who shall be Greatest

Work and Wages or Life in Service - a continuation of *Little Coin, Much Care*

Alice Franklin

No Sense Like Common Sense or Some passages in the life of Charles Middleton, Esq - written by William in Mary's name. Charles was the name both of Mary's brother and of one of her children and Middleton was the second name of Claude, the child for whose death she never forgave herself.

Love and Money, another story with a moral, was based in Heidelberg. It contains the names of people she knew while she lived there, according to her autobiography. It can be assumed that the story is based on real characters.

Which is the Wiser?

My Uncle the Clock Maker - actually written by William, and set in his native Derbyshire, about ten miles from Nottingham.

Two Apprentices - based in Uttoxeter during the Napoleonic Wars. One apprentice is *"good"* while the other succumbs to *"temptation"*, a common device of Mary's. The characters are named after people who really did live in Uttoxeter.

My Own Story or the Autobiography of a Child - about Mary's early life. Its style and vocabulary are not what we would expect a child today to read. Mary's life is glamorized and she writes of her parents' devoted love for one another which is incompatible with comments in her autobiography. There is a villain of the piece, a relative who is out to destroy the respect and local standing of Samuel and his family. She describes the things he does to irritate the family and the conflict Samuel feels between his natural anger and his religious principles

Stead Fast Gabriel - gives a similar impression to *Little Lord Fauntleroy*: a bit goody-goody. It shows the friction between country children and children from a mining village.

In 1847 Mary published her book of Ballads and in the preface she remarks, *"The love of Christ, of the poor, and of little children, always were and will be ruling sentiments of my soul."* James Britten considered that her best poems were published in this book; *Lilian May, an Easter Legend, The Sin of Earl Walter, The Abbey Garden*, and *Willie o' Wyburn*. He also felt that *The Fairies of Caldon Low* should be better known and he considered *The Poor Man's Garden* a very beautiful poem.

THE FAIRIES OF THE CALDON LOW
A Midsummer Legend

"And where have you been, my Mary,
And where have you been from me?"
"I've been to the top of the Caldon Low
The midsummer-night to see!"

"And what did you see, my Mary,
All up on the Caldon Low?"
"I saw the glad sunshine come down
And I heard the merry winds blow."

"And what did you hear, my Mary,
All up on the Caldon Hill?"
"I heard the drops of water made,
And I heard the corn-ears fill."

"Oh! tell me all, my Mary,
All, all that ever you know,
For you must have seen the fairies,
Last night on the Caldon Low."

The Traveller on the Hill-top

"Then take me on your knee, mother;
And listen, mother of mine.
A hundred fairies danced last night,
And the harpers they were nine.

"And their harp-strings rung so merrily
To their dancing feet so small;
But oh! the words of their talking
Were merrier far than all.

"And what were the words, my Mary,
That then you heard them say?"
"I'll tell you all, my mother;
But let me have my way.

"Some of them played with the water,
And rolled it down the hill;
'And this,' they said, 'shall speedily turn
The poor old miller's mill.

"'For there has been no water
Ever since the first of May;
And a busy man the miller will be
At dawning of the day.

"Oh! the miller, how he will laugh
When he sees the mill-dam rise!
The jolly old miller, how he will laugh,
Till the tears fill both his eyes!'

"And some they seized the little winds
That sounded over the hill;
And each put a horn into his mouth,
And blew both loud and shrill:

"'And there,' they said, 'the merry winds go,
Away from every horn;
And they shall clear the mildew dank
From the blind old widow's corn.

"'Oh! the poor blind widow,
Though she has been blind so long,
She'll be blithe enough when the mildew's gone,
And the corn stands tall and strong.'

"And some they brought the brown lint-seed
And flung it down from the Low;
'And this,' they said, 'by the sunrise,
In the weaver's croft shall grow.

"'Oh! the poor lame weaver,
How he will laugh outright,
When he sees his dwindling flax-field
All full of flowers by night!'

"And then outspoke a brownie,
With a long beard on his chin;
'I have spun up all the tow,' said he,
'And I want some more to spin.

"'I've spun a piece of hempen cloth,
And I want to spin another;
A little sheet for Mary's bed,
And an apron for her mother.'

"With that I could not help but laugh,
And I laughed out loud and free;
And then on the top of the Caldon Low
There was no one left but me.

"And all on the top of the Caldon Low
The mists were cold and grey,
And nothing I saw but the mossy stones
That round about me lay.

"But coming down from the hill-top,
I heard afar below,
How busy the jolly miller was,
And how the wheel did go.

"And I peeped into the widow's field,
And, sure enough, were seen
The yellow ears of the mildewed corn,
All standing stout and green.

"And down by the weaver's croft I stole,
To see if the flax were sprung;
But I met the weaver at his gate,
With the good news on his tongue.

"Now this is all I heard, mother,
And all that I did see;
So, pr'ythee, make my bed, mother,
For I'm tired as I can be."

Britten himself chose to quote "The Fisherman's Song":

Going out

Briskly blows the evening gale,
Fresh and free it blows;
Blessings on the fishingboat,
How merrily she goes!
Christ He loved the fishermen:
How He blest the fishing-boats
Down in Galilee!
Dark the night and wild the wave,
Christ the boat is keeping;
Trust in Him and have no fear,
Though He seemeth sleeping

Coming in

Briskly blows the morning breeze
Fresh and strong it blows;
Blessings on the fishing boat,
How steadily she goes!
Christ he loved the fishermen;
And He blessed the net
Which the hopeless fishers threw
In Gennersaret.
He has blest our going out,
Blest too our returning
Given us laden nets at night,
And fair wind in the morning.

The 19th Century Novel and the Howitts

The nineteenth century saw changes in style and in the popularity of the English novel. In the eighteenth century the reading of novels had been frowned upon, an idle and frivolous pastime. The Victorian period brought us many good writers and it was Charles Dickens who made the English novel respectable, popular and prolific. Mary started her writing during this period of change. She associated with many of the famous names of that time, including Dickens, Mrs Gaskell, Tennyson, Wordsworth, Elizabeth Barrett Browning and many others.

Mary, like other writers, was influenced by her background. Before her marriage she had mixed casually with the gentry through the people she met when accompanying her father on his work, but the Uttoxeter Quakers did not attend the social events of the town or the big society balls which were held in the White Hart Inn, now the White Hart Hotel. The idea of personal and business advancement through social contacts and marriage was quite against their principles. Quakers only married within their faith, and anyone who did otherwise was dismissed from the Society of Friends. Mary would neither have experienced nor been an onlooker at such events, so it would be difficult and possibly against her principles to examine such things in detail.

This is not to say that the Bothams did not entertain visitors, many of whom would have come to talk in Uttoxeter, in a room hired at the Red Lion Inn in the Market Place. But Mary implies that as a small child she stayed out of the way on these occasions, though she would have had some contact with the visitors later. It must also be remembered that Mary was brought up, in a country market town, to speak in the quaint archaic Quaker fashion and she would not be as familiar with the speech and social graces of the time as her contemporaries.

During this period ordinary people gave people nicknames and children would chant them in public. Quakers would have been obvious targets for this treatment, because of their appearance. To the Uttoxeter Quakers, with their strict adherence to the Quaker Dress, fashion was irrelevant. So it is not surprising Mary does not mention the dress of the characters in her books. Quakers were also conscientious objectors, and their failure to 'do their duty' during the Napoleonic Wars could well have led to lingering bad feeling among the general public. It is quite likely that Quakers were ridiculed and if this was so Mary would have understood the feelings of the less fortunate.

Mary had grown up with her mother's stories about the people she had met when working for the chaplain to George III, like Samuel Johnson, Garrick, and many high-ranking Anglican clergymen. Both Anna and Mary read anything and everything they could get their hands on; Mary even managed to get hold of literature secretly after she decided at about the age of fifteen that she wanted to be an author.

It is worth comparing Mary's background with that of the Brontë sisters and Jane Austen, all of whom were daughters of Anglican clergymen. For much of the seventeenth and eighteenth centuries, it was common practice for a younger son of the gentry to enter the church. The members of the clergy and their families were therefore considered respectable members of society, they would be invited to dine with their well-born parishioners and would attend local balls. Some members of the clergy were absentee vicars and rectors, leaving the parish work to a curate. This enabled the vicar or rector to follow the pursuits of the gentry, such as riding and hunting. The Brontë sisters may well have had a secluded life, but there would have been visitors to the Vicarage of gentle birth, and in the absence of their mother the daughters would have had to 'stand in' on these occasions. Jane Austen and the Brontë sisters were able to mix with and observe the society of 'social graces'.

Jane Austen's novels often contain young military characters, handsome and gay in their dashing uniforms, personifications of the glory and the heroism of soldiers. This sentiment would have been completely foreign to Mary Howitt's upbringing and religion. Jane Austen's brothers were serving officers in the navy and she would also have known all the anxieties of a family with loved ones at war. Elizabeth Gaskell with her broader upbringing was not afraid of writing about soldiers, or indeed about any other branch of society. Mary's Quaker conscience would not have allowed this, nor would it have allowed her to describe wars, although she was prepared to write about facts. She refers to the children drilling like soldiers in Balance Street, which she could see from her playroom window, but never uses soldiers as characters in her tales.

Mary Ann Evans, who wrote under the name of George Eliot, was the daughter of an estate manager who would have had to work in close consultation with his gentry employer. No doubt Mary Ann would have been in a position to observe what the family of her father's employers did, how they behaved, and how they spent their time. Mary Ann Evans was self-educated. She lived in Warwickshire and visited rural areas in Staffordshire and Derbyshire, observing the lives of the country folk in all the areas she visited. Like the others, she wrote about what she knew, from all levels of society.

Elizabeth Gaskell's family were Unitarians. Very educationally minded, the Unitarians had schools for both boys and girls which gave a wider teaching than just religion. They did not stick to the Bible alone for reading and writing, but taught singing, natural history and ancient and modern languages. Literature in the wider sense was valued, and Elizabeth, who taught in the Sunday School, read widely. Unitarianism appealed to several writers, including Coleridge, who had considered taking up the Ministry in 1799. Lamb and Hazlitt were also attracted to the denomination, as was Mary Howitt herself at one period of her life. Elizabeth Gaskell's father was a Unitarian minister and she would have received a much broader education than Mary Howitt or the daughters of the Anglican clergy, who would learn music, singing, drawing, embroidery etc. She married William Gaskell, a Unitarian minister in Manchester, and like any other minister's wife she helped him in his pastoral duties. She visited the sick, the needy and the poverty-stricken, and tried to alleviate their suffering. Often the clergy were the only educated people in the area so if a doctor, who had to be paid, could not be afforded, the minister often advised on sickness or found someone to nurse the sick.

Mary Howitt and Elizabeth Gaskell were very fond of corresponding with one another, exchanging ghost stories and the like until Elizabeth's death in 1865. Mary never published these stories, possibly because her father would have nothing to do with such ideas, and prohibited them from hearing about them, except that Nanny Woodings told them to the children without their parents' knowledge. Everyone in Elizabeth's circle told ghost stories and Elizabeth published some of hers in 'Old Nurse's Story', written for Charles Dickens.

Elizabeth produced a lot of work for Dickens, all of which was negotiated through Mary, who would write to Elizabeth requesting the article. In October, 1849 Mary wrote to Elizabeth requesting a piece for the editors of *Saturns Union Magazine* in America. Elizabeth sometimes stayed with the Howitts and there is no doubt that William and Mary did much to encourage her work. Elizabeth was also a great friend of Charlotte Brontë and it is quite likely that there was some exchange of information or interest between them all.

It is often stated that Elizabeth Gaskell took up writing at her husband's urging after she lost her only son in 1845, but it is also thought that her account of Clopton Hall may well have been written much earlier, prior to 1845. William was impressed with Elizabeth's work and had encouraged her to write further. When she had completed *Mary Barton* it was William who trudged around the London publishing houses until he found one that would accept it for publication in 1844. Other short stories followed *Life in Manchester, Libbie Marsh's Three*

Eras, The Sexton's Hero and *Christmas Storms and Sunshine,* all written under the pseudonym Cotton Mather Mills Esq. In 1848 William wrote to an unknown person, asking if they had read *Mary Barton* and stating that the book had been written at his suggestion and that the authoress had never written a book before.

Household Words

Elizabeth Gaskell had met the Howitts in 1841 when they were all on a tour of the Rhine, before her marriage [VS] and the friendship was to last the whole of Elizabeth's life. After the publication of *Mary Barton* she was asked to contribute to *Household Words*, a magazine for which William and Mary also contributed articles; none of the articles gave an author's name. On 20th February, 1850 Mary wrote to Elizabeth requesting work which was to be 'in' three weeks in advance and for publication in the 30th March edition. William and Mary's son Alfred was very amused when his father's story *The Miner's Daughter* was attributed to Currer Bell or Elizabeth Gaskell; in America it was attributed to Dickens himself.

On 20th February, 1850, Mary received a letter from Charles Dickens from his address in Devonshire Terrace, saying,

I address this note to Mr Howitt no less than to you. You will easily divine its purpose, I dare say; or at all events you would, if you knew what companions of mine you have ever been.

You may have seen the first dim announcements of the new cheap, literary weekly journal I am about to start. Frankly, I want to say to you, that if you would ever write for it, you would delight me, and I should consider myself very fortunate indeed in enlisting your assistance.

I propose to print no names of contributors, either in your own case or any other, and to give established writers the power of reclaiming their papers after a certain time. I hope any connection with the enterprise would be satisfactory and agreeable to you in all respects, as I should most earnestly endeavour to make it. If I wrote a book, I could say no more than I mean to suggest to you in these few lines. All that I leave unsaid, I leave to your generous understanding.

And so began *Household Words*, a journal that was successfully published for many years. During this period William and Mary were very close to Charles Dickens. In 1845 Dickens was impressed by Brice Castle School, where William and Mary had sent their two sons, Alfred and Charlton, the only school he had seen where education was treated as a broad system of moral and intellectual philosophy [VS]. Charlton was also educated at the London University School, which was a dissenting public school run by the Unitarians and free of Anglicanism. It excelled in the teaching of science and banned corporal punishment, very unusual and progressive in Victorian society.

Alfred Lord Tennyson corresponded with the Howitts for many years and stayed with them in 1847 after they returned from Germany. Another friend was Miss Eliza Metyard, the daughter of a prominent Shrewsbury surgeon, who, like other women authors, had disguised her name to thwart male prejudice. Her pseudonym was 'Silver Pen'. She stayed with the Howitts and was among the guests at a Christmas dinner which included Dr Garth Wilkinson, Mr Doherty and Mr La Trobe Bateman. Miss Metyard was interested in social and political reform, which she continued to the end of her life. Mary wrote to her that she wanted to write about Protection of Women but felt Saunders would be too frightened to publish.

Mary wrote mainly for children and very prolifically at that. She had the qualities of silent and accurate observation along with a good memory. She often deals with Uttoxeter and its environs in articles, as well as her own life. Some of her poetry books are beautifully illustrated with wood cuts, and there are several little collections of her poems, many about nature, with representations of birds, animals, trees and flowers forming decorative curves or 'L's around the pages. Some of the books in this series, bound in gold-tooled leather, were reprinted at least seven times and many went to America. *The Spider and the Fly* is a poem by Mary Howitt, with a moral, like many others:

THE SPIDER AND THE FLY

"Will you walk into my parlour?" said the Spider to the Fly:
"Tis the prettiest little parlour that ever you did spy;
The way into my parlour is up a winding stair,
And I have many curious things to show when you are there."
"Oh no, no," said the little fly, "to ask me is in vain,
For who goes up your winding stair can ne'er come down again."

"I'm sure you must be weary, dear, with soaring up so high;
Will you rest upon my little bed?" said the Spider to the Fly.
"There are pretty curtains drawn around, the sheets are fine and thin,
And if you like to rest a while, I'll snugly tuck you in!"
"Oh no, no," said the little Fly, "for I've often heard it said,
They never, never wake again, who sleep upon your bed!"

Said the cunning Spider to the Fly: "Dear friend, what can I do
To prove the warm affection I've always felt for you?
I have, within my pantry, good store of all that's nice;
I'm sure you are very welcome - will you please to take a slice?"
"Oh, no, no," said the little Fly, "kind sir that cannot be,
I've heard what's in your pantry, and I do not wish to see!"

"Sweet creature," said the Spider, "you're witty and you're wise;
How handsome are your gauzy wings, how brilliant are your eyes!
I have a little looking-glass upon my parlour shelf,
If you'll step in one moment, dear, you shall behold yourself."
"I thank you, gentle sir," she said, "for what you're pleased to say,
And bidding you good-morning now, I'll call another day."

The Spider turned him round about, and went into his den,
For well he knew the silly Fly would soon come back again;
So he wove a subtle web, in a little corner sly,
And set his table ready, to dine upon the Fly.
Then he came out to his door again, and merrily did sing, -
"Come hither hither, pretty Fly, with the pearl and silver wing;

"Your robes are green and purple, there's a crest upon your head:
Your eyes are like the diamond bright, but mine are dull as lead!"
Alas, alas! how very soon this silly little Fly,
Hearing his wily, flattering words, came slowly flitting by:
With buzzing wings she hung aloft, then near and nearer drew, -
Thinking only of her brilliant eyes, and green and purple hue,

Thinking only of her crested head - poor foolish thing! At last
Up jumped the cunning Spider, and fiercely held her fast;
He dragged her up his winding stair; into his dismal den
Within his little parlour - but she ne'er came out again!
And now, dear little children, who may this story read,
To idle, silly, flattering words, I pray you, ne' er give heed:

Unto an evil counsellor close heart, and ear, and eye,
And take a lesson from this tale, of the Spider and the Fly.

The Traveller on the Hill-top

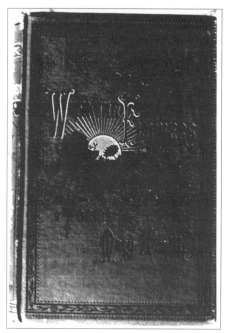

With the Flowers, by Mary Howitt, a typically ornate binding of the time.

At the time Mary started writing, people thought that children were miniature adults. Mary obviously disagreed, at the beginning of *My Own Story, or The Autobiography of a Child*, published Aug. 30th, 1844, she wrote:

It has often been a subject of regret that so little is known of the workings of a child's mind during its earlier years. Little of this, however, can be known, excepting in cases of great precocity in children; and then the case is not an ordinary one, for children do not reason at all, they only receive impressions. They feel things keenly, kindness or unkindness, joy or sorrow - but they neither reason nor reflect - the reason and the reflection come later, and then we draw inferences, and understand the connection of one thing with another. We stand then, as it were, at the proper distance to take in a general view; we stand like the traveller on the hill-top, and look over the landscape which we have left behind us. We see there, in a clear perspective, the house in which we were born; the trees around it, or the neighbours' houses; we see here sunshine, there shade; there the hill of difficult ascent, which was painful to our feet, and there the green and sunny valleys where we wandered with the companions of our joy, and gathered the gay flowers of every season.

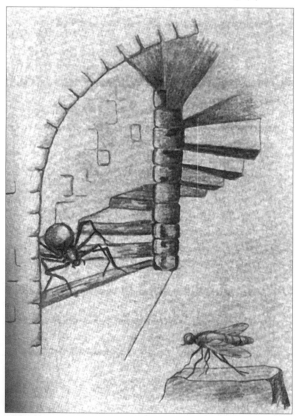

The 'Spider and the Fly' a well-known childrens' poem by Mary Howitt. Drawing by Mary Noon.

CHAPTER EIGHT
NATIONAL PROBLEMS AND THE HOWITTS

The 19th century was a period of great change. The Napoleonic Wars, which caused much disruption of trade, finished in 1815. Soldiers returned home, many severely wounded and unable to work. Jobs were scarce; the Industrial Revolution had put large numbers out of work, the corn laws and several poor harvests had made the price of food, particularly bread, very high - the cost of wheat between 1800 and 1820 varied from 57/- and 126/- per quarter. At the same time wages had declined. A man earning 33/3d. in 1795 received only 5/6d. in 1830. Food was often aldulterated, flour with alum, for instance, and milk was often contaminated. Poor diet made people prone to disease.

1845 was the first year of the Irish Potato Famine - and the Irish were unable to import English wheat. Many emigrated to the United States to escape the famine; some got no further than Liverpool where the average age of death was 22 years, in constrast to a rural area like Rutland, where it was 41 years. The Church of England was struggling with its Parish Relief - the claims on its purse were more than they felt able to give. The Overseers of the Poor tightened the amount of money they gave to their poor. During the 1830-40s there arose a general awareness of the plight of these people. In 1832 there was a Royal Commission on the Poor Law; Chadwick sat on that Commission. In 1834 the Amendment Act abolished outdoor relief; the Act it amended dated from 1601! "Less eligibility" was introduced.

In 1833 a Factories Act limited the working day for pauper apprentices to 12 hours. Children under 9 years old were forbidden to work and those 9 to 13 were limited to a 9-hour day. Factory Inspectors were introduced. In 1842 women and boys under the age of 10 were prohibited from work underground in mines and inspectors were introduced. By 1844 another factory act reduced the age for children to 8 years and women were now restricted to 12 hours of daily work. Three years later the Ten Hour Act restricted women and children to 10-hours.

A contemporary engraving showing the attack on the Stockport workhouse and taking of food, after the Poor Law Amendment Act of 1834.

In 1816 a Select Committee on Madhouses revealed the appalling conditions. Diseases such as cholera and dysentery were rife in the squalid industrial towns. Chadwick's famous report on the Sanitary Condition of the Labouring Population led to a Royal Commission of Towns being set up in 1843. 1845 saw the setting up of the Lunacy Commission to supervise asylums and in 1847 the first Medical Officer of Health was appointed. 1832 saw the first electoral reform allowing urban middle class men the vote, accompanied by local government reform three years later.

In many urban and semi-urban families, both parents worked outside the home; universal education was not the norm and young children could no longer be sent out to earn money for the family. Children were therefore left at home on their own with the hazards unsupervised care brings. The Howitts felt that conditions could be improved by self education and produced *The Howitt Journal*. Others likewise sought to improve the plight of the poor through literature; Charles Dickens, Charles Kingsley, Elizabeth Gaskell, amongst others.

Journals and Bankruptcy

In 1846 William became an editor and part-proprietor of *The People's Journal*, which aimed at *"removing abuses"* and the *"general betterment of the working classes"*. He had previously been a contributor and now joined John Saunders, a well-known poet, novelist and dramatist. On April 11th he signed an agreement whereby he was to match the funds invested by Turrell, Saunders's partner and brother-in-law, in return for a one-half share. William paid £800 for half, while a second half was to be the return for his and Mary's services to the journal. Saunders continued as editor; all he invested was his skill and time and he kept no books! Saunders and Turrell also defaced the original agreement (Saunders was to say the agreement had only been for a one-third share).

Mary was angry with her sister Anna and Daniel Harrison because they criticized some of the articles:

What canst thou mean by thinking The People's Journal is not Christian in spirit? - there is no attempt to set the poor against the rich, but on the contrary, to induce them to be prudent, sober, independent; above all to be satisfied to be workers, to regard labour as a privilege rather than a penalty, which is quite our view of the case.

This idea of improvement within one's class was the view of the Christian Socialists and of people like Charles Kingsley of *The Water Babies* fame, who were not in sympathy with the current gospel of '*get out of your class at any price - be boss, where once you were an under-paid worker*'. Mary was sure of the paper's high aims and that it might be *"an instrument for good"*. This may have been so, but it was evident that this did not apply to William's co-editor and proprietors, who were soon denounced as *"scoundrels"*. No accounts had been kept, and everything was in chaos; Mary hoped they could get out of it without loss.

To William, it became clear that he must start a paper of his own - a Howitt Journal. Mary supported William in his aim of helping the working classes, *"and as we considered sin to be the result of the defective education of mankind, we aimed at universal progress by the mental, moral, and physical elevation of the human race; believing that with the growth of the mind, and its freedom from adverse circumstances, religion would come of itself."* [GW] *The Howitt Journal* was first published in January 1847. William was the sole proprietor and Mary the joint editor. They enlisted the help of Dr Samuel Smiles, author of *Self Help* and other works aimed at educating the lower classes, and together with other *"gifted and popular writers, we sought, in an attractive form, to urge the labouring classes, by means of temperance, self-education, and moral conduct, to be their own benefactors."*

The issues came out in weekly parts price 1/-, postage 2d and each six months' collection could be bound later on as a set. The circulation was 30,000 (including both weekly and monthly sales) though the sales fell because of Saunders's intervention. It was published in London by William Lovett of 171 Strand, London. William James Linton was chief engraver. He was one of the best engravers of the period and always breakfasted with the Howitts.

The Howitt Journal (1847-1848) was a vehicle for information on such topics as Health, Wages of the Working Classes and Living Conditions of the Working Classes. They published the results of the Registrar General's tables of mortality and the causes of illness. Journals like theirs were available for working people to read at local educational institutes. Uttoxeter's only nineteenth-century local historian, Francis Redfern, was self-taught, and it was due to the Uttoxeter Literary Institute and similar that men like him were able to acquire knowledge.

Another well-known writer of the day involved in the *Journal* was Dr Thomas Southwood Smith (1788-1861), who practised as a Unitarian minister in Edinburgh while he studied medicine. He helped found the *Westminster Review* in 1824, *The Penny Cyclopedia*, the Useful Knowledge Society and The Health of Towns Association. He visited the inner city poor, where he saw much poverty, poor housing and the illness and death that went with them. His works included very valuable papers on epidemics and sanitary improvements.

Mary was a member of the Health of Towns Association and her articles in the *Journal* may well have been to further the Association's aims. 1842 saw the Publication of Chadwick's report on the Sanitary Condition of the Labouring Population, which led to the Royal Commission on Health of Towns in 1843. This is a typical extract from Howitt's Journal:

COMMON LODGING-HOUSES, AND
A MODEL LODGING-HOUSE FOR THE POOR

It has long been notorious that the common lodging houses in London, and in other large cities, for the itinerant poor, are of the most wretched and contaminating description. They are generally situated in densely populated neighbourhoods: small, ill-ventilated, filthy, and crowded to suffocation, they engender disease of the most virulent kinds; the poisonous miasma of which, wafted upon every breeze, is carried into the dwellings of the rich as well as of the poor, spreading death and desolation all around; as witness the following incident which occurred in London only the other day:-

"Death from Impure Air, - An inquest was held on Thursday by Mr Payne, city coroner, at the Red Lion, Shoe-lane, on the body of a man unknown, who died suddenly in a common lodging-house, in Field-lane, Holborn. The deceased, it appeared, had occupied a bed in the lodging-house, 26 Field-lane, for which he paid fourpence per night, for the last three months. On Friday night he returned to his lodging about six o'clock, and complained of a pain across the loins. He went early to bed, and during the night he was heard to laugh hysterically, and in the morning was found a corpse. The only 'property' found upon him was four duplicates, in a tin box, and a halfpenny. Dr J. Lynch said that on going into the room he found a very offensive smell of animal exhalations, as if there had been several persons sleeping in it. He stooped down at the first bed, and found the body of the deceased. Many of the lodging-houses were built over cesspools, and the impure air breathed in the confined apartments had just the same effect upon the vital parts as inhaling the noxious vapour of burning charcoal...but he died in a fit, no doubt caused by breathing impure air. He (Dr Lynch) had no hesitation in saying that death in the present case was accelerated by want of proper ventilation. In some of them (lodgings) eight or nine persons slept where accommodation was afforded for only two...it is a well-known fact, that out of 100,000 children born, 50,000 died solely from inhaling impure air. Fever is constantly breaking out in these houses....

These lodging-houses are also the prolific hot-beds, and the nurseries for every species of wickedness and crime; yet the poor, from dire necessity, are compelled to use them, and to pay for their filthy, abominable, and dangerous accommodation, a price very far exceeding what might afford them decent, and in their circumstances, comfortable lodgings.

108   **The Traveller on the Hill-top**

Efforts have long been in operation, and in operation successfully, to raise the industrious working classes to a proper estimate of themselves, and to improve their moral, intellectual, and physical condition. That great work is going on prosperously and will prosper.

But the poor, the very poor - the wandering, half-naked, diseased and friendless outcasts, of which there are always many thousands in London, and tens of thousands throughout the kingdom - are still neglected; they are constantly prowling on our streets, picking up a mean, a criminal, and a precarious living; and when evening comes, without sympathy, without hope, without the means of instruction and improvement open to others, they have nowhere to hide their miserable bodies, and their aching hearts, but in those dens of infamy, the common lodging-houses...."

As well as temperance the Howitts supported sanitary reform, free trade, free opinions, and the abolition of obstructive monopolies. They upheld the belief that there should be schools for every class of the population and they recognized *"those great rights which belong to every individual of the great British people"* [L&R].

Mary asked Eliza Metyard to write on women's issues, including the Protection of Women question. Women's liberation was not a new social issue for the Howitts. They had helped with the publication of David Love's work *The Life of David Love,* the autobiography of a working class man under the title *John Ashmore* in 1823. This book talks about single women being educated in economy and household management. The subject continued through *The Howitt Journal*, and, indeed, concerned Mary for long after the *Journal* ceased to be. She and Eliza worked on committees with Octavia Hill, Harriet Martineau, Elizabeth Gaskell, Barbara Leigh-Smith, etc., all of whom had contributed to *The Howitt Journal*. Mary was an avid supporter of the Whittington Club, an organization set up by Douglas Jerold, the publisher, who wanted to encourage women as well as men. It was revolutionary in its day, promoting among other things the notion that women should sit in Parliament. Mary was secretary of the Club during the working of the Married Women's Property Act, which was set up by Barbara Leigh-Smith (later Bodichan), who also advocated free education for girls as well as boys, and at one time she was even involved with a group who advocated 'free sex'.

Ebeneezer Elliott commented on *The Howitt Journal "a shrewd pithy letter: 'Men engaged in a death struggle for bread will pay for amusement when they will not for instruction. They woo laughter to unscare them - that they may forget their perils, their wrongs, and their oppressors, and play at undespair. If you were able and willing to fill the journal with fun it would pay.'"* [GW] This might have been proved true, had the working class been able to afford to buy, or indeed been able to read, the weekly three halfpenny magazine. Mary ruefully commented, *"Our magazine proved, like its predecessor a pecuniary failure"* [GW]. The Howitts were nearly made bankrupt, and their letters at the time relate to loans or gifts of money from relatives and friends.

The Confidence Trick

In the spring of 1847 the Howitts made the acquaintance of Edward Youl, a bespectacled, dark-haired man of about thirty. A Cambridge graduate, he had decided to devote his life to literature as a change from teaching the Classics. He told them confidentially that he was *"struggling with poverty for conscience's sake."* The only child of a pawnbroker who had made a fortune but died intestate, he would, he said, rather starve than claim such ill-gotten gains. He told them that he had married a not very well-off girl of the Society of Friends.

As usual, the trusting Howitts believed his story and allowed him the freedom of their home. They liked his prose and obtained a job for him with John Cassell at a salary of £200 per annum, writing for the *Standard of Freedom*. For this he only needed to work three days a week but he became lazy. A bad time-keeper, he was dismissed, despite repeated warnings. William had him reinstated at least once, but eventually he had to leave.

William and Mary did not wish to abandon Edward and his wife, though Mary was not impressed with her either. They found work for both of them. She was to work as an actress in Hull with their friend Charles Kean, the actor, and Mr Linwood, the owner of the *Eclectic Review*, was to visit the Howitts at Lower Clapton with a view to offering Edward a job. But Edward turned out to be a confidence trickster and rogue. On the previous Friday evening Mary received a visit from a Mrs Copeland, of 11, Upper Stamford Street, Blackfriars, *"a respectable woman"* who had called to collect rent due. She informed Mary that *"a gentleman named Youl had taken her rooms for poor Mrs Howitt, who was in such destitution that she was compelled to make private application for relief to the nobility, adding I was very sorry for you, ma'am I am sure, but when letters, evidently containing money, and sealed with coronets, kept coming, and I never got my rent, I made so bold as to learn your address at the British Museum, and was surprised to find you living in so good a house."* [GW]

Although a warrant was issued for his arrest, Edward managed to slip the police and got to Hull. His wife wrote to Mary on the Sunday saying her husband would explain everything and would they forgive him because her prospects would suffer along with her husband's. The following day he wrote a begging letter in Mary's name to Macaulay, who sent him £10. A private detective traced him to either Leeds or Liverpool. Alfred was sent to find him. Unfortunately, Alfred was at that time a bit of a "dandy". He enjoyed dancing and was very taken with one of his cousins, the daughter of Mary's sister Anna, and as a result he missed Youl who boarded a boat for America.

Mary found Youl had obtained money on her behalf from Lord John Russell, Lord Lansdowne, Lord Denman, Lord Mahone and Lord Brougham, who wrote from Cannes forwarding £20 for her and requesting Lord Russell to settle a pension on her. Later she discovered that Sir Robert Peel had sent £50 for her.

> The forged letters returned to me were written in a crawling, exaggerated strain. In acknowledging a donation from the Bishop of Oxford (Wilberforce) [a brother of William] I was made to say, "I went down on my knees and thanked God who had moved his lordship's heart to such noble kindness to me." [GW]

In April 1850 Mrs Youl visited the wife of Dr Muspratt in Liverpool, saying that her husband was the person who had falsely obtained money and that she had only just found out. Her husband had deserted her and she had pawned everything she had, including her wedding ring.

> Many years later, John Cassel found himself sitting opposite Youl in an eating house in New York! Though he was in a different guise, Cassel recognised his voice and features. Youl denied ever having been in England, but Mary tells us that, in March 1870, one Robert Spring, alias Sprague, alias Redfern Hawley and a host of other aliases, was tried and convicted in the Court of Quarter Sessions in Philadelphia for false pretences and experts believed this man and Youl were identical. He had been in America, "the distracted father of a large family." [GW]

The mental strain on the Howitts must have been severe, coming at the same time as their problems with *The Howitt Journal*. During these troubles the family moved again, this time to 28 Upper Avenue Road, St John's Wood, a detached house which was small and cold.

William, because of his involvement with the Co-operative Movement, was invited to speak all over the country on the topics which he had advocated in his recent Letters on Labour. He had warm friends and supporters of all social classes. The previous year Mary had written about the Leigh-Smiths, whose acquaintance they had made during a visit to Hastings, where the Leigh-Smiths had a country house. Mr Leigh-Smith was MP for Norwich and was described as a *"good Radical and supporter of Free Trade and the abolition of the Corn Laws."* The Howitts joined Mr Leigh-Smith with a party to Cambridge, including Professor Pulsky and his wife, Professor Kinkel and Herr Kroff from Prague, refugees from Europe.

The Women's Movement

In the middle of the nineteenth century The Married Woman's Property Act was an important political issue. Until it was passed in 1882 any property, investments or money a woman had on marriage automatically went to her husband, as did anything she inherited after her marriage. This was how John Botham had been able to mortgage his wife's property when he was short of money. In fact, a woman owned nothing in her own right except by inheritance at her husband's death.

Throughout their lives, women were treated as the property of men. A girl belonged to her father and he could do what he liked with her. This is why the bride is still given away by her father in marriage; at that time he literally did give her away to her husband, who then 'owned' her. She had no legal status. A wife was her husband's chattel; in wills and on tombstones it was often written 'wife and relict of' or 'the relict of' and the husband's name followed, and the wife was not necessarily mentioned by her own Christian name.

A mother had no rights over her own children, and should she leave her husband she forfeited them. Divorce was expensive and required an act of Parliament. Proceedings had to be brought by the husband, and it was always assumed that the woman was the guilty party. No proof of any kind was needed. A woman on her own had no means of supporting herself and it is comparatively recently that women have achieved equal rights to vote. In 1918 women over the age of 30 years and with certain educational and property qualifications could vote, in 1919 they could stand for Parliament. It was not until 1928, only just over seventy years ago, that women of all classes could vote at the same age as men.

Writing was however to a degree an acceptable pursuit, as was involvement with charitable causes outside the home. In these ways women could make themselves noticed respectably. Mary Howitt achieved recognition as a woman in her own right, despite her restricted upbringing and the social attitudes of the time. William was very much in favour of women having rights of their own and encouraged Mary to develop her own career.

The Petition of Elizabeth Barrett Browning, Anna Jameson, Mary Howitt, Mrs Gaskell and others was presented to Parliament early in 1856. It aimed to alter the law regarding married women's property rights and earnings. There were just under 3,000 London signatures, including William Howitt's, and another 2,000 obtained in Westminster. Unfortunately, the most significant change it produced was that divorce was made easier for men. There was little benefit to women, though they did gain limited property rights.

Mary's friendship with the Leigh-Smiths brought her into close contact with women activists. Barbara Leigh-Smith (1827-1891), later Mrs Leigh-Smith Bodichon, was the daughter of Benjamin Leigh-Smith, MP, who was very actively involved in the movement, and also a friend of Mary's son Alfred. Her grandfather had been a follower of George Fox, an emancipator and a great abolitionist. Barbara married Dr Eugene Bodichon who supported her in her causes. She was also a close friend of Mary's daughter Annie and a first cousin of Florence Nightingale. Although not acknowledged as a women's activist, she was a supporter of many reforms. Mary also supported women's causes but unlike Barbara she could not give financial support. Instead she wrote articles for magazines and for women's groups.

Many middle class girls at the time were not sure that they wanted marriage, with incessant childbearing and an interminable round of social functions. They did not have the freedom to choose their husbands, relying instead on the leniency of fathers and guardians. Anything that went wrong was blamed on the woman, whether it be an unhappy marriage, rape, or venereal disease. Pioneer women sought equality with men in the field in which their interest lay. They did not want superiority to men. Florence Nightingale did not want to take over the medical profession, she wanted to form a group of women knowledgeable of medicine and trained in caring, a quality which she felt was native to them.

In 1830 the unhappily married Caroline Norton, granddaughter of the playwright Sheridan, sued her husband, Lord Melbourne, for adultery. The jury threw out the case. She had left her husband and started writing to support herself (her husband tried to claim her earnings from her). One of her early pamphlets helped the passing of the Custody of Children Act of 1839, which enabled innocent mothers to receive the custody of their children. Until then, fathers had complete control of their children; they could, and in one case did, tear a baby from its mother's breast to have it adopted. Caroline Norton's sad case stirred the hearts of many women and people like Barbara Bodichon who worked for the emancipation of women. It was inevitable that she should ask a fellow writer, a Quaker who believed that all people were equal in the sight of God, to help with her cause.

In 1857 Barbara Bodichon founded and endowed Girton College, Cambridge, the first women's university college. Emily Davies, a pioneer in women's education, was the first principal. Although the students sat the same examinations as the men did, Cambridge refused to confer on women full membership of the University (*ie* award them the same degrees as male graduates received) until 1947!

Spiritualism

The Howitts were still experimenting with spiritualism in the 1850s though their son in Australia did not approve and urged them to be careful. Their type of spiritualism was what was called "The Christian" branch - they used Bibles. They discovered automatic writing and spirit-inspired painting, which had come to England from America. Mary's childhood interest in ghosts, hobgoblins and brownies continued and both Mary and William had presentiments and dreams. This was nothing new for Mary; after all, her father had returned to Uttoxeter from the Forest of Dean shortly after her birth because of a dream and presentiment.

Elizabeth Barrat Browning, a friend of Mary's for fifteen years, was also a spiritualist, and attended seances, at one of which Mary received a message from her dead son Claude. By then she was experimenting with spiritualism at her own home in Highgate. Robert Browning was not keen on William and disliked their wives' friendship. To Mary's great sorrow he brought about its end in 1856. During the 1860s and up to 1875, William wrote articles for the *Spiritualist Magazine*, about a hundred in all. He also corresponded with Charles Dickens on topics such as spiritualism, mediums and ghosts, sometimes in the pages of *All The Year Round* and in the *Spiritualist Magazine*.

In 1850 Harriet Beecher Stowe's book *Uncle Tom's Cabin* was published and stirred feelings on both sides of the Atlantic. William did not consider the book to be of any significance as a work of art, but he and Mary promoted it as the subject matter was close to their hearts. They very much wanted to meet Harriet Beecher Stowe and on her visit to England in 1852-3 they had their desire granted. Mary served on thc Duchess of Sutherland's committee which received Harriet. Mary was now mixing with titled people, but she never felt at ease, disapproving of titles because of her Quaker beliefs. Of Mary, Harriet Beecher Stowe said she was *"just such a cheerful, sensible fireside companion as we find in her books - winning love and trust the very first moment of the interview"* [VS].

Artistic Renewal

Mary and William appear to have sought the acquaintance of well-known writers, and the Great Exhibition of 1851 gave them an opportunity to further this aim. Here they met General Sheriden, among others. Nevertheless, there are several letters in existence in which Mary declines invitations that would have enabled her to meet other authors and notable people. On one occasion, in an undated letter to a Mrs Gilbert, she declines an invitation sent on a Friday to meet Dr Raffles of Sunday School fame on the Monday morning at Miss Greaves's. She asks that Miss Greaves be made aware that they are much obliged for the invitation but they both have business which cannot be put off.

Always interested in new movements and ideas, Mary became acquainted with the Pre-Raphaelite Brotherhood in 1848. They were unconventional, expressing in their art liberal ideas which might seem opposed to the Howitts' way of thinking, but nevertheless the Howitts included members of the brotherhood in their circle of friends. Inspired by the Italian artists who preceded Raphael, they devoted themselves to the pursuit of truth and beauty. They portrayed their subjects exactly as they appeared in nature rather than following the time-honoured formulae taught by the art schools and supposedly derived from the style of the great 16th century Italian painters, especially Raphael. In this style figures had to conform to lifeless attitudes with accepted rules of picture composition. Dark and gloomy colours were used in the belief that they resembled the works of the old masters.

As well as painters, the Pre-Raphaelite group included sculptors and writers. They were all young, in their twenties when Mary met them. Amongst them were Buchanan Read, the American, Leigh Hunt, Holman Hunt, who is known for his painting *The Light of the World*, and Edward La Trobe Bateman, described by Mary as *"endowed with an exquisite feeling and skill for decorative art"*. Dante Gabriel Rossetti, Christina Rossetti, John Everett Millais, who exhibited at the Royal Academy, the poet Hazeldell and William Allingham Woolner, the Irish poet and sculptor of the bust of Tennyson in Westminster Abbey, were also among the group.

Describing to Meggie what she called *"one of their crushes"*, Mary referred to the women's "wild hair" and the fact that they were uncrinolined. Such women were considered completely unrespectable and of very loose morals; they did not conform to the rigid standards of etiquette of the Victorian period. This all fitted in with their idea of 'natural beauty', and some women envied them their freedom of movement at a time when the fashion was for corsetted, wasp-like waists and dresses which prevented the wearer from bending at the waist or lifting her arms - all for the sake of fashion and the current male ideas of feminine beauty.

Mary went on to describe their homes. There were pictures all over the walls and sketch books lay on the tables. They used rich, free-flowing colours which Mary thought beautiful. Conventional decor was subdued and it is therefore not surprising that Mary was moved. These were romantics, people with new ideas which were sometimes shocking. Mary told Meggie she felt out of place in such a group of young, like-minded people.

The Royal Academy exhibition of 1850 was the beginning of the end for the Brethren. Public opinion was against them and they could not stand up to another public debate about their work the following year. They disbanded, though John Ruskin had some sympathy for them and consequently their style became fashionable a few years later.

The Howitts rented Clive Vale Farm in Hastings and in 1852 Edward Lear, the writer of nonsense verses, took rooms there (he was relieved to find there were no dogs!). He was introduced to William Holman Hunt, who arrived in August of that year for a "short holiday" with William Rossetti. Holman Hunt felt the cliff scenery of the place was just what he wanted for his work. The picture *Strayed Sheep* was executed during this holiday.

Prince Albert, the Prince Consort, took a great interest in 'the arts'. He wanted the general population to be educated in art. It had been said that art *"appealed as pure, noble, and harmonious, to the mind rather than to the eye or ear. The general public was wholly uneducated in the art."* It led to the 1851 Exhibition, organized by Prince Albert, the Society of Arts and other interested people.

William Wordsworth.

Charles Dickens

Elizabeth Barrett Browning

Elizabeth Gaskell

Four of the literary figures who had important friendships and business associations with the Howitts.

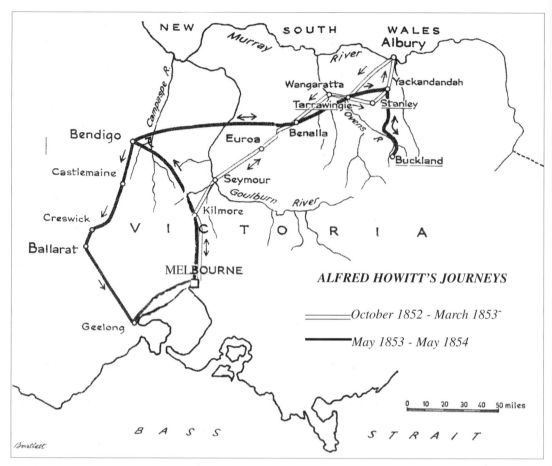

Alfred Howitt

CHAPTER NINE
LINKS WITH THE ANTIPODES

Godfrey Howitt, William's youngest brother, and educated by William, eventually qualified as a doctor in Edinburgh in 1830. He set himself up in practice in Leicester, as honorary physician to the Nottingham General Hospital and to Nottingam City Infirmary. On 6th April 1831 he married Phebe Bakewell, sister of John and Robert Bakewell of Nottingham, at the Friends' Meeting House, Castle Donington. They were to have three sons and a daughter.

William had fought for Godfrey to study medicine, and Godfrey continued to turn to him for advice and help. He left university in debt and his new practice meant more financial outlay - his specially made furniture, for instance, was expensive. But the practice did not produce enough patients. He was clearly frustrated; he wrote telling of a well-established doctor who charged much more for his professional services and yet had plenty of patients. As early as July 1825, he mentioned in a letter to William the possibility of going to another country where medical men were wanted. The seeds of his emigration had been sown.

Godfrey and his family arrived in Australia in April 1840. He was one of the first doctors in Melbourne. He bought land at the corner of Collins and Spring Streets, where he practised until he moved to Caulfield in 1869. He was an early member of Port Phillip's Medical Association, a council member of the University of Melbourne (founded 1853) from 1853 until 1871, the first honorary physician at Melbourne Hospital and the Benevolent Asylum, a founder member of the Entomological Society in London, a member of the Edinburgh Botanical Society, and also in the same year, 1854, the first Vice-President of the Philosophical Society (later the Royal Society of Victoria). Like the rest of his family he was a keen naturalist, especially interested in botany and entomology. A palm he planted was still in the Royal Botanical Gardens in Melbourne in 1971. When he died in 1873, having been predeceased by Phebe in 1868, he left his large library of books on botany and entomology to the University of Melbourne, along with a substantial sum of money, £1,000, which provided natural history scholarships. There are still doctors among his descendants in England.

William and Godfrey Howitt's brother Richard also emigrated to Australia, though he later returned to England. He, too, settled near Melbourne, in an area he called Wilford after a favourite place near Nottingham. He bought 40 hectares of land in what is now a suburb of the area known as Alpington. Whilst he farmed sheep, he was also a keen naturalist, spending a lot of time in excursions into the bush. Godfrey's letters are so different from those of Richard, who left England with him. Both men wrote on their paper in two directions - a common practice early in the nineteenth century when writing materials were scarce and expensive. When they had filled a page they turned the sheet of paper 90 degrees and over-wrote across the previous lines. Godfrey's handwriting is open and larger than that of Richard, who writes reams in a tight and fairly small hand.

Richard does not appear to have been an easy man; his letters to his parents are full of self-justification. He wrote to his parents to tell them of a disagreement with Mary, possibly about Anna refusing his hand, because he wanted to get his side of the story to them before Mary. He did not find Australian life conducive to his happiness. He was also unlucky, contracting dysentery three times in a short succesion. He bought a farm next to Godfrey, stocked it with many sheep and then saw the price of the animals start to fall. Even in his early letters from Australia he implies that he does not intend to stay there. In fact, he returned to Nottinghamshire after three years and lived more or less as a recluse, occupying himself with

116   **The Traveller on the Hill-top**

the farming he loved, along with writing poetry. Some people considered Richard's poetry to be superior to that of other members of the family, including William. He wrote *Impressions of Australian Felix*, a book of poetry, about his Australian experiences.

The Australian Visit

1851 was the year of The Great Exhibition and the occasion prompted Mary to write her feelings about it:

> On brilliant Sunday morning, in the spring of 1851, my husband and I, walking down the fields from Hampstead, with all London lying before us, suddenly saw something shining over in the distance like a huge diamond, the true mountain of light. It marked the first Great Exhibition in Hyde Park, a new feature, not only in the fine view, but in the history of the world. We met a humble Londoner evidently on his way to Hampstead Heath. William said to him, "Turn round and look at the Crystal Palace shining over in the distance." He did so, and exclaiming "Oh! thank you, sir; how wonderful!" stood gazing as long as we could see him.

> Some reader has, without doubt, still fresh in his recollection the gay, animated appearance of London in this spring of 1851. The evidence of the approaching Exhibition was apparent on every side: houses and shops cleaned and repainted, hotels for "All Nations" and coffee-houses of the "Great Exhibition" opened right and left; huge wagons, piled with bales, slowly moving along to Hyde Park; and, standing in bewilderment at the corners of streets and by omnibuses, were foreigners, with big beards and moustachios, in queer felt-hats and braided coats; whilst elegant Frenchwomen, in long cloth cloaks with picturesque hoods, and plain drab bonnets with rich interior trimmings (a new style of dress, beautiful from its severity), might be seen in Regent Street and Piccadilly, acting as a foil to Oriental magnates in gold embroidery, flowing silk, and gorgeous cashmere.

> How crowded, that spring, was the private view of the Portland Gallery by lords, ladies, artists, priests, and distinguished foreigners! J. R. Herbert, R. A. grave and thin of countenance and spare of form, walked bareheaded at the side of the portly, benign Cardinal Wiseman, and with reverence pointed out various pictures to him. Then came a low buzz movement of excitement in the throng, which contained the Archbishop of York and the Bishop of London, when Cardinal Wiseman, Dr. Doyle, Roman Catholic Bishop of Carlow, Father Gavazzi, and Mazzini were seen grouped together examining the same painting. "How very odd!" was the general remark; and my husband added, "The fine arts may truly be said to form neutral ground!"

1851 was also the year gold was discovered in Australia and the newspapers were full of it. William wanted a break from writing and saw this as an opportunity to have the rest he needed, to make some money and to gather material for further writing on his return (indeed, the trip resulted in six volumes). It is interesting to speculate how much the Great Exhibition with all its excitement and foreign visitors influenced Williams's decision.

He decided to travel with his sons, Alfred and Charlton, and Edward Bateman, to whom his elder daughter Annie was engaged. Edward was the son of the Howitts' Clapton friends; the engagement was broken off after he had been in Australia for some years, but nevertheless he remained one of Alfred's friends. William looked forward to visiting his brother, Godfrey, and seeing what future the country offered his sons. Both Mary and William felt Europe was over-populated and that there was not much future for young men in England. How little things change.

When William got an idea into his head he implemented it immediately, and his visit to Australia was no exception. He tried to make his arrangements quietly as he did not want to attract unwelcome travelling companions (though he was unsuccessful in this). He also had to deal with opposition from his family, Mary anticipating all sorts of catastrophes. He had not got enough money for the expedition, and what were Mary and his daughters to live on? He ended up borrowing money to finance the trip and for financial "adequacies" at home. Mary and Annie were to earn their own livelihoods, Mary by writing and Annie by her writing, drawing and painting. In fact, as well as keeping themselves Mary and Annie worked hard so that they could pay off William's debt!

William took with him his mining tools, two folding beds and a chair, pans, crockery and cutlery, firearms, thigh-high boots and many colourful shirts (this shows how much he wanted to participate fully in what he understood to be the Australian culture and how far behind the Howitts were leaving their Quaker attitudes). He also took a light cart which, in the event, proved too heavy for the wet, muddy conditions of Melbourne.

They sailed on the Kent, which had returned to Britain from Peru with a cargo of guano. Elizabeth Fry's son, brought up a Quaker, had chartered the ship. Alfred became disillusioned with him and also disapproved of what he had seen in the office. The Kent had been inadequately cleaned and this was to cause more discomfort for the passengers than normal. Guano does not carry a pleasant aroma. It was, however, a better ship than most carrying passengers at that time. The Howitts witnessed one ship being towed by five rowing boats full of passengers! Sea travel at this period was extremely hazardous and fraught with dangers. Illness and the lack of fresh food and water created problems for the passengers.

Alfred and Charlton boarded the Kent at Gravesend on 4th June, 1852 but William decided to have more time with Mary and did not join the ship until it arrived at Plymouth, which they reached by train. The ship was becalmed and eventually sailed on 10th June with 17 cabin passengers and 252 "intermediates", who travelled in an area which was partitioned off but still public. Alfred described the bedlam on board. His bull terrier, Prince, objected to being housed with the pigs, there was baggage all over the place with people falling over it, and children raced around crying. The Howitts were cabin passengers so Alfred and William were able to work together on translating *Geschicte der Magie,* published in Leipzig in 1844. It appeared in English as *The History of Magic* and had a big influence on the emerging interest in magic and the occult in England.

The Howitts proved to be very good sailors when they met with a storm in the Bay of Biscay. They finally arrived at Port Phillip (3 miles from Melbourne) on 20th September, after a voyage of 102 days. They were not very impressed with what they saw in Port Phillip: Melbourne's docks. The dock was teeming with people, theft was rife and the Howitts lost some of their luggage. It was raining hard and the area was a quagmire, with rotting carcasses lying in the streets. There had been heavy tree-felling for building, for fuel and for props for the mines. The shoulder-height stumps were considerable obstacles. Everyone dressed informally, regardless of wealth. At the time of their arrival there were 90,000 immigrants on their way to Australia, Germans, Chinese, as well as British, all hoping to strike it rich. When they had disembarked they took a boat to Melbourne to stay with Godfrey, leaving all their baggage on board. It took them a good month to get their goods unloaded from the ship.

William was impressed by the town of Melbourne itself and said it reminded him of Nottingham. He had acted satisfactorily for the people on board ship and was soon well known in Australia for sorting out problems he saw in mining areas. William always felt obliged to sort out other people's grievances. He was so overwhelmed by the obvious corruption and the over-inflated prices of food and land, that he wrote pages about it in *Land, Labour and Gold.* All this was the result of the discovery of gold. People had left the town to prospect, and the price of labour had risen accordingly. The Howitts hired men to carry out services such as transporting goods and found they were always charged far in excess of what the company quoted, the extra money being pocketted. Prices of goods were highly inflated. A horse which would cost £10-£15 in England fetched £70-£100 in Melbourne, and butter was being sold at

An engraving of Melborne around 1870

3/- a pound. Some lodging houses were no more than a portion of a stall. Godfrey's own house had gone up in value about 100-fold. A London house at that time cost £1000-£2000 but in Melbourne £4000-£6000 was being charged.

The Howitts aimed for the Ovens Gold Field, some 250 miles from Melbourne. The party, which included one of Godfrey's sons, Teddy, had horses but they were led much of the way. William was now nearly sixty years old but he walked extensively, often in the burning sun with temperatures soaring to 120-130 degrees Fahrenheit at mid-day. Some of the terrain was very steep and rugged but there is no indication that this caused the group to mount their horses for any length of time. Some wet areas had to be charged at so as not to be bogged down. They took down someone's wire fence and went across the fields, presumably putting the fence back again afterwards - after all, William had grown up in the country.

William's party had to suffer the company of other groups who wanted to tag along. Some of them did not have good horses, and they unhitched William's horses so that they could take the place of the poorer horses in difficult terrain. This made William cross as his horses were being overused and were tired when he tried to get his own cart across.

On their way to the Oven they recalled the visit of a burglar to a sheep station. He was a gentlemanly type, said to have been a titled escaped criminal from Liverpool. He went into a house where there were only three women at home, the men being out with the sheep, and stole the contract notes following the owner's sale of his former sheep station (he felt he would be able to forge the signature and get it cashed) and all the valuables, always appearing to know where to look. Then he asked the daughter of the house to play the piano, then to sing, and afterwards, when it was dinnertime, ordered them to serve him with their dinner. He sat down with a couple of his friends, while others of the band of bush-rangers were outside guarding the house. The story ends in the fairytale fashion of justice being done; the thief was killed and several of his gang badly wounded. This story is one of many from Charlton's note book which William turned into *A Boy's Adventure in the Wilds of Australia*. This book is full of information about the flora and fauna of the area. It describes a sheep-station, mainly light open forest with no undergrowth, grass growing beneath the ubiquitous large eucalyptus trees and sheep grazing beneath the trees.

They improvised when cooking. Roast beef was hung from a string tied to a spade handle stuck into the ground over a fire suitable for roasting an ox. This would be followed by good solid pudding, a "billy" of tea and good bread. Charlton brewed his own yeast in a glass bottle corked down and hung on the sunny side of the tent and he proved to be a first class baker. On the trek to Oven, Charlton picked up young birds and every stray or lost dog. Seldom had they fewer than nine or ten of them. They had made it a rule to eat wild animals, to be self sufficient; Alfred used to kill them. Possums, as common as rabbits, were very good to eat and were given to the dogs as well, and the dogs would go out at night to catch them.

The party washed their own clothes in the river. They complained about the heat of the sun; the dry heat burned their hands so much that they wore gloves. But the main complaint was flies, flies and more flies. They attacked the provisions, especially the meat, and in the heat they attacked any wound or sore, which would soon become septic.

The Howitts arrived at the Oven gold field in October 1852, after two months' travel - "What a journey!" is William's judgement of the trip. They must have looked comical setting up their tent slightly away from the other miners and their families, laying a cloth on the ground for a carpet, placing William's folding chair upon it and erecting two folding beds.

As usual, he was ready to take charge of the situation without giving anyone else the chance to sort out their own affairs. This he had done on the ship on behalf of passengers and now he spent a lot of time learning about the miners' lives and taking on board their grievances. He discussed politics and prophesied the Russian threat to Austria - the Crimean War. His sons soon settled and mixed quite happily with the other prospectors, but William was too old to adjust. He did not like the noise of the camps and he was always wanting to see something new.

The water was of such poor quality that William ended up with dysentery, which nearly cost him his life. This was the scourge of travellers to Australia. The party had gone prepared with medicine supplied by Dr. Godfrey Howitt, and they sent a letter to Godfrey. He sent them medicines and directions for treatment, but for a week William lay

in a most wretched condition. The intolerable heat had run into thunder, deluges of rain, and cool weather; but still the frightful complaint continued unabated, and my strength every day was sinking. The grating and dissonant croakings of the bullfrogs in the creek, the loud screaming of the curlews, and the uncouth sounds of opossums and flying-squirrels, made the nights dolorous.

They discovered that they were near the farm of a wealthy squatter called Forlonge. Alfred rode over to the farm and Mr. Forlonge moved the party and their tent, erecting it near a hut in which Alfred and William slept, while the others stayed in the tent. Mr Forlonge had lived in the hut before he built himself a better place. It was wet and hot but here, with good food and attention, William's life was saved.

As soon as William had recovered they were off on the road again. They went to Reid's station where they met up with Thomas Woolner, the sculptor and poet, and Edward Bateman, who was nephew of the Lt. Governor of Port Phillip and still engaged to William's daughter Annie at the time. It was on this journey that Alfred first came into contact with aborigines. Many aborigines had never seen a white man or a horse, and they could be very frightened, thinking the white man was a god. Alfred and William carried revolvers and were prepared to use them. Apart from those who worked with the settlers, the aboriginal tribesmen did not often come into the open but they were very good at creeping up to a camp under cover of dark to steal. William sat in his chair at night with his revolver on his knee, guarding their supplies, as food was scarce. People also put tins etc. in the tent openings because of thieves (not always aborigines).

William was very pleased with the way the boys worked looking for gold down by the river. They had read in the newspaper when they first landed of the large size of the gold nuggets that Australia was realising. One nugget weighed 100lbs, a party of four dug up 84ozs in a day and a party of two dug up 60ozs in a day - not the usual hard grind one hears about in the American gold rush. Following their visit to the Oven gold fields they found gold at Nine-mile Creek, which was soon over-run by diggers. They then moved on to Bendigo, where they again were successful (though to a lesser extent).

William and his sons walked right across Victoria and into New South Wales. Sometimes they would walk for weeks on end, twenty miles a day, day after day. In scorching heat, they waded through rivers and dug for gold. Such was the stamina of William that he discounted his dysentery. Even when he was seventy, he often wrote for sixteen hours each day and always walked for four or more miles a day! He had always been physically active: in Nottingham he swam three times a week in the Trent, breaking the ice if necessary just by jumping in. He was obviously a very hardy man.

Towards the end of their stay, William left the boys mining and visited Sydney. It had some fine public buildings, a good library and literary taste, but William preferred Melbourne, which was a mining town. He also went to Tasmania, then known as Van Deimans Land. He left Tasmania on 8th July 1854; the ship had to be laden at least 12 hours before it was due to sail so that the authorities could search it for convicts.

By the time the Howitts left to return home the price of gold was falling, but they still managed to sell their mining gear at a profit. Neither Charlton nor Alfred were pleased about returning to Melbourne. Melbourne had no dances!

Alfred had decided not to make the expensive return voyage to his homeland, though he was very uncertain as to whether or not he was doing the right thing. Even William admitted he was sorry to be leaving and this feeling seemed to intensify when he returned to England and Europe. It is interesting that neither *Land, Labour and Gold* nor *A Boy's Adventure in the Wilds of Australia* contains anything about the return visit to Melbourne, William rejoining his sons, the farewells to Godfrey and his family, or the farewell to Alfred. The sailing of the ship is just incidental in *Land, Labour and Gold*.

Mary's Problems

After William and her sons had left England, Mary and her two daughters moved house once again, this time to The Hermitage, situated at Highgate on the West Hill just above Millfield Lane. Mr Bateman, the father of Edward (Annie's fiance), had found these premises, which consisted of a small three-storeyed house and a lesser tenement which he felt had potential. Dante Gabriel Rossetti lived there, and when he decided to visit and stay with his cousin, Mr La Trope, he sub-let it to Mary.

There was a long sloping garden with lovely elms and a large ash tree. To make the house more presentable, the landlord had painted the interior woodwork a dark green and put bad stained-glass and 'grotto' work into the cottage. The Howitts stayed at The Hermitage until 1857, when it was sold and its new owners decided to demolish it.

Mary found this period very difficult. She had been used to having William around to sort out all their business problems, and he also read through all her translations. Now she was left to rely solely on her own interpretation. At this time she was having problems with work for Frederika Bremer, the Swedish authoress who had been compared to Jane Austen. She was a prolific writer; Charles Kingsley, George Eliot and Elizabeth Barrett were all impressed with her work. Mary had been awarded a medal by the Literary Academy of Stockholm for her translation of three of her novels and three novelettes.

Miss Bremer was sending her work which had been transcribed by a young girl. She and Mary had agreed to certain alterations and omissions. This worked well until Miss Bremer published a disclaimer in *The Times* distancing herself from the "mistakes and misconceptions" [VS] and also claiming that if she and Mary had been physically nearer these things would not have happened. *The Times* carried Mary's reply on 24th December and in its edition of 24th January the paper assured the English public that Mary would continue to be an almost perfect translator.

There is a lost letter that explained Miss Bremer's action to which Mary had referred, along with confirmation that the disagreement had been patched up in private letters to interested parties. Miss Bremer then wrote about matters close to Mary's heart; the abolition of slavery, social and economic reforms, emancipation of women, and Swedish parliamentary reform. Mary and Miss Bremer had other problems as well. A man by the name of Mr Clarke was pirating publications, hastily taken from German editions with only slight alteration to Mary's text.

We printed the Bremer novels at our own risk, when such became the rage for them that our translations were seized by some publishers, altered, and re-issued as new ones at a shilling each. The men in our printer's office were bribed from America, and in one instance the pirated sheets appeared before those we ourselves had sent over. Cheap editions ran like wildfire through the United States; and the boys who hawked them in the streets might be seen deep in 'The Neighbours', 'The Home', and 'The H. Family'. [GW]

The Howitts agreed that the author, not the publisher, had the right to choose who did the translations. Clarke was not the only pirate. New York library holds letters from William that relate to some pirated versions of Mary's work which had been bought by a Mr Putram. He withheld the £60 his agent had promised to pay William for his *The Hall and the Hamlet* and Mary's *The Children's Year*. The reason given was to keep up the reputation of the States.

Throughout this time Mary kept herself busy with various social and religious committees. She often dreamt of William and her spiritualist leanings led her to give credence to these dreams. On one occasion she dreamt that William was either very ill or dying. There was no way she could allay her fears; she just had to wait for a letter. At one of her meetings she overheard someone referring to her husband. A London newspaper had said that William Howitt had made a remarkable recovery. Mary was aware that everyone who went to Australia was ill at first, but William had been extremely ill. In fact he had nearly died, though later he denied this saying he was "as hearty as a roach".

William and Charlton returned to England on 7th December 1854. William wrote for many London newspapers and magazines about his experiences, describing such things as the criminals and thieves, the profiteering, the various religions (such as the Mormons), the spiritualists and the mediums. Indeed, in 1853 he had written an article for *The Times* describing the bush, which was said to be more vivid than any other. He published *Land, Labour and Gold*, an interesting period piece on the colony and the best ever written on the subject, *Tallangetta, The Squatter's Home* and in 1855 *A Boy's Adventures in the Wilds of Australia*, for which Charlton's notebook was used. William also wrote a piece for *Household Words* about the two days he spent in Rio de Janeiro on his journey home. After this had appeared, many wished that he had travelled more extensively in Europe, like Dickens and Trollope.

Alfred Howitt

Mary's second son Alfred had arrived in 1830; *"the baby throve, though expected with much anxiety after the still-births and miscarriages which tended to become more frequent with Mary."* [L&G]. Her philosophy in raising her children was that there should be no rules, only kindness and truthfulness. Her son Alfred was happy-go-lucky, a bit of a dandy despite his mother's Quaker sensibilities; he once referred to a social event to which his brother Charlton would not have gone. Alfred's sister Meggie described him as being lithe and active in mind and body and more of a Botham than a Howitt. Mary had difficulty understanding him; he was not a man to show his emotions. When the time came he had no plans for a career, nor was he an academic. Both of Mary's sons had worked in London offices and during periods of great anxiety over them she must have turned her thoughts back to what had happened to her brother Charles, only to become more concerned.

Alfred corresponded regularly with his good friend Joe Todhunter in New Zealand. His humorous, informative letters show that he had had a good education, something his mother felt was lacking in her family. His sketching was also very proficient.

Alfred was adventurous and attracted to danger - he thought nothing of rounding up wild bulls and being thrown from his horse to land spread-eagled in the bushes. His letters from Australia worried his mother sick and she kept asking him to return to England to get a safe and respectable joh. He loved Australia - the carefree life, the mode of dress and the lack of convention. He worked for a time in the *Standard of Freedom* office and taught himself German in the evenings. Mr. Cassell, the proprietor, was against strong drink and advocated coffee instead. Alfred had no intention of settling down, though, and did not remain with the *Standard of Freedom* for long. He moved around from one job to another, seeking adventure rather than financial security. He farmed in both conventional and unconventional ways and returned to known mining areas to seek out new sites. During the whole of this restless period he indulged his love of exploring.

Alfred farmed in partnership with his uncle Godfrey and when his mother urged him to return to England he told her that he felt obliged to stay. He had to supervise men, working with them to clear woodland, fence fields, make sheds and pigstyes - in fact, build a 110-acre farm from nothing. Unfortunately prices for vegetable crops were falling and little money was made. But by 1857 Alfred had decided that Australia was to be his permanent home and by 1858 the farm had begun to pay, and he was off on his explorations again.

The conditions of the roads were appalling; they were steep and rough and sometimes no more than 5 miles could be covered in a day. The period spent with his father had taught him how to survive in the wild, and he lived off the land - something few white people knew how to do. As he travelled around the Gippsland district of which he was so fond, he sent reports to Melbourne with sketches and maps and he collected botanical specimens and animals which he caught and skinned. He sent these back to Melbourne for the new natural history museum.

He taught himself minerology, a subject which he was later to study in great depth. He had the help of his sister Annie in England, who contacted appropriate people for advice. She gave dinner parties for small groups to spread the news about her brother's knowledge and she sourced some of the latest equipment on the market when he could not obtain it in Melbourne.

Alfred learnt to be a highly disciplined explorer. He had to face temperatures of up to 114°Fahrenheit with hot winds and even, once, 145°. Water shortage was the worst problem; to alleviate his thirst he chewed bullets until they were flat. In the heat the smallest wound became a sore and brushes and combs warped.

In 1859, Mary was pleased to hear that Alfred had returned safely from his arduous journey to the area north of Lake Torrens, which consisted of *"parched desert, bare, broken, flat-topped hills, dry watercourses, and soda springs, whose waters effervesced tartaric acid. He, his men and horses were consumed with thirst in 1860 as he opened up for the Victorian Government a fine mountainous district of Gippsland, which included the profitable gold-field of the Crooked River."* [GW]

Alfred was also a geologist and Gold Warden in North Gippsland. In May 1860 he was appointed leader of a prospecting party to Gippsland by the Government Prospecting Board. The Government had the idea that if prospectors came other settlers would follow to supply goods and services. This time Alfred had to contend with very low temperatures - the panning dish froze to the ground whilst he lit his pipe. The rations ran out, there was nothing to kill and the rivers were too cold for fish. He made bridges over streams, cut scrub and made roads. He named mountains, streams and gullies after men in his party or prominent men in Government. He climbed the highest mountains in the Victorian Alpine chain; once, when stranded on an icy slope with the gold washing dish in his hands, he slipped and shot down the hill because he had inadvertently sat on his dish which acted as a toboggan, speeding his descent. His party named it Mount Howitt. He enjoyed telling his grandchildren this story.

The Royal Society of Victoria sponsored the Burke and Wills expedition. They invested a lot of money - £5,497 alone was spent on 27 camels and their transport with Afghan sepay drivers from India to Melbourne. The baggage weighed 21 tons! Alfred was very critical of the preparations: he felt that the knowledge of the party members was not sufficient for what they were to do and that they did not have the correct equipment. Robert O'Hara Burke was a police inspector from Galway who did not know the area.

While in the bush, Alfred had joked that should the Burke and Wills expedition need a search party it would be him who led it! In Autumn 1861 he was in Melbourne when he was asked to do just that. He and his group were to travel south to north across the continent, through an area he was already familiar with. Alfred had finished his work at Crooked River - there were now 600 residents with eating houses on the road and, later, hotels, stores and butchers where a line of coaches was to be put together from Port Albert to Sale.

On September 13th, 1861, Alfred and his large party came to Burke's depot at Cooper's Creek, and found papers buried in the cache, informing them that Burke and Wills after reaching the Gulf of Carpentaria on February 11th, returned on April 22nd and were terribly disappointed to find themselves (although after date) abandoned by those whom they had left in charge of the depot. A search, which was immediately commenced for the missing explorers, ended in the discovery of the sole survivor, King - a melancholy object, wasted to a shadow, who had been living for upwards of two months with a friendly tribe of aborigines. Weakness, or overjoy at his rescue, made conversation with him difficult, but he was at length able to explain the course of events. Gray had been accused of shamming illness by his companions, had died of exhaustion on the return journey. The impetuous Burke, after reaching Cooper's Creek, and when, being without provisions, their strength gave way, taking the narrator with him, had made a desperate attempt to push on for aid to the cattle station at Mount Hopeless; leaving the gentle submissive Wills behind with a supply of nardoo seed, which pounded into flour and cooked as Porridge, afforded a slight nourishment. Burke succumbing ill the effort, told King when he was dying to put his pistol in his right hand and leave him unburied as he lay. After obeying the injunction, the survivor returned to Wills, whom he found a corpse, with the Wooden bowl near him in which he had prepared his last meal of nardoo, and of which, poor fellow, he had written it was not "unpleasant starvation".

Wills breathed his last in a native hut erected on a sandbank, and King had carefully covered the remains with sand; but as Alfred discovered that they had been disturbed, probably by dogs, he carefully re-interred all the bones that could be found, read 1 Corinthians XV over them, and cut an inscription on an adjacent gum-tree. He found Burke's skeleton in a little hollow, lying face upwards in a bed of tall, dead marsh-mallows, and shaded by a clump of box-trees; under it a spoon, and at its side the loaded and capped revolver. He consigned it to the earth, wrapped in a British flag, and cut an inscription of a box-tree to indicate the spot. [GW]

Alfred organized this expedition and returned without loss. They asked him to return with a fresh team to bring the bodies back to Melbourne for a civic burial. One hundred years later, Alan Moorehead wrote,

He moved easily and confidently through the primeaval world, and he possessed a quality that is very much lacking in the determined, embittered world of Australian explorers and he had a touch of humour. There were no disagreements in his camp, he was very much the leader, and because of his knowledge of the bush they were all eating and living well. The condition of the horses and the camels had actually improved since they left the Darling.

The news of Charlton's death in 1863 in New Zealand shook Alfred. It was a turning point for Alfred; he noticed a difference in his thinking and outlook on life. Around this time he was appointed Police Magistrate, Warden Crown Lands Commissioner and coroner in the Omeo district, a 150-square-mile mountanous area in the state of Victoria. He was immediately liked; he did not wear uniform and he mixed with the ordinary men. Alfred hated fuss of any sort, including being entertained by community officials. He would far rather be in his old housecoat.

On 21st January 1863 Alfred William Howitt married Maria, daughter of the late Judge Boothby, Chief Justice of the Colony, who had been a friend of the family in Nottingham. Alfred had met the nineteen-year-old Maria on a business visit to Adelaide, when he had been entertained by the Judge. Mary Howitt was pleased to hear of this union, and also that Alfred had " *a settled post under Government in his favourite district, Gippsland. It promised for him a happy and most useful future, which, under a merciful Providence, has hitherto been fulfilled."* [GW] Maria ('Liney') took over the correspondence with Mary. The letters which passed between England and Australia demonstrate that they understood one another well.

Alfred and Maria were to have five children: Charlton, born 1865, Mary, born 1866, Annie, born 1868, Maude, born 1870, and Gilbert, born 1872. Alfred believed that all his children should be well educated, girls as well as boys. When he was offered the post of Permanent Resident for the Northern Territory, he declined with the comment that he could not see Liney being Governor's lady at Government House.

Alfred had promised that after his marriage he would stop exploring, but in fact he continued his investigation of rocks, flora and fauna for the rest of his life. He even took his wife and his 8-year-old son on a 360 mile ride. From the time Alfred arrived in Australia he made notes on what he saw; these were the material for the very important articles and books that he was to write from now on. He developed many of his ideas whilst riding around his administrative area. He spent the 1870s studying eucalyptus, insects, flies, ants and beetles for one English naturalist, and he collected the teeth of native animals for another.

He was directed to Beechworth to do a temporary job there. Refusing to mix with the rest of the community, he spent his time co-ordinating the notes he had taken over many years. The outcome was the first geological survey of north Gippsland, an area of 200 x 250 miles. This prompted a request for a fuller survey.

During the course of 1874 he reorganized his geological notes and in 1875 published a paper about the geology of land he had surveyed - the Geological Survey of Victoria Progress Report number 2. In the September he purchased geological scientific equipment, including the new slicing machine. He also made some of his own machinery from quite primitive materials. From 1879 his geological work was recognized in Australia and abroad. He received many accolades in honour of the work and knowledge that he had acquired. In 1895 he was unanimously chosen to be one of three Commissioners for Audit. It was a life-long blue-ribbon appointment, free of all Parliamentary influence, with a salary of £1,000 p.a.

The father of Australian anthropology, he had his first meeting with the aborigines in 1854. *"The worth of two trips cannot be over-estimated,"* he said. He learned the different languages of the tribes and they taught him how to survive in the bush; how to catch and cook game, and how to locate frogs deeply buried in set clay (if squeezed they gave up their water). They made him a member of their tribe and allowed him to attend their secret religious rituals.

Charles Darwin's *The Origin of Species* had been published in 1859 in a storm of controversy. Alfred strongly supported the ideas it promoted, but some academics in England took the attitude that the Australians could not possibly understand the issues. Some people could not believe that our ancestors could have resembled such a primitive tribe as the aborigines. The undercurrent that had been present for some time was now in the open, and open for wider discussion.

In the course of his anthropological work, Alfred came across much opposition. In 1868 he took an interest in the Central Board for the Protection of the Aborigines and was honorary correspondent. In 1872 he started corresponding with Lorimer Fison in Fiji and with Dr Lewis Morgan, an American ethnologist. He corresponded with Darwin himself in 1874. After 2 years' work, Alfred Howitt and Lorimer Fison published the book *Kamilaros and Kurnai* in 1880, Part I by Fison and Part II by Howitt. Macmillan Press in England had undertaken the work, after Annie's intervention. The open-minded American, Morgan, who had suggested the joint venture, wanted it published in his country but this could not be done for several years. Piracy still reigned and Alfred suffered its effects, just as his mother had.

1883 and 1884 saw seven more papers, two written in collaboration with Fison. He was also a fellow of the Geological Society of London and the Anthropological Institute in London. In 1884, Annie paid a visit to her mother in Rome. Whilst she was there she was taken ill and died. This was a tremendous shock to Alfred. She had given him so much encouragement and shown such deep interest in his work over so many years that he felt her loss deeply. In fact, he nearly gave up his work altogether. She had shared his joys and sorrows and his frustrations despite the physical distance between them. Both of his daughters had helped with his work and his family had at times accompanied him on his expeditions, but from this time on his daughter May tried to fill the gap Annie's death left.

Between 1891 and 1907 Alfred wrote *The Native Tribes of South-East Australia*. He retired in 1901. In 1903 he was awarded the first Mueller Medal and honoured with the fellowship of the Royal Anthropological Institute. He was also awarded the Clarke memorial medal by the Royal Society of New South Wales. That same year he visited London with his daughter May. On this occasion he wanted to see about the publication of *The Native Tribes of South-East Australia*, which was carried out in London. He was not prepared to let the Australians meddle with his work. He met members of his family and friends, including Joe Todhunter and Octavia Hill. They visited Paris and Heidelberg to see the changes in those countries too. He spoke at the British Association at Cambridge and accepted an honorary doctorate at that University - a real honour for a colonial. He was now Dr Alfred Howitt.

In 1905 Melbourne University awarded him a doctorate. In 1906 the Premier asked him to leave his home and return to Melbourne as Commission Chairman, looking into the working and ventilation of Victorian Mines. He was very reluctant to go. Still apparently a fit man, he still felled trees and caught cuttle fish to make French Polish for his cabinet making, for which he used native timbers. In 1907 he was made president of the Adelaide branch of

Alfred's sketch of the homestead at Cape Schank

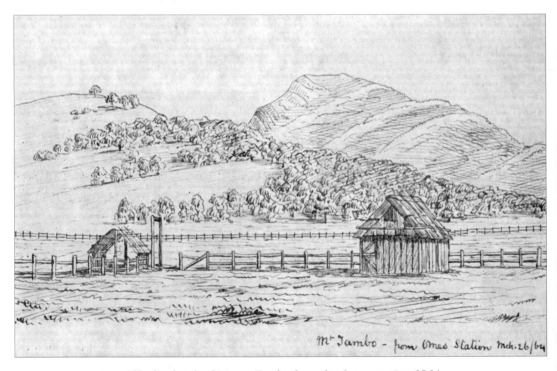
Alfred's sketch of Mount Tambo from the Omeo station 1864.

the Australian Association for the Advancement of Science. At the end of his life Alfred reminded people that his work had started long before the Aborigines had mixed with white people and that their customs and culture were therefore changing.

After a short illness, Alfred died on 7th March 1908. He left his rock collection and geological notes to the University of Melbourne, his scientific library to Queen's College and his botanical collection and writings to the National Herbarium in Melbourne.

West Hill Lodge and Annie Howitt

In 1857, before William and Charlton returned, the Howitts had moved house again, this time to West Hill Lodge. This house was not far from The Hermitage, still on the Highgate Hill, and with its flat roof, they had a magnificent view over London (then much smaller than today) and "its environs". This house was *"hidden from the road by a screen of clipped lime trees, which afforded Florence Nightingale a pleasing open-air retreat; when, spent in the service of her country, she occupied in great retirement West Hill Lodge during the spring and early summer of 1859."* [GW]

The years at West Hill Lodge were happy ones. One of the Howitts' neighbours was Miss Burdett Coutts, the great heiress of the long established bank for gentlemen and the army. She was also a founder of the feminist movement and financial supporter of many schemes for social and economic reform. The Howitts did not leave West Hill Lodge until 1866, so they would still have been in residence when Florence Nightingale was there. Mary's good friends, the Leigh-Smiths, were uncle and aunt to Florence.

From West Hill Lodge Anna Mary, or 'Annie', the eldest daughter of William and Mary, married Alaric Alfred Watts, a clerk in a Government Office, in 1859. He was a writer and the son of Alaric, an editor of *The Literary Souvenir*, and Zilla Watts, one of Mary and William's great friends from their earliest writing days. Annie had had disappointments. She was involved in spiritualism and psychic disturbances, as were Alfred and his father Alaric Watts. There was another common interest in as much as Alaric Watts had also known bankruptcy. Annie had studied art on the Continent. She wrote poems and literature, illustrating her own and her mother's work. Her paintings included miniatures and portraits. She painted her parents, the Wordsworths and others; this had entailed travelling with her father specifically to do the portraits. She had displayed work in galleries of repute.

Mary very much admired her daughter's skills, though others felt she would have drawn and painted better without the inspiration of the spirits! However, Annie felt moved to paint a large painting of Boadicea. Ruskin, who did not believe in women writing or painting for a living, said that a panoramic magnification of Boadicea was totally beyond the tools of her experience, and that she should stick to painting peacock wings. Annie was so distressed by his remark that she resolved never to paint again.

Charlton Howitt in New Zealand

Herbert Charlton Howitt, though sometimes referred to as 'Herbert' in historical records, was known as 'Charlton', a family name. Unfortunately, there are very few surviving records of his time in New Zealand, and some of those have been lost. Additional information, however, may be obtained through the Todhunter family correspondence held in Christchurch Museum, N.Z., which contains some letters from Mary to the family. The Howitts had become neighbours of the Todhunters when they moved to The Elms.

Charlton was born in what was to become a year of calamities. Mary's fourth son arrived early in a very cold 1838. Mary said,

"A few days after the child was born, I found it next to impossible to keep myself warm, though, like Harry Gill, I was covered up with flannel. I felt a chill pass through me; I rolled up and tried to get rid of the shiver and earnestly besought the Almighty that it might not be the forerunner of a terrible illness. I cannot soon forget how hard a thing I felt it would be to die."

Soon she had a gathered breast and a starving baby,

"and in the midst of the trouble, our housemaid was taken ill with erysipelas and had to go home; then our man was kicked by a pony and nearly killed, and lastly, the monthly nurse, who on my account and the baby's was staying a week longer, was taken ill and left at an hour's warning. Thou may think how like Job's calamities all these things came upon us, especially when thou recollects that it was such pain for me to nurse the baby that I have cried at the thought of it.'

A wet nurse was eventually found in a neighbouring cottage and Mary finishes the letter,

"the baby has grown fat and is sleeping now like a little dormouse. He is unlike the other children; he has not a particularly good forehead, which of course, we must attribute to his being born in Surrey, for the Surrey and Sussex people are well-known to be the greatest fools in England. Poor little child - well if he is to be the dunce of the family, I hope he will be the most fortunate, for I am beginning to think extraordinary intellect does not do much good for a man who has to make his own way."

Charlton had the makings of a survivor, and a survivor he was to a greater or lesser extent, depending on your opinion.

In 1860, when he was 22, Charlton wrote to his parents to ask if he could pay them a visit to discuss "business". They were on holiday, at Well House in Niton on the Isle of Wight that spring. On Saturday, 21st April 1860 he set out to walk from Cowes and Mary and William met him three miles from Niton on the Newport road.

The "business" was his desire to emigrate to New Zealand. An opportunity had just arisen for him to settle in the Province of Canterbury with some friends who had the respect of his parents. William and Mary considered the suggestion overnight, and the following morning they agreed to his going. William's own hankering after Australia may well have had some bearing on their decision.

"Charlton, we resolved in our minds, was a born naturalist, with every taste and quality needful for a settler in the wilds. As a child he had made the most extraordinary unbudgettings about his pet bees, guinea-pigs, and bantams. At fourteen he had especially enjoyed the voyage to Australia for the sake of the whales, the mollemoke he caught, and the little flycatcher, which out at sea had spent one day on deck. He had delighted in the strange sights and sounds of the bush, the curious insects, flying squirrels, duck-billed platypus, and so forth." [GW]

Charlton had initially thought of going back to Australia and disappointed his brother Alfred when he chose New Zealand. New Zealand was newer to the British than Australia, though both had been discovered by the Dutchman Tasman in 1642 and James Cook had visited both places from 1769 to 1770. Australia was sent its first convicts in January 1788, and from 1794 onwards there was a steady stream of people wanting to settle there. It was only in the 1840s that New Zealand had its first settlers. Charles Heaphy and Thomas Brunner were pioneer explorers of those early times. Up until then there had only been sealers, whalers and traders. Christchurch is flat and was rather boggy. Two men had been responsible for its development: John Godby and Lyttleton, after whom Christchurch port is named.

So when Charlton went to New Zealand it was a new land, although towns such as Christchurch had already been pegged out ready for the building of houses. The buildings in existence were wooden, the planks placed horizontally one above the other. They were mainly bungalows in the North Island, but Christchurch had started building two and three storey buildings, some with balconies, some with towers; in fact, they were very like English houses of the period.

Charlton Howitt before he went to New Zealand, and with George Dobson in New Zealand in 1863.

The New Zealand rainforest.

When Charlton, Alfred and William had landed in Melbourne, it was already a settlement; the town merely grew as a result of the gold rush. But the South Island of New Zealand was only just being settled by Europeans. Later in the century, around the 1860s, '70s and '80s, there was the Christchurch Beautifying Association who imported some of our garden birds and animals and paid to lay out gardens like those in England, including a botanical garden. They planted native European trees and they imported a huge fountain, cast at Ironbridge, similar to one in the museum there. These Victorians tried to make Christchurch like their old homes in England.

In contrast, Charlton was to explore native sub-tropical forest, uncharted terrain and rivers. The explorers of that country were young men, mostly in their 20s, hungry for adventure and a new life. The Maori wars were still to come but there were fewer Maoris in the South Island because a Maori chief from the North Island had tried to annihilate them. These native tribes were friendly towards the white man, many of whom would not have survived without their help. In the early part of 1840 the Maoris had signed the Treaty of Waitangi, which gave them the rights and privileges of British subjects. What a different environment Charlton found himself in from that he had experienced with his father and Alfred, who was still in a country where European influence was longer established, in a country of extremes of temperature, where wildlife was abundant. New Zealand had no known mammals of its own, only birds.

Charlton had relished the strenuous parts of the Australian journey. The harder the challenge, the more he enjoyed it. He liked the solitude and thick forests, and his notebook was all about animals and botany, to judge by the book his father wrote using it as source material. After he returned to England he kept himself in training, in the hope of eventually emigrating. Like Alfred he had received a good education, but he was not really interested in formal learning. He would far rather garden, do some farming or make tools.

Alfred's friend Joe Todhunter, an indigo merchant in London, had heard very good reports from another friend, Edward Dobson, one of the Wakefield pioneers who arrived in the first of three ships to reach Lyttleton, New Zealand in 1851. Dobson kept sending glowing reports of the Wakefield Settlement to his sister Rosie. Joe, who had considerable business experience, felt that he could further his business out there, so he bought from the Trustees of Canterbury Settlement in London some land at Pigeon Bay on Banks Peninsula which had prospects for timber and farming. He then set up a firm with friends, including two brothers and a cousin of the Montgomery family; William, Henry, and Alex Montgomery and a James Kay. Thus Todhunter, Montgomery and Kay was formed to work in New Zealand for five years. Later Joe Todhunter sent his much younger brother Charlie out to join them.

Charlton, who had had an office job working for Ebbw Vale Co. in London, decided he wanted to farm in New Zealand. He was offered the post of manager of the farm which Todhunter, Montgomery and Kay had purchased so he went to work on a farm in Lincolnshire to gain some experience before he left England. Joe felt that Charlton was mature and sensible beyond his years and wanted him to have a share in the firm.

Charlton sailed for Christchurch on The Minerva in November 1860 as a paying passenger, and arrived on 27th February 1861, to find that Alex Montgomery had spent considerable sums of money, beyond what had been agreed, on enterprises he had never seen through. There was a ship in the process of being built, a rusty saw mill, no animals on the farm, and the fields were not laid out.

Eventually Annie Todhunter, Alex's fiancee, and Charlie Todhunter sailed with their aunt, Eliza Gill to New Zealand. When they arrived at Lyttleton on 16th June 1861 Charlie was horrified at the situation, and they were all concerned about Annie's future. On their arrival Alex took them over rocks to Pigeon Bay, about twenty miles from Christchurch, and over a range of hills. Mrs.Gill was very surprised by Alex's action. They spent the night with James Kay and his wife in their little wooden bungalow. Charlie and his aunt discussed the situation and many letters flew between New Zealand and London, but Annie was left to make up her own mind as to whether or not she married Alex. Joe wrote to Charlton,

"I was much grieved and vexed at your bad accounts of Montgomery and his undertakings as well on your account as for others. I hope you will be plain with Charlie and Annie, and let them know all when they arrive. It is very sad...and to you most disappointing. I am quite satisfied that you have acted wisely and with sound discretion..." [TP]

Initially the Todhunters thought they would take a small house in Christchurch, where Charlie would get employment and Annie would teach the piano, though it would have been difficult to get pupils and they decided a dairy farm would be more sensible.

Charlton tried very hard to earn the company extra revenue to pay off the debts incurred, although Joe had covered them temporarily. He was also requested to take care of the legal part of the dispute and took Alex to the magistrate. Joe wrote to Charlton on 26th September 1861, *"I will take care you don't lose any money or advantages I promised."* [TP] No record of legal action can be found, however, and Alex disappeared with the West Coast Gold Rush. Some members of the family were relieved because they quite liked him.

Charlton was legally settled on the farm but he had not purchased it as there was a problem with the sale. He was selling timber and growing peaches and other fruit, and hoped shortly to finish building the house. In December 1861, in a letter to his mother, Charlton talks about clearing the bush land, setting potatoes and making butter. On one occasion Charlie found that Charlton had been injured by cows when trying to stop them escaping; the seriousness of the injury was minimised and ignored by Charlton. He enjoyed the mountain and forest scenery, the different varieties of animal and vegetable life which he found in New Zealand, the *"Switzerland of the Pacific"* as he called it. In later life Mary reminisces, saying,

"Still affecting all primitive modes, and wishful to redeem a neglected property in a bay near Lyttelton, he dwelt for some time alone in a slab hut built on the slope of a clearing by a mountain torrent surrounded by a happy family of cats, dogs, and bipeds, for he had acquired the Maori faculty of calling about him the native birds."[G.W]

There is an undated letter from Mary to Joe commiserating about Annie's disappointment, relating to the marriage that may or may not take place to Alexander. She compares it with Annie Howitt's broken engagement to Edward Bateman. Neither of the marriages took place. In this letter there is a reference to Charlton which is a bit obscure. Mary says,

"As regards Charlton however it is much less important than for dearest Annie. Charlton is young and active and has a brave heart and an undaunted spirit which will go on cheerfully even through difficult times, but for poor Annie so much is involved...Charlton and Charlie are both young and full of the true courage of life, and this strange, sad experience in a new distant land will bring them no doubt together...These are the times when it is proud of what stuff men are made, and I feel sure that these two youths will be a credit to us all and, I trust, a comfort to dear Annie and Mrs. Gill." [TP]

When spring came again, Charlton wanted to get back to the country. He was up before dawn, and even farmed by moonlight. He also worked at the saw mill when there was a ship waiting to be loaded. After a good harvest Charlton was dissuaded from his isolation. There is one passage written in the autumn of 1862 which says how thin and ill he looked through overworking himself and this was when he decided he would give up farming. Charlton loved his farm, *"the most beautiful spot he ever saw."* Mrs Gill was very impressed by his knowledge of birds and shrubs and which berries could be eaten. He also gained the respect of Maoris for whom he gave lodging on their way to the West Coast.

Charlton made friends with William and Henry Montgomery, who were working at the quay. They wanted him to go into partnership with them as a solution to reorganizing the business, but this would still leave Charlton with huge debts. Joe, in London, continued to be a great support. He gave his brother power of attorney to act on his behalf and later allowed Charlton to borrow money to purchase a farm if he wished. The company had to be reformed and William and Henry took up partnership with Charlie. In a letter Mrs Gill says of William,

"we are inclined to endorse Charlie's favourable opinion of him, he impresses me with confidence in his good sense and honesty of purpose he is a better educated and more intelligent man generally than his brother, more agreeable socially, he is a great reader, and seems to be a kind hearted and well-disposed man - like his brother he is a great talker but has a much larger range of subjects, he is very quick and shrewd....I should like to be present when Charlton hears of your generosity in making good his losses - Charlie thinks he will at once decide to settle down on the forty acres - the way of life is so much to his taste." [TP]

Charlton went back to Christchurch where the rest of the Todhunter family were living and where he must have had a role in the new company. He and Charlie had become extremely good friends, but he was still sorry to leave the friends he had made at Pigeon Bay.

At this time prospectors were beginning to come south from the Buller river down to the Grey river valley. The Provincial Government decided to make a rough track along the old Maori route over the Hurunui Saddle wide enough to allow a walker with swaggers to get through. The Saddle is also known as Harper's Pass and lies more or less at right angles to Arthur's Pass, named after Charlton's friend and colleague Arthur Dudley Dobson. From 1865 onwards, the Pass took most of the east-west overland travellers during the summer months of February to April, and since 1923 has been the route of the Trans-alpine railway.

The rivers rising on the west side of the New Zealand Alps are not to be trifled with. Rainfall is high; in summer the snow melts and many of the rivers have cut deep canyons. The river beds are very wide, and even in a wet period the river may appear little more than a stream. The river Buller can rise 20 metres rapidly, flooding the road that runs along the side of the gorge high above the river bed. The annual rainfall on the surrounding alps is 120 inches. The rivers are surrounded by dense sub-tropical forest, in shallow soil that washes away in the rains bringing mud slides, sometimes blocking rivers and causing water diversion, or rapidly rising new lakes. Early travellers had to chop down very large sub-tropical ferns, trees and hardnesses with their bush hooks. The bush hook was an elongated blade sharpened on one side, slightly wider than the long thick 'broom' handle to which it was attached.

When Charlton returned at the end of the winter he arranged to go with George Dobson on a surveying exploration (Dobson, a road engineer, was murdered in 1866 by an infamous bush ranger gang). Mrs Gill described in a letter Charlton's return from Wellington; his first port of call had been to his friends at Pigeon Bay, where he stayed for about a week. He had brought back *"a fine collection of ferns for his garden"*. Mrs Gill did not have much faith in their survival and thought they ought to be kept as dried specimens. At this time he used to go riding with Annie Todhunter and planned in August 1862 to take her to the hills in search of more ferns but this trip did not materialize. Visitors arrived, one of whom knew Alfred well - Mrs Holmes, the wife of a railway contractor.

The planned outing was delayed until the next day. They were just setting out for their ride when a note came summoning Charlton to Government House on *"important business"*. The Provincial Government had observed his hardworking qualities and his freedom from colonial vices and they wanted him to lead the northern exploration in search of gold. Mrs.

The Traveller on the Hill-top

Gill wrote on 13th September 1862 that the greatest event of the month had been Charlton's unexpected appointment as leader of the Northern prospecting party. *"He only had a few hours to decide and would not do so without consulting Charlie and William Montgomery so he went straight to the quay"* [TP]. They returned quickly, the decision having been made. Charlton was expected to be ready to depart the following Monday!

When the matter was settled he started making preparations very energetically, getting pack horses and arranging about provisions, tents, etc. The government was to provide a dray with provisions, tools, tent and baggage as far as wheels could go and two horses. They would pay Charlton 15/- a day; other members of the party, chosen by him, would get 10/- a day and find their own provisions. They were to be away for three months, and should they find a payable gold field each person would receive £250. Many men wanted to join the exploration party and despite the difficulty in finding suitable men, Charlton had chosen a team by Saturday evening. He had been recommended a couple of men by Arthur Dobson and a Mr Ollivier; *"all were of the working class, all accustomed to up-country life, and two I think had been on the gold fields"* [TP]. The government, however, had done nothing about pack horses by Monday morning so Charlton returned "the firm's" grey, Hawkeye, and he purchased another horse hiimself. Mrs Gill carries on, saying,

> *"A good deal of Pigeon Bay rust has been rubbed off him, to the improvement of manners, appearance and temper; in sterling qualities he is infinitely superior to most of the young men about town....Mr. M. is loud against the Government sending out prospecting parties, and predicts the ruin of the province should they succeed. I believe many of the older colonists are of the same opinion. Mr. Grosvenor Miles, to whom Charlton gave his letter of introduction the other day, said he hoped Charlton would return as he went...judging from the accounts from Otago, it would be a great evil. Lately a new goldfield was discovered in Otago, and a perfect mania seems to have seized upon people here. Vessels to Dunedin were crowded, and last week hundreds returned disappointed. Poor Charlton was rather troubled at the thought of the diary he will be obliged to keep for the satisfaction of the Government folks, and thought writing it would be the hardest part of his duty, but W. Montgomery told him it need only be a sort of 'log', not very formidable, and suggested that he should take one of Alfred's reports as a model."* [TP]

On Tuesday, 9th September, quite a party set out from the government buildings: *"Whitcombe, Bray, two chiefs - G. Dobson and two others"* [TP], together with cart horses and equipment and Charlton with his 'swag' strapped in front of him. They set off for Taylor's station. *"Mr. Dobson, Mr. Whitcombe and George's [Dobson's] surveying party were going north next day to Waitoke Gorge, sixty miles from Christchurch."* [TP] Charlton was to set out in a westerly direction across the mountains, with provisions to be deposited at the last *"station"*. Charlton was pleased to be able to join these other men because he felt he would get some instruction in the geology of the ranges and other relevant information. Seated on his tall horse with his opossum rug strapped in front of him, Charlton was bright and as cheerful as the day.

> *"Mary D. was one of the party as far as Rangiora, and Annie mounted the pony and accompanied them some miles on their way. They were quite a procession defiling over Papanui bridge, the equestrians and surveyors' carts laden with tents and baggage."* [TP]

Charlton was asked to examine the rivers Hurunui and Teramakau, in the northern part of Canterbury Province. In the September he began following the Hurunui, still a difficult route though the Canterbury Provincial Government had spent over £4,500 'improving' it. It ran 58 miles from Christchurch to Waitohi Gorge, only about a third of the way across to the west coast. He made pathways, erected flags as signals to indicate passable fords, and built huts for shelter along the horse track, using wood he cut from the natural, undisturbed bush. He had also been asked to find suitable settlement sites on the West Coast.

In a note to Charlie written on 20th September, Charlton said he was making use of the opportunity to send them a note:

"I am well and getting on all right. This is a most splendid country to look at, but most tremendously rough. The river Hurunui runs through a fine grassy flat with high mountain ranges on each side, the tops covered with snow, and most of them with bush. The grass here is something wonderful, there being no stock here it has grown until it is almost impossible to get through until burnt. The horses are thriving well on it. We camped for two days at Waitoke Gorge and prospected for Mr. Dobson's edification. Made a start on Sunday morning and arrived here on Monday night, the road not half so bad as I expected. We have been out prospecting some large creeks coming in above the lake. We had to wade up them for about ten miles, it being impossible to get along the banks in most places, as they are straight up and down or else covered with bush. Yesterday we went up one, but were obliged to come back, as it had been raining all day and it was too wet to camp out. To add to the pleasure, coming back one of the men slipped off a rock into the water. I was laughing at him when the bank gave way with me into a great hole nearly overhead, the water being at freezing point. You may imagine the feeling." [TP]

He went on to say that there was a great abundance of water birds, duck and water fowl there and also white cranes which he was trying to catch.

By the end of September, Charlton had looked for signs of gold around the Hurunui Valley to the Waitohi Gorge to the Saddle and came to the conclusion that if gold was to be found it would lie on the western watershed. In October he and his party faced sleet and rain which forced them to build a whare for food storage and shelter. In November, he was cutting forest, opening up country around the Hurunui river. He wrote from Upper Teramukau to Mrs Gill, who was going to Melbourne on her way home. By now, Annie had broken off her engagement to Alex Montgomery and they were planning to return to England. Charlton hoped she would deliver a letter to Alfred, who was expected to be at the home of their uncle, Dr Godfrey Howitt., and asked to be remembered to Charlie and Annie. He wrote of continual rain, the river carrying logs and scrub rising to such a height that it looked like a great sea. He met areas where he could not ford rivers and had to make detours, back through the bush. His party had had enough. When they were nearly to the coast, mainly due to the abominable weather, his men became disillusioned and persuaded him to turn back.

RAIN

It rained and rained and rained
The average fall was well maintained
And when the tracks were simply hogs
It started raining cats and dogs
After a drought of half an hour
We had a most refreshing shower
And then most curious thing of all
A gentle rain began to fall
Next day but one was fairly dry
Save for one deluge from the sky
Which wetted the party to the skin
And then at last the Rain set in.

Anonymous

By 27th November, he was in Christchurch. Mrs Gill wrote stating that they had left their house in Columbo Street as their lease had expired and moved to a boarding house for the remainder of their stay. Charlton had returned on foot, travelling just under 140 miles in four days, but he appeared fresh and well and none the worse for the experience, except that his clothes were dilapidated. He had undertaken this feat because he did not want to miss his friends, before they departed. The three young people went out riding and reached Sumner, where the Dobsons lived, before dark. Men, horses and baggage arrived after a few days. Charlton was very busy but found time to talk to his companions about his expedition:

"the inclement weather, only 14 days free from rain, the grandeur of the mountains, the different forms of vegetable life, the hospitality of Mr. and Mrs. Taylor at whose station the provisions were deposited. The three Maoris, Jacob, Gainui, and Solomon, joined their company and travelled with them a few days on their way to the West-coast to baptize native children, Charlton giving them food and shelter at night, for which they were very grateful. Conversing among themselves, his name was often repeated, with signs of approval." [TP]

The Maoris had tried to persuade him to travel across the Saddle and go down to the coast with them, and told him how they intended to stop at the navigable head of one of the rivers, possibly the Grey, and make a canoe of plaited flax which they would then use on the rapid water. They described the difficulties and dangers and how to manage their "bark by poling."

Charlton told how, while he and his men were working on the track, a younger brother of explorer Mr Whitcombe and Mr Money arrived in a poor state of health and starving. Charlton shared his tent and provisions with him for several days. When Whitcombe got into the *"current of a mountain stream"* Charlton rescued him by means of a pole. The track had been opened wide enough to allow a horse to get through and over the Saddle, but at times the only way down was to slide, and that included the horses!

Charlton looked forward to his next assignment. He was bright and happy despite not having found gold and having had to stop at a point when he thought he was coming to an area where gold might be. Before his friends departed on Sunday 14th December, he suggested a walk into the Little Bush - an old Maori camp on the top of the ranges above Sumner. When they had ascended to 1,100 feet above Sumner they looked to the north and saw the tall dark forests of the peninsula, the bay and the sloping downs, Lyttleton harbour with its shipping and the little town just below with the Pacific to its east. To the north and the west stood the Canterbury plain, the great Waimakiriri river which meandered from the mountains to the sea It was a beautiful day and the sun illuminated the view. Whilst they stood under the trees, Charlton made a peculiar sound through his fingers; the birds flocked into the branches and as he continued with the sounds they began to sing (the party members did not consider their song to be as harmonious as those of English birds!).

The next day, accompanied by Annie, Charlton joined Arthur Dobson, who was in his tent at Heathcote, to help him with a survey for the railway to Christchurch.

On his return to Christchurch he was chosen as the "most fitting person", to lead an expedition to open up communications between the Canterbury plains and the newly-discovered gold and coal areas on the west coast. In January 1863 he was instructed to follow the river Teramakau through dense forest to the western beach, thus opening up a route from the Hurunui plain to the mouth of the Grey or Teramakau rivers.

He set out with five men, but soon sent two back as not being suitable or sufficiently fit for the task ahead of them. He and the remaining three marked out and cut a 40-mile track through Harper's Pass and down to Teramakau. It rained and rained. In the Hokitika region the average rainfall is 118 inches (3,000mm), falling on 144 days. The rivers and waterfalls were in full spate so the men lived soaked to the skin. At one point they were unable to see where to put their feet when walking down a ravine. At another there was nowhere where they could safely erect their tents and they had to arrange their sleeping position so as to avoid falling into the ravine. Here and there were huts that had been set up by others as base camps which were used as safe havens and usually contained emergency food supplies.

River Buller

In June the party made camp on Lake Brunner. Charlton's last letter home was written from there on May 26th, 1863:

"My dear Annie,

"I received your kind letter of the 8th of January, some four days back. Many thanks for all your kind wishes. You will see from the dates that I am still on the West Coast, still engaged in cutting the track to the mouth of the Grey River, the native name is Mawjera. This track has taken much longer than I expected, and the winter has now set in, so that there is no way of getting back to the settled part of Canterbury by the way we came, on account of the snow. The only way being to walk up the sea beach to the River Buller, where there are diggings and to go from there by vessel to Nelson. I hope, however, that we shall be able to manage to stay here all winter to get finished. We have to catch what birds and eels we can to make the flour last out as long as it will.

"I do not know when I shall be able to send this but expect to find a vessel at the Grey by which I can send it.

"A very sad accident happened here a short time since to a friend of mine of the name of Whitcome, a surveyor.

"As there is now a very great excitement at Canterbury about the West Coast, he was sent by the Government to find out if it is practicable to get through from a river called the Rakara, which runs out on the West Coast about 20 miles south of the Teramakau. He took an old Swiss with him who had been here before, and whom I had seen here.

"After very great hardships they managed to reach the beach at the mouth of the Hokatika, having found it quite impracticable for any sort of track.

"Having finished their last biscuit - they only had 3 biscuits each a day whilst travelling - they were anxious to get to the Maoris living at the mouth of the Teramakau.

"When they got there the Maoris were all gone, and there was no means of crossing the river. The Old Swiss wanted to walk up through the bush 4 miles up the river where some more lived, but poor Whiteome had had so much of the bush that he was unwilling to do so much, as 10 miles further along the beach, there is the mouth of the Grey where they were sure of getting plenty to eat, and very likely to find a vessel to take them home. They therefore looked about, and found the bottoms of two canoes without the sides which are sewn on. These they lashed together, and although The Old Swiss was very unwilling set off to cross. No sooner were they in the middle, then the canoes filled, and they were almost immediately carried down to the breakers in the sea.

"Poor Whitcome jumped off to swim to shore, the old man kept hold, and was carried out to sea, every wave that came turned the canoes over and he had to climb up into them again. Thus he passed the greater part of the night expecting every minute to be swept from the canoes, which turned over every two or three minutes. At last, when he had given up all hope, he felt them touch something. This turned out to be the shore. After some trouble he managed to reach the beach where nearly dead, he buried himself in the sand. He said 'he was so old he would have been glad to die'.

"The next morning he walked along the beach, and found himself about a mile from the Teramakau on the side from which they had set off. Soon he found his swag, then the canoes, then the body of poor Whitcome. He stayed all that day scratching a hole in the sand in which to bury the body. He recovered most of the things, watch, thermometer, and papers, and so set off up the river to the Maoris. These 4 miles took him a day to walk. All this time he had nothing to eat. When he reached the Maoris he found them nearly without any food. He obtained about 10 pounds of potatoes and with these he set off up the River. He stayed one night at the diggings where there were only 4 Maoris, who had only a wood hen amongst them, and which they shared with him. He then set off to find us, and was two days and a half on the road, during which time he had nothing to eat. When he found us he was very weak. We gave him plenty to eat and enough to carry him to Taylor's Station, took him across the lake in a canoe, and as the horses had to go to Taylor's got him to take them.

"I don't think I ever saw a man more pleased in my life. He said when he was going away upon the horses 'When I did come to you, I was poor and miserable, I did have nothing to eat, and I was nearly dead. Now I have plenty to eat, and I have a horse to ride, and one to carry my swag. I am like one gentleman.'

"After all this do not go and frighten yourselves about me as I take good care. I like this country. I have some thoughts of coming and living on a little plain called Pahtidu, close to Lake Brunner. I am sure this country will go ahead. The only drawback to the plain is that it is rather far from the beach and the weather is so wet on this side of the Island There is, however, plenty of timber, coal and gold, and nobody knows what else yet.

"Grey River 10th June, 1863

"I have just come down to the beach to bring down a man who has been lost in the bush and nearly starved.

"We had to carry his swag and get him along as well as we could, as far as the diggings, when I expected to find Maoris and go down the river in a canoe. However there was no one there, so we had to leave him with what flour we could spare, and come down here through the bush to send someone for him.

"There are plenty of stores here now the Government, having sent a vessel round, so that all is right for the winter, so far. The Maoris are in a high state of delight, as they have now plenty to eat, they have been very badly off there having been so many people here all the crops are eaten. The Government has besides sent them presents of seed wheat, potatoes, pigs, fowls, ducks and goats, none of which animals they posessed [sic]. When we got to the beach we caught up three Maoris - 2 men and a woman going to the Grey. As soon as they saw us they began to shout 'Tena koi Hauite, Nui, Nui, te plom ta kai te Nawheru', which means 'How do you do Howitt, plenty of flour, plenty of food at the Grey'. They were most tremendously pleased, and were going to buy flour. When I had seen them last they had come to Lake Brunner to catch eels, as there was nothing but a few potatoes at the beach. They have bought two tons of flour, besides a great stack of tea, sugar etc.

"They tell me that there has been another battle in the North Island, and a lot of Maoris are killed. They say that they don't like the war, and that it is no good to fight the white men.
"Your affectionate brother "C.H."

A contemporary Victorian engraving of a Maori canoe.

Soon the wind rose and the heavy winter rain began. James Belgrave Hammett, the cook for the party, kept a diary in which he recorded the weather. At one point they had to strip and carry their belongings on their heads as the river water was neck high. On 9th June he noted that he was tired of being wet through. They arrived at Lake Brunner on 23rd June and there is no further mention of rain until 28th June, when it was blowing hard. By 3rd July rain had really started, and Hammett made comments like *"still raining heavily"*, *"rain still continues"*, *"rain still pouring down as if the gates of heaven were open for another flood"*. It was so wet he could not light a fire.

The camp they came to had been raided and its supplies were gone, so on 27th June Charlton, Robert Little and Henry Muller went in search of food. Previously, Charlton had lived on eels caught on this lake from his canoe (which he had made from green wood as there was no dry wood around) - besides the eels, there would be flour in a watti on the other side of the lake. Hammett, the cook, was left behind to take care of the camp because he was injured, having dropped an axe on his foot. While he was waiting some Maoris came by and said they had heard that Mr. Howitt was dead. When his companions had not returned by the 3rd of July Hammett became worried and set out to find them. He walked round the lake and eventually found Charlton's swag, which had been washed up on the beach. It was rolled up in a little calico tent which was normally used for travelling around. The men had disappeared; no bodies were ever found.

Mary had had an uneasy feeling, and when the New Zealand Government notified her of Charlton's death it came as no great surprise. The letter she and William received, dated 14th September 1863, reads as follows:

"Sir,

"It is with the deepest sympathy that I have to inform you of the disappearance of your son Mr Charlton Howitt under circumstances which leave no room for doubting but that he has been *drowned in Lake Brunner near the West Coast of the Islands with two of his men whilst crossing the lake in a canoe.*

"The published journal of the only survivor of your son's party which will be forwarded to you contains all the information which can at present be gained respecting this unfortunate occurence. I may however add that I do not think it possible for (Howitt) to have done more than he did and that Mr Townsend, the Government Agent at the mouth of the Grey River dispatched a party to the Lake without delay to renew the search.

"Mr Charlton Howitt was first engaged under government during the past year in examining the rivers Hurunui and Teramakau in the Northern parts of the Canterbury Province for the purpose of ascertaining whether these rivers contained gold. This exploration was conducted with so much energy and perseverance under great difficulties that on his return to Christchurch he was selected as the most fitting person to take charge of an expedition to be sent to cut a horse track through the dense forests on the West Coast to open up a communication between the Canterbury plain and the auriforous country in the Teramakau District. This duty was faithfully performed under many hardships and discouragements and but a few miles remained to be cut when the fatal accident occurred which has deprived the Government of a valuable servant and saddened the hearts of all who knew him.

"It is a melancholy satisfaction to be able to reflect that with Mr Howitt's name has been added to the sad list of pioneers whose lives have been sacrificed in the attempt to open up the West Coast. His work remains and will long be gratefully remembered.

"Mr Todhunter had kindly undertaken to forward to you Mr Charlton's papers and all his detailed informations respecting his last journey with a map showing the route taken by him and should I ascertain any further particulars any time it can be forwarded.

"I have the honour to remain with sincere sympathy and respect

"your obedient servant

"E.Dobson, Provincial Engineer, Province of Canterbury, NZ

Meggie was in Sweden when the news of Charlton's death reached the family. Her mother wrote, *"Charlton had been instrumental in saving several lives and if there was no human aid near to save him when in peril, there were angels' hands to lead him up to a higher, safer existence. Thank God, that he has been given us to love and rejoice in; that he had done good work; that he has saved life not taken it; that he has been a pioneer through tractless wastes, opening paths for civilisation and peaceful human existence."* [SG]

He was twenty-five when he died.

On 14th September 1863 Charlie wrote his mother from Christchurch, saying she will have heard from Joe *"of the sad intelligence of the loss of poor Charlton. It will indeed be a severe blow to his parents and all who knew him. Poor fellow, he suffered much without murmuring, and always showed himself a good friend to those in need."* [TP] He continues, saying that Charlton must have saved many lives while over on the West Coast. *"The papers that were recovered in his swag are merely a few home letters and memoranda, so I did not send them by this mail, but intend sending them with his other things."* [TP]

He says the Government felt his loss very much and that they promised to institute every possible search for the bodies and would *"pay some proper mark of respect to his memory"* [TP]. He pays tribute to good Mr. Dobson who had helped so much, assisting in making enquiries and how Mrs.Dobson was going to write to Aunt E. Mrs Gill, in one of her letters dated 1863, said how much she had liked Charlton.

"Charlton always ranked in my affections next to my own sons and I feel his loss deeply he was so simple and good and self sacrificing that we have every reason to hope that he is only removed to a higher sphere of usefulness. His parents were very much pleased with the Dobsons very kind letter of sympathy bearing testimony to Charlton's worth of character." [TP]

In February 1864 Charlie set out with George Dobson, R A Sherwin and others from the West Coast to look for his friend. After a difficult journey the search party reached the Little Hohono river, where Charlton's last camp was, about 20th February. It rained all night and it took them four hours to light a fire! The tent leaked and the place was full of mosquitoes and sandflies. They searched for Hammett's tent and raft, but gave up without success at the end of the day. On the 24th they reached the watti, where they found some clothes and sugar belonging to Charlton. They brought one of his shirts back with them.

The lake is approximately ten miles long and about seven miles wide, surrounded by dense bush. They waded round it for five miles before they camped on the beach. The bush was too thick to penetrate. They were quite sure Charlton must have drowned when the canoe capsized and sunk. The lake was full of enormous eels weighing up to 50 lbs each; these must have been what Charlton was fishing for. They are scavengers, and the Maoris said they would strip the flesh off a dead body within 24 hours. Charlie no longer expected to find any remains, but he and Dobson did find Charlton's tent, which contained his diary and notes. On March 4th Charlie arrived back at Christchurch. Charlie wrote a letter:

"I fear the reports are too true....Poor Charlton's has been most severely felt here by all who knew him, as also by the Government, as he proved himself so thoroughly efficient and untiring in the performance of his duties. I shall not write to the Howitts, as I am sure you will kindly break the sad news to them far better than I could do by letter....the few papers recovered in his swag will be forwarded home by first opportunity, as also his chest and anything that belonged to him." [TP]

He communicated everything about Charlton to his brother Alfred in Australia and included a map of the area Charlton was working on. Mary and William asked Charlie to have Charlton's books, which contained many Jules Verne-type adventures.

Charlton is remembered with eight other explorers - Thomas Brunner, Charles Heaphy, John Rochfort, James and Alexander Mackay, Henry Whitcombe, Charles Townsend, and George Dobson - on a memorial erected in 1923 on the west coast in the Karoro Cemetery, Greymouth.

The Greymouth monument.

Restlessness

1858 saw the beginning of much travelling for the Howitt family. They visited Wales several times, and in between they went to France, Switzerland, Germany, the Tyrol and Italy, as well as different parts of England. Mary said they were familiarising themselves with habits, customs and beliefs such as *"second-sight, good and bad omens, presentiments, and apparitions"*. She said of Wales *"the Chester and Carnarvon Railway had already brought along the sea coast of North Wales an influx of tourists and wealthy settlers, demanding and introducing the necessities of advanced civilisation."* [GW] Of the quarry men she said,

> How I respect the grave, earnest quarry-men, clad in buff moleskin waistcoats and trousers, similar in colour to the outer coating of the rock, and blue and white striped shirts of the same tone as its freshly hewn inside; often with splendid faces of the rough, stony kind, and hair and beard like rock growths, of the gold-brown hue of late autumn ferns and heather. Men of fortitude and piety these, who to the utmost of their ability support the temperance movement, their schools, chapels, land, ministers; the latter belonging to their own class, and often dating their spiritual vocation from early work-days in quarries! [GW]

In 1862 William published his *Ruined Castles and Abbeys*. Mary had a story about life in Heidelberg published in 1864. This may well tell us about her own life in Heidelberg.

The Orchard

The Howitts moved to The Orchard in Claremont, near Esher - *"our favourite old neighbourhood"* - in 1866. The exiled Empress Eugenie of France lived there at the time and Mary was in contact with some of the royalty who visited. Mrs Annie Watts, wrote to her sister Meggie on 25th August 1867 that *"after 4 o'clock we went to Claremont, which Prince George was especially anxious to see, that he might describe it minutely to his Queen, who dreads the thought of residing at Claremont, from the belief that she should die there."* The Prince thought Claremont beautiful and yet he felt a *"great melancholy about the place"*.

Anna's husband Daniel Harrison had, through his endeavours, become a prosperous merchant dealing mainly in tea. The firm he founded, Harrison and Crosfield, moved to London in 1854 and is still there today. Mary was pleased to have her sister living near her.

In the spring of 1859 Mary, William and Annie visited Thorpe, Ilam and Tissington in the Peak District, and called on the Watts, the Russells and other friends, including Sir Henry and Lady Fitzherbert at Tissington Hall. They had a happy reunion with the much-loved Richard Howitt. Her daughter, Annie (Watts) wrote in the Reliquary of 1862,

> Most people living in the Midland Counties have heard of "Dressing" of the Holy Wells at Tissington. The fame of this pretty village, with its fine wells and ancient festival, has, through the writings of Home, extended also beyond its provincial locality, and has stimulated the curiosity of many a mind alive to the poetry of village festivals and antique association.
>
> Tissington might be taken as a perfect type of a thorough old English village, a village which Washington Irving would have loved to describe, and which at every turn reminds you of Birkett

The Traveller on the Hill-top

Foster's clever woodcuts illustrative of rural England. It lies amidst rich pasture fields and meadows, now, at the commencement of June covered with lush grass and myriads of flowers. All breathes the most entire peace and plenty; flocks and herds feeding in their abundant pastures, and filling the air with their lowing and bleatings. The peasantry well-grown, and some of them remarkably handsome, have an especially contented and well-to-do aspect, speak a broad dialect and possess a thoroughly Old English air.

Tissington has an old hall of grey stone, one of the ancestral seats of the Fitzherbert family, built in the style of the Elizabethan era, a place stately with its emblazoned coat of arms above the portal, and its handsome old stone gateway festooned with roses, its pleasant gardens, and park graced by well-grown trees, amidst which conspicuously stands forth a long and fine avenue of magnificent limes, forming in one direction an especially pleasant approach to the hall and village...

Annie goes on with a detailed description of the Hall, the village, its houses,the pond and famous wells, The Tree Well, The Town Well, The Hall Well, Hand's Well:

flow into an oval-shaped stone basin, standing upon an oval pedestal; this well is situated in front of a cheerful cottage gardens, somewhat higher up the street; and, the fifth well, called "The Coffin Well", is the most neglected of all the wells in appearance: it lies apart from the village street in a grassy spot, neither garden nor field; cottages face it on one hand, whilst on two sides elder trees and thorns overshadow it. It has a dreary character of damp and gloom well befitting its name.

Annie and her parents would have no difficulty in recognizing the village today.

In remoter time, probably at the era of the Reformation or the Commonwealth, there appears to have been a cessation of the custom; but it was revived by the inhabitants of Tissington as a mark of gratitude towards God, after a season of terrible drought, in which all the neighbouring country suffered severely, Tissington alone escaping, through the supplies of water in the Holy Wells.

This morning, the first of June [Tissington Well dressing is on Ascension Day, a Thursday] *the morning before the important day of ceremonial, we walked over to the village, expecting already to see signs of the morrow's festivities; and we were not mistaken. It was a damp, hazy morning, the grass heavy with the thunder rain which had fallen in the night, a morning when "the spen-grey" forgot to play, and the mist hung on the hill...*

That particular year it was very wet, everyone returning from the evening ceremony soaked to the skin. With her artistic education, Annie would have appreciated the fine details and colour sequences used in the arrangement of the flower petals.

The architectural character of the shrine was Gothic - brilliant arch within arch, until your eye reached the central device, which, in this instance, was a representation of a temple, formed of blue, yellow, and white flowers upon a green ground. The central arch bore, as motto - red upon white daisies - "Christ is Our Peace." The three pinnacles were each surmounted by a disc covered with floral mosaics; the centre representing a white dove with outspread wings, whilst the other two displayed crosses of white, yellow, crimson, and green.

The over-all colour scheme was golden and crimson, using white, yellow, crimson and green,

a rich combination which harmonized most beautifully with the dusky green of the yew-tree behind it....with a narrow border of yew-twigs interspersed with flowers; this edging of green seemed to blend the rich colours with the green background of trees, by shadowy and soft gradation, so that the whole appeared to melt into one mass of beauty.

She continues with details of the procedures of this ancient celebration explaining that from time to time it had been neglected and then restored. She describes the church and the hymns:

cornet, flute, harp, sackbut, psaltery, and dulcimer must walk in procession to the different wells in proper order, and with proper decorum the appointed passages of Scripture read, and the hymns sung, accompanied by the aforesaid "cornet, flute, harp, sackbut, psaltery and dulcimer"...

Meanwhile the hospitality of the village had begun. Not a stranger present but was invited to partake of the plentiful viands prepared throughout the village, from the sumptuous board spread in the great dining-hall of the Hall itself, to the humbler, but not less hospitable table of the village farm-house, where, instead of continental wines, you were regaled with home-made cowslip, currant, gooseberry, and elder-flower wine, each so sparkling and excellent as to induce the most temperate to repeat their libation in compliance with the village injunction, the oftener filled the more welcome!

With her daughter, Mary visited Caldon Low, the place that inspired her to write *The Fairies of Caldon Low*. They record how crowded the trains were when they visited Ashbourne for Dovedale which was also very crowded for a Sunday. Regretfully this beautiful railway line has now gone. William remarked,

It is wonderful how much the country has become cultivated since I was here before. All the cornfields are now on the top of the highest hills, where only there was heather, and where the people thought oats would scarcely ripen. Now it is nearly all wheat; and oat-cakes are almost exploded [sic]. We sometimes get some baked as a luxury.

The oatcake of Staffordshire and Derbyshire is unique; large and soft like a pancake, it can be used as such but traditionally was cooked with bacon in a frying-pan or on an enamel plate under the grill. They are still produced.

In the spring of 1860 William and Mary, accompanied by Meggie and Sister Elizabeth (a woman who looked after the children) went to the Isle of Wight. They spent their time walking, enjoying the varied scenery; they met Sydney Dobell who was suffering from *"rheumatism of the heart"*, and who had spent the winter on the island. He was considered to be the most *"intellectual of the Spasmodic Poets"* [VS]. Mary was impressed by his understanding of nature in miniature. William and Mary had thirty years earlier taught themselves the finer details of nature but did not idolize nature to the extent that Dobell did.

In a letter written to William on 25th August 1859 from Mayfield, where her daughter Agnes lived with her husband Joseph Simpson, Mary mentions an interesting evening she had spent at the Swinscoe wakes. The wakes consisted of *"an entertainment of tea, a penny-reading, and music given on occasion of the wakes in the primitive, high-lying Staffordshire village, which, after a long ascent from the Idyllic spot, lies in quite another climate and region with stone walls and bare hill-tops."*

William, now in his sixties, appeared as fit and healthy on his return to this country. On one occasion, while he was visiting the north of England, his brother Richard paid him a visit. William walked twelve miles to meet his brother off the train and must therefore have walked the twelve miles back again. His tour of Australia had given him an urge to travel and see more of the world: *"These Australian experiences fostered in each of the three travellers their innate love of Nature, which in my husband's case made him always ready to start off to the mountains, the sea-side, or the continent, fulfilling, wherever it might be, his literary occupations in the quiet and refreshment of fine scenery."* [GW]

In another letter dated 31st May 1869 Mary gives an amusing description of the Epsom Races in her usual humorous style:

I do not think such miserable May weather was ever known; so intensely cold that one is obliged to wear winter clothing and have fires in every room. On Saturday there was such a bitter frost that scarlet-runners and tender summer growths are nipped, and everybody mourning over their gardens. The last tolerable day here was Wednesday, the Derby day, when we arranged to go over to the Oldham's for an early tea, and then walk to the Epsom road and see the folks returning.

We did so and very much amused we were. We took our seats on a bench by the roadside. There are several in that locality, probably put down for this purpose. We had the bench to ourselves, with the exception of one man, so nothing could be more comfortable. The whole road was crowded with people like ourselves, come to be amused; mostly on foot, sitting and walking about, and some in carriages drawn up at the roadside. At about half-past five the people began to return, in every possible description of vehicle, from the grandest four-in-hand to the coster-monger's cart; nearly all half-drunk, merry and wild as could be, many in green veils and blue veils; with wooden dolls stuck all round their hats, and with dressed mechanical dolls in their hands, which sneezed and laughed and made all sorts of noises; or the pea-shooters, through which they shot peas at the people as they passed. Those shot at the Pater he collected, brought home with him, and has planted, to see what his winnings at the Derby turn out. Some had on false noses, others women's hats; the women wearing the men's. One man in a carriage wore a woman's nightdress and a mob-cap, as ridiculous as possible; some were biting big loaves of bread; others had bladders in their hands. All were laughing and shouting. The man who sat on the bench by us said "They have no vice in them, only fun." Your father and Mr Oldham, two old men with white beards, seated side by side, were an everlasting source of amusement. Sometimes they were lovingly saluted as "Father" or "Grandfather"; sometimes they were pitied - "Poor souls! because they had no father!" There were hundreds of sporting betting men in white hats with or without veils; hard, worldly, cold, business faces of the most repulsive character. One set of these men sitting in the body of a drag were playing at cards. It was altogether a strange revelation of life with which one thanks God one has nothing to do; and one wonders what will become of these souls in the other world. What a revolting hell it must be to which they naturally gravitate! Nevertheless we vastly amused ourselves. We counted upwards of five hundred carriages in about two hours. And the women in them! Eight out of ten were fat, jolly women, used to jovial living. Many of them we imagined to be butchers' wives and landladies. It was very diverting, but having once seen it, we shall never care to go again.

Meggie Howitt

Mary's younger daughter Meggie had also started writing, and had decided to follow the footsteps of Frederika Bremer through Egypt, Palestine and Greece - quite an adventure in 1869. No mention is made of a chaperone, though a young lady would not have travelled alone. She was later to write the official biography of Miss Bremer.

When in Rome she was invited to write the life of the artist Overbeck by his niece. To prepare herself for this task she read voluminous correspondence, including letters and books on Church history and disputed points of doctrine. As a result she coverted to the Roman Catholic Church. Mary, who helped Meggie with her work, also became interested. She met several priests, and through them and her reading her sympathies and beliefs changed.

In 1869, Mary and William visited their beloved Wales for the last time. They continued to spend their time in the garden they had created in Claremont with the help of their crotchety old gardener, Seeker. He cared for the garden as they wished, encouraging the birds *"who swarmed in the big chestnut by our chamber window, chattering from daybreak,* [and] *demolished the peas wholesale..."* [GW]

After a while they became restless. Mary wondered whether they were growing tired of "manual labour" or just getting old; whichever it was they decided to visit Italy.

We wanted to see Italy before we died, so we let the Orchard for twelve months, from Lady Day 1870, to some desirable tenants, and started for Switzerland and Italy; anticipating, with the rapid flight of time, soon to find ourselves back in the old and still beloved spot. [GW]

Mary's autobiography is based on letters. In 1868 Anna, her daughter Agnes Harrison, and Agnes Alderson, Emma's daughter, visited Mary. During their visit Mary read over their *"chronicle of our ancestors and of our early life"* and gave *"notes and suggestions...for future guidance"*. Anna and her family had always hoped to write a family history and they were very upset when Mary acquired many of the family letters in order to compile her own autobiography. She had kept many that she had received from family and friends and had had Anna's family return many of those which she had written to them. Sadly, she died before it was finished and the two volumes were completed by Meggie.

The Traveller on the Hill-top

Contemporary prints of the Epsom Derby, Snowdon in Wales and at the bottom of the page Dovedale near Ilam and Tissington in Derbyshire

Rome

Marienruhe in the Tyrol as it appeared in 'Good Words'.

William and Mary Howitt

CHAPTER TEN
THE TYROL AND ROME

Franco-Prussian War

In the spring of 1869 Mary, William and Meggie, together with William's great-niece and a young lady friend, left to visit Brussels and the site of the Battle of Waterloo, on their way to Italy. Mary wrote to Anna saying they would return within the year, but as it transpired the sisters never met again. By July they had reached Lucerne, where the crops were withering in a drought. They heard that Prussia wanted Prince Leopold of Hohenzollern to take the Spanish throne which would cause a rift between France and Germany and perhaps war. On July 16th they reached Zurich in very sultry weather, which was broken by violent storms:

That same midnight came the much-desired rain, pelting down amid vivid lightning, with but little thunder, yet attended by a tramping of feet and a curious movement in the country road of Flutern [near Zurich], where our old-fashioned pension was situated, followed by a loud knocking at the street door. Verily a rude awakening to us; for war being actually proclaimed by France to Prussia and the Swiss Confederation ordering the active force of the militia to the frontier, our landlord, with other householders, was required to lodge for the night soldiers arrived from a distance.

The next day, Sunday, we saw on the drill-ground the preparations for departure. A private distributed wallets to the line of his comrades. Young sunburnt peasants in regimentals sat resting on their knapsacks, or strapped the Swiss arms - the silver cross on the red field - to each other's coat-sleeves in a brotherly, helpful way, which would have extended from Prussia to France and from France to Spain if Europe were truly Christendom. In the evening the perpetual rub-a-dub-dub of drums and the shrill sound of fifes ascended from the gas-lit city to us on the height as of Flutern. [GW]

Like their fellow tourists, English and American, William and Mary were uncertain what they should do. Italy was considering joining the war, but they did not want to go back to Belgium either and so they decided to stay in Switzerland. Mary described the atmosphere:

A nameless apprehension seemed to have settled on mens' minds, even in Zurich; and one locksmith, we heard, worked night and day, making iron coffers to contain the money and valuables their purchasers wished to bury. [GW]

They met refugees from Germany and a Danish couple with whom they became friends and Mary wrote several little anecdotes about their time in Switzerland.

In September Victor Emmanuel's troops entered Rome, and the Howitts felt it was safe for them to proceed there. They took longer than intended, arriving on 22nd November and one month later, on 22nd December, the city was declared the capital of Italy.

After such a journey it is not surprising that the Howitts were more than willing to stay on in Rome, which they found so agreeable. Indeed, they never did return to England.

Our tenants in England were desirous of continuing their lease of the Orchard, and we to stay on in Italy, where the climate had something so soothing, so exactly fitting to old age. I prized in Rome the kind, sympathetic friends given to us, the ease of social existence, the poetry, classic grace, the peculiar and deep pathos diffused around; above all the stirring and affecting historic memories, for every stone and monument spoke of famous classic or Christian deeds, of the blood of martyrs and the virtues of saints. [GW]

For the rest of their lives they spent their winters in Rome and their summers amongst '*the most beautiful of scenery*', in Mayr-ain-Hof on the outskirts of Dietenheim in the Tyrol. The family became so fond of the area that eventually Meggie built a house at Meran called Marienruhe (Mary's Rest) where she lived herself for a while after her parents died..

Rome

Disaster struck Rome in the week following Christmas. The Tiber rose and flooded the city; after five days *"the muddy, yellow waters of the Tiber"* had gone down sufficiently for the inhabitants to realize the damage. *"In the middle of the streets mud lay ankle-deep - thick, slimy mud, that adhered like ointment to everything it touched, and left a yellow stain behind."* [GW] It grieved Mary to see the beautiful buildings of Rome damaged by the water and mud.

On New Year's Eve the King visited the flood-affected parts of the city, leaving money for those who had suffered. Mary described his arrival:

> On Saturday, at four o'clock in the morning, we heard, as we lay in bed, a distant shout and a roar as of driving carriages. Up we jumped, and looking from our windows saw, in a sudden illumination of Bengal light, the long expected ki ıg, amid shouts of "Evviva il Re!" flash past in a state equipage, followed by other carriages and torches. [GW]

While in Rome the Howitts met Margaret Foley, *"the gifted, generous-hearted New England sculptress"*, and *"her tender-spirited young friend, Lizzy H-"*. Margaret was to be a life-long friend of the family, spending much time at their summer home at Mayr-am-Hof in the Tyrol.

> We vastly enjoyed our Robinson-Crusoe life at Mayr-am-Hof, wrote Mary, where a godly routine of prayer and labour hallowed the entire household. Margaret Foley, a born carpenter and practical inventor, set to work, and so did my husband, and made us all sorts of capital contrivances; thus, with fine weather out of doors and a roof over our heads, we lacked nothing. [GW]

Neither Mary nor William really took retirement. They continued to write for the Spiritualist magazines, the Tract Society and various papers and magazines as they felt moved so to do. William, who continued in his religious beliefs until the end of his life, wrote *The Holy Sparrow*, published 1871. In it he makes scoffing remarks about the sparrow who splashes in Holy water and is then able, by fluttering its wings and tail, to *"absolute all things"* [VS]. He wrote articles on vivisection, cruelty to animals and the consumption of nicotine by the young, for the magazine *Social Notes* around 1878. Some social issues do not change! At about this time William was called a *"cantankerous writer who quarrels with everybody"* by Crabb Robinson [VS], who wondered how he could have acquired *"that sweet woman his wife"*. Towards the end of his life he commenced a book of the life, message and work of George Fox, but unfortunately he died before he had completed the work.

Mary had become the official correspondent for *The Leisure Hour*, the paper published by the Religious Tract Society, continuing the work she had been undertaking for so long.

Golden Wedding Anniversary and Final Years

On April 16th, 1871 William and Mary celebrated their Golden Wedding Anniversary with a visit to the mouth of the Tiber with friends, including Margaret Foley. They seemed revitalized. About this time, when both in their seventies, they climbed with a party of friends and family for six hours high into the Tyrolean pastures and spent the night on the hay in the senner's hut, in order, *"to see more of how these good peasants lived."*

Mary, William and Meggie had become involved with the local version of the English Ragged Schools, which were being organised by the wife of the resident physician at the American Embassy in Rome, along with Mrs Marsh, the wife of the American Ambassador.

Visitors came from all over the world to the Howitts' house in Rome. Alfred visited from Australia, which gave them great pleasure, and so did their other children from England. Old friends came, such as Samuel Smiles, who had known the Howitts since the middle of the 1840s and many of the young people they had befriended during the later part of their life in England - writers, artists, sculptors and reformers, people of different religions, Quakers,

The Traveller on the Hill-top

Unitarians, members of the Spiritualist movement and numerous Roman Catholic pilgrims. There were also American guests, including Louisa May Alcott of *Little Women* fame and her friend Mrs Abbey Patton (née Hutchinson), Ralph Waldo Emerson and Henry Thoreau.

People who did not know the Howitts personally also called on them, such as Joaquin Miller, a biographer. Whether he wanted to collect material for a biography about them or just to meet them while visiting Rome is not clear. Others definitely came with the aim of seeing Mary herself. Moncure Conway, for example, was writing a history of demonology and wanted to gather information from her.

One visitor was Dr Elizabeth Blackwell, one of the pioneering women of the nineteenth century. She overcame great difficulties to train as a physician at a time when most medical colleges were closed to women and medicine was not a decent occupation for a respectable woman. Born in Bristol, she emigrated to New York in 1832 and finally succeeding in getting accepted to train as a doctor and then practising there. The qualification was not accepted in Europe but she returned and retrained at St Bartholemew's Hospital in London. Dr Blackwell came from a Quaker background and had a great interest in public health and the rights and welfare of women. One of her main objectives was to encourage other women to train as doctors; Elizabeth Garratt Anderson was one of her students, who later opened a hospital for women, run by women, in London - the only one of its kind in England. Sadly it was closed in the late 1980s. Elizabeth must have had much in common with the Howitts.

Mary mixed with the Scandinavian and the English communities.She also knew the biographer of Anna Jameson, her niece Geraldine Macpherson, George Duncan, T. B. Read, who was similar in age to Mary, Augustus Hare, the family of Marion Crawford, the British Consul, Joseph Severn and the Earl of Camperdown, who left his collection of autographed Howitt books to the Boston Athenaeum in Massachusetts.

For about seven years the Cistercian monks at Grande Trappe had tried to drain an unhealthy swamp, and at William's suggestion Alfred Howitt was asked to send eucalyptus seedlings from Australia. The trees flourished and the swamp was successfully drained. The eucalyptus crop was found to be a very successful business enterprise, thus substantially helping the monastery. (William also suggested that Dr Bodichon, who was a French Algerian and husband of their friend Barbara Leigh-Smith, should introduce eucalyptus trees to Algeria. The Grove of the Fontane which Dr Bodichon planted was still growing in 1947.)

Family Deaths

William died on 3rd March 1879 from bronchitis and haemorrhage. He was buried in the Protestant Cemetery in Rome, near the grave of the poet Shelley. Because he had never received Holy Communion in the Church of England, the Anglican Priest was unable to perform the ceremony and it was Dr Nevin, the Rector of the American Church, who said a few prayers and made a kind but ambiguous address. He hoped to discourage others from placing themselves outside the community of the Established Church.

Mary started writing for *Good Words*, the Catholic magazine and when she decided to write her *Reminiscence of my Later Life* she realized that her memory was not always accurate. She was anxious to give a true record of her life so she wrote to her sister Anna to ask her help. Anna had kept a journal and so they were able to compare notes. Between them, they clarified dates and events. Mary's daughter Anna Mary (Annie Watts) was asked to sift through old papers still stored at Esher.

In 1881 Anna, aged 90, moved to Bournemouth for the milder weather. In April 1882, while Agnes and her husband were staying with her, she took to her bed. She asked to be read

Chritianas passage through the Valley of Humiliation and the Valley of Death from Pilgrim's Progress, and afterwards calmly and cheerfully said, *"I am weighed with no more anxieties. I am ready to go."* On the 10th April she asked to be read Mary's poem about their Balance Street garden, before dying peacefully.

Mary and Meggie had moved into Marienruhe, their new home in the Tyrol, in 1881, and it was to this house that Annie, now in her 60s, came for a visit in May 1884. Unfortunately, while she was there she contracted diphtheria. She died on 23rd July 1884 at Dietenheirn and was buried in the Roman Catholic cemetery near Mayr-am-Hof. A special dispensation had to be made because she was a practising Anglican.

Mary had an attack of bronchitis while at her summer home but, to her friends' surprise, made a remarkable recovery, although on leaving them for the winter she said that they might not meet again. She wanted peace and contemplation and to visit the holy places, and felt that Tyrolean society might be too much for her.

Conversion

All her life Mary had fought with herself to find a religion that would give her spiritual peace. She eventually found it in the Roman Catholic Church, which she joined on 26th May 1882, a few years after Meggie. She had made two stipulations before her conversion; that she be buried with her husband in the Protestant Cemetery and that she be allowed to keep her English Bible, which she had used all her life. Her biggest doubt - over the Virgin Birth - had been overcome. In a letter to her niece, Mary Harrison, Mary wrote,

Well you know from my letters how the subject of religion touched me deeply and how I read and sought and found nothing positive. Meggie used to say I should never be happy till I joined the Church - the true Church. But one night I was going to bed in that room (pointing to the door) when something within me said "the End is come and thou art not saved". Horror, hopelessness and darkness took hold of me. I trembled so that the bed shook under me and at last I got up and came in to Meggie's room. "Something strange is going on in me, I have hopeless fear and dread and I cannot lie still." She got up and got me brandy. I took it because she poor dear had brought it, but she could not silence that voice repeating through everything "The End has come and thou art not saved." In the morning we talked and I read the books Meggie gave and then I met Father Robiano. I had been so prejudiced against him as a Dominican; but when he came in, tall and white in the robe of his Order, a strange feeling came over me; it might have been the figure of our Lord. Then came my baptism and I was received into the Catholic Church. Oh Mary, my dear, if you would thus be received you would have such peace and you would feel so safe. [L&R]

Mary Harrison visited her aunt in her Austrian home in 1887. It cost her £32-11s-6d to travel from Bournemouth to Meran, spending two nights on the way. Travelling was difficult for her because she used crutches as a result of having been dropped by her nurse when she was about a year old. She was carrying many parcels, including the homoeopathic medicines which she prescribed for herself, her family and her patients. In her unpublished diary she wrote,

My dear aunt is just what she ever was; she is now as positive about her views as she used to be about spiritualism, which she now says was the greatest misfortune that ever befell them. She is constantly anxious I should become a Catholic until I determinedly said I couldn't, she wanted me to remain here [Marienruhe in Tyrol] *till next autumn and then go with her and Meggie to Rome, and there, in the time honoured city, to acknowledge the truth as it has been since the days of the Apostles the only truth that was given to Peter. She says all this with her old energy and emotion."* [L&R]

Farewell

Mary was last seen in public on 8th January 1888, with the Duke of Norfolk at the Papal Jubilee. He took her to a private entrance and later escorted her out of the Papal Palace, where she had an audience with Pope Leo XIII, kissed his ring and received his blessing. Mary was now content. She had decided to stay on in Rome so that she could be buried with her husband. She died on 30th January 1888 in her 90th year. The special dispensation was granted to allow Mary to be buried beside William in the Protestant Cemetery.

Mary may not have been a dynamic or dramatic writer, but she had talent, much sympathy and understanding and an easy way of writing. She achieved her aim of making children's literature more readable, of making it more understandable to them. She tried to educate them through her books, encouraging them to broaden their understanding of the world. She was restricted in what she wrote by her upbringing and her early religious teaching, although she had a vivid imagination and she may well have used her imaginative gift more if she had been able to break through the barrier of her restrictive childhood.

William and Mary Howitt had introduced Scandinavian literature (including the Icelandic sagas) into Britain and America and were responsible for collecting nearly all the classical fairy tales of the English-speaking world. In *Poets and Poetry of Europe* (1870), Longfellow says that he acquired all of his information on Danish and Icelandic literature from their works. He had at first been critical of the Howitts' Scandinavian works, so he must have changed his mind.

She was a person well loved and respected in her lifetime, not just in her own country but throughout Europe, America, Australia and New Zealand at least. Her achievements should be long remembered, especially in her home town of Uttoxeter. Wherever one looks in contemporary biographies her name appears, usually as a person who has helped the subject of the biography in some way. Those libraries which hold her books are very pleased to be the custodians for her works and wish they were used more often.

A black bas-relief monument to Mary and William was erected at Nottingham Castle, next to Byron's monument in the poets' arcade. It can still be seen today.

It was not until six months after her death that the family heard that Mary had joined the Roman Catholic Church. Her son Alfred, in Australia, feared what damage might have been done to his son when he stayed with his grandmother, and even Annie and Alfred Watts, who were still spiritualists, had been unaware of her mother's conversion!

Meggie continued to live in Austria until just before the First World War, sharing a house with a friend. She had been educated in Germany, England and finally in France, and she was fluent in five languages. She fled the War in a hurry, leaving most of her books in Innsbruck. She disposed of the family papers and, as a British citizen, she was able to return to England. She had continued to visit Germany and the Netherlands after the War and in 1925 she had had an audience with the Pope. She had spent her life caring for her parents, after which she cared for the sick and the poor, entering the Bridgettine Order. She lived in Launceston, Cornwall until her death on 8th April 1930, in her ninety-first year, and was buried in the Bridgettine Convent of Syon Abbey. At the time of her death, she was working on the biography of St Bridget of Sweden, the foundress of her Order. Amice Lee describes her thus:

a straight, active, little figure with gracious, slightly foreign manner, with outstretched hands and a merry smile she welcomed us. Her vigorous mind, deep affection and keen sense of humour were unchanged by age or illness. [L&R]

Obituaries

There are obituaries to Mary which can still be read, such as the following from *Staffordshire Advertiser,* Saturday, February 4th 1888:

Mrs Mary Howitt died on Monday morning at Rome, as her husband did nine years ago. She had gone thither from her usual home in Meran to spend the winter. Mary Botham was the daughter of a prosperous Quaker at Uttoxeter and was born in 1799. In 1823 she married William Howitt and began the career of joint authorship which made the names of William and Mary Howitt sound pleasantly in the ears of a wide circle of readers. In the very year of their marriage the young people published a volume of verse, the preface of which said:- "Poetry has been our youthful amusement and our increasing daily enjoyment in happy and our solace in sorrowful hours. ** Living chiefly in the quietness of the country, we have watched the changing features of nature; we have felt the secret charm of these sweet but unostentatious images which she is personally presenting, and given full scope of these workings of the imagination and of the heart which natural beauty and solitude prompt and promote." Eleven years afterwards Mrs Howitt issued a dramatic poem styled The Seven Temptations, and a tale named Wood Leighton followed. She also wrote largely and with signal success for young people. She accompanied her husband to Germany, and while there translated largely from Swedish and Danish. She, in fact, first made Fredericka Bremer known to English readers, and in 1851 she produced along with her husband the Literature and Romance of Northern Europe. She did not go with Mr Howitt to Australia, but on his return they recommenced their joint literary labours, settling themselves at Highgate. Mrs Howitt, besides the work she accomplished along with her husband, produced a Popular History of United States, and a three volume novel called The Cost of Caergwyn, and also continued to bring out works for children. About 1872 the Howitts left England and settled in Italy. In 1879 Mrs Howitt lost her husband, who died in Rome on 3rd of March of bronchitis, the same malady that has now proved fatal to the survivor. Five years later another great sorrow darkened Mrs Howitt's declining years, the death of her eldest child, Mrs A.A. Watts, the accomplished author of "An Art Student at Munich". The brave old lady, however, did not drop her pen, and even last year she contributed to "Good Words". She had died regretted and honoured by all who knew her for her kindliness, her sincerity, and her love of all that was beautiful and of good report.

Many years ago Mr and Mrs Howitt had withdrawn from the membership of the "Society of Friends", though retaining an attachment to the spirit of writings of the fathers of the sect. About the year 1873 they became converts to Spiritualism. After the death of her husband, Mrs Howitt followed the example of her daughter and joined the Roman Catholic Church. Her presence in Rome at the date of her death is explained by Papal Jubilee celebrations. She is said to have been the first of the Jubilee pilgrims presented to the Pope.

An obituary to Mary which is a sixteen page booklet by James Britten dated 11th July 1888, and which was reprinted from the magazine *The Month* and sent to Agnes Simpson by Anna Mary starts "*A name which was at one time a household word in every home where there were children, and which carries us back past the beginning of the present century, has this year been added to the number of those who have passed away."*

Britten says *My Own Story* was a *"Manifestly true and life like picture of childish days"* and suggests Samuel Botham was like his father John and that he was respected by his children rather than loved by them. In the last letter Mary wrote to Britten, dated 16th January 1888, she wrote of her blessing in the Vatican and the unspeakable peace and joy it had imparted to her - the feeling was of being in her Father's house.

Dear, dear friend, I wish you were here that I could talk over with you the wonderful and gracious event of the last week. Many mercies are connected with it which will remain with me to the end of my days, as signal tokens of Divine love. Dear friend, I do not think that we have any idea what is the condescensions of God, until some merciful deliverance from perplexity or suffering suddenly reveals it;

Britten says that the British Museum Catalogue has forty pages listing Mary's works, commencing with *The Forest Minstrel* by William and Mary Howitt in 1823.

There is evidently more of the wife than the husband in this little book, and this, I believe, was the case with other works published in both names.

He sums up,

The name of Mary Howitt is one which has inspired the living respect and esteem of all, and those who had the privilege of knowing her intimately cannot fail to sorrow deeply for her loss. Her courtesy of manner and the genuine honesty and extreme simplicity of her character, together with the great power she possessed of entering into the feelings and interests of others, won the hearts of all who came in contact with her. Her humility was most striking; she would never listen to a word of praise, and when any one alluded to her fame as an authoress, she would say, "My writings are of a bygone age, and no one cares for them now; there have been so many better writers since my time." After she became a Catholic, she used to speak of herself as a baby in the faith, learning day by day fresh truths and discovering new beauties in the faith she had adopted. Her whole countenance would become suffused with the peace and joy she had found in the one true fold, and she used to yearn after the souls she loved who were still outside it. The Penny Catechism was her constant companion, and she would have liked everyone she knew to possess a copy of it.

Mary was much respected and honoured in her lifetime. She had made children's literature more readable and interesting. Her fame spread throughout the English-speaking world and thousands of children grew up knowing her name and loving her poems. Now she is forgotten. If her poems are printed they do not carry her name, and even the residents of her home town have gradually forgotten how famous she was and what she gave to the world.

The Traveller on the Hill-top

Acknowledgements and Bibliography of sources

"Autobiography"	Mary Howitt
"Around the Forest"	Ralph Anstis
"Something about Coleford and the Old Chapel"	1877

"Articles from Gloucestershire Society for Industrial Archaeology Periodicals"
Papers and articles at Forest of Dean Heritage Centre

"Coleford, The History of a West Gloucestershire Forest Town"	Cyril Hart
"Hastings & Men of Letters"	Gerald Brodribb
"Mary Howitt" obituary	James Britten
"Ackworth School"	Elfrida Vipont
"Laurel & Rosemary"	Amice Lee
"In Their Several Generations"	Amice Lee
"Kaleidoscope" Journal	British Library
"Victorian Samplers"	Carl R. Woodring
"Come wind, Come Weather"	Mary Howitt Walker
Letters to Rev. & Mrs Gaskell	John Rylands University Library
Howitt Collection	Heanor Library
Howitt Letters	Nottingham Archives Dept.
Howitt Family Letters	Derbyshire County Record Office, Matlock
Howitt articles and books	Nottingham County Library

Assorted published extracts relating to Charlton Howitt supplied by Christchurch Museum and Archives and the New Zealand Library & Museum Services

Papers and visit to H.C. Andersen birth house and Museum — Odense, Denmark

An assortment of Anthologies containing Mary and William's poems

"Howitts Journal"

"History of Uttoxeter"	Francis Redfern
"In the Steps of Francis Redfern"	W. Torrance

"Lives of Nottinghamshire Worthies and of Celebrated and Remarkable Men of the Countye from the Norman Conquest to AD1882, "The Howitts" — S.P. Hall

"Social Development of English Quakerism, 1655-1755	Richard T. Vann
"The Quakers & the English Revolution"	Barry Reay

Todhunter family correspondence extracts taken by kind permission of Christchurch Museum
Mary Howitt's Letter by kind permission of John Ryland's Library, University of Manchester ref: English MS 414
Extracts from "Kaleidoscope" reproduced by kind permission of British Library
Extracts from "Laurel & Rosemary" reproduced by kind permission of Oxford University Press
Writings for the People: Radical Women & Cultural Politics in the 1840s & 1850s   Helen Rogers
William Howitt's description of Nottingham riots and all quotations from "Good Words" are reproduced by kind permission of Nottingham County Library
Family letters reproduced by kind permission of the family.
Illustrations of the Uttoxeter Meeting House by permission of the Society of Friends
Illustrations for "The Spider and The Fly" and "The Fairies of Caldon Low" drawn by my daughter, Mary Noon.

Bibliography of Mary Howitt (or mainly Mary)

* date unknown or various

1856-1862	Popular History of England from Edward II	7 editions
*	Drawing Room Scrap Book	Editor for 3 years. Pub: Fisher
*	Pictorial Calendar of the Seasons	
*	History of Magic	Translation of Ennemoser
*	Alice Franklin	Baker's Dozen
*	Who shall be Greatest?	Baker's Dozen
*	Which is Wiser?	Baker's Dozen
*	With the Flowers	
*	Opinions on Colonial Matters	
*	Frederika Bremer's works - 18 vols	Translation from Swedish
1823	Forest Minstrel	
1823	Pedestrian Tour of Scotland	
1830	Antedivian Sketches	Poetry

1834	Sketches of Natural History	
1836	Wood Leighton	
1838	Birds and Flowers and other things	Poetry
1838	Colonization and Christianity	Treatment of colonies by Europeans
1839	Hymns and Fireside verses	
1840	Hope on, Hope ever, or The Boyhood of Felix Law	Baker's Dozen
1840	Strive and Thrive	Baker's Dozen
1840	Gypsy King	
1841	Sowing and Reaping, or What may become of it	Baker's Dozen
1841	Student Life in Germany, by Dr Cornelius	Translation from German
1842	Work and Wages, or Life in Service	Baker's Dozen
1842	Little Coin, Much Care	Baker's Dozen
1843	Love and Money	Baker's Dozen
1844	The Two Apprentices	Baker's Dozen
1844	A German Experience	
1844	Otto Speckter's Fable Book	Translation from German
1844	Life and Adventures of Jack of the Mill	
1844	History of Magic - 2 volumes	
1845	Only a Fiddler, by Hans Christian Andersen	Translation from Danish
1845	Improvisatore, by Hans Christian Andersen	Translation from Danish
1845	My Own Story	Baker's Dozen
1845	Fireside Verses	
1845	Life in Delecarlia, by F. Bremer	Translation
1845	Impressions of Australia	
1846	Wonderful Sories for Children, by H.C. Andersen	Translation
1847	The True Story of Everyday Life, by H.C. Andersen	Translation
1847	The Heir of West Wayland	
1847	Ballads and Other Poems	
1847	Childrens' Year	
1848	The Childhood of Mary leeson	
1848	Scenes of Country Life - 2 vols	
1849	Our Cousins in Ohio	Baker's Dozen
1851	Genevieve: Tale of Peasant Life	Translation from French
1852	The Literature and Romances of Northern Europe	Many editions
1852	Popular History of the U.S.	
1852	The Desolation of Eyam and Other Poems	
1852	Pictures of Life, by Adelburt Stifier	Translation from German
1853	The Dial of Love	
1853	Stories of English and Foreign Life	
1855	Birds and Flowers, and other country things	Poetry
1856	The Picture Book for the Young	
1860	The Man of the People - 3 vols	
1861	Littlesea, or Lost and Found	
1861	Little Arthur's Letters to his sister Mary	
1862	Ruined Abbeys and Castles of Great Britain	Many editions
1863	The Poet's Children	
1863	The Story of Little Cristal	
1863	The History of the Supernatural in all ages and nations	2 vols
1864	The Cost of Caergwyn	
1864	Mr Rudd's Grandchilden	
1865	Tales in Prose for Young People	
1867	Our Four-footed Friends	
1867	Woodburn Grange, a Story of English Country Life	
1868	John Oriel's Start in Life	
1869	Vignettes of American History	
1869	The Northern Heights of London	8 vols
1871	A Pleasant life	
1871	The Mad War Planet and Other poems	
1872	Birds and their Nests - Poems	
1875	Natural History Stories	
1881	Tales of All Seasons	

156 The Traveller on the Hill-top

1881	Tales of English Life	Includes Middleton and the Middletons
1886	Reminiscences in my later life	Published in Dickens journal
1889	An Autobiography	

A Bibliography of William Howitt (or mainly William)

* date unknown or various

1824	A Poet's Thoughts at the Internment of Lord Byron	
1833	Popular History of Witchcraft	Many editions
1833	Vidication of History of Priestcraft	
1834	Popular History of Priestcraft	
1834	Sketches of Natural History	Many editions
1835	Three Death Cries of a Perishing Church	
1835	Pantika, or Traditions of the Most Ancient Times	
1836	The Book of the Seasons	
1836	The Boys' Country Book	Many editions
1838	Colonization and Christianity	
1840	Sowing and Reaping	Baker's Dozen
1840	Visits to Remarkable Places	Many editions
1841	Student Life of Germany	
1841	The English in India	
1842	The Rural and Domestic Life of Germany	
1843	No Sense Like Common Sense	Baker's Dozen
1843	The Wonderful History of Peter Schlemighl	Translation from German
1844	Wanderings of a Journeyman Tailor, by Holthause	Translation from German
1844	My Uncle the Clockmaker	Baker's Dozen
1844	Jack of the Mill	
1845	Edinburgh Tales	
1848	The Homes and Haunts of British Poets	
1848	The Hall and the Hamlet	
1848	The Rural Life of England	
1850	The Steadfast Gabriel	Many editions
1850	The Yearbook of the Country	
1851	The Heir of Wast-Wayland	
1851	Madam Dorrington of the Dene	
1852	The Literature and Romances of Northern Europe	
1857	John Cassell's Illustrated History of England	Many editions
1857	Tagllangetta, the Squatter's Home	
1859	A Country Book	
1860	The Man of the People	
1862	The Ruined Abbeys and Castles of Great Britain	Many editions
1863	The History of the Supernatural	Many editions
1864	Stories of Stapleford	
1867	Woodburn Grange	
1869	The Northern Heights of London	
1875	The Story of a Happy Home	
1873	The Religion of Rome	Translation from Italian
*	The English Peasant	
*	The Wind in a Frolic	

The Traveller on the Hill-top

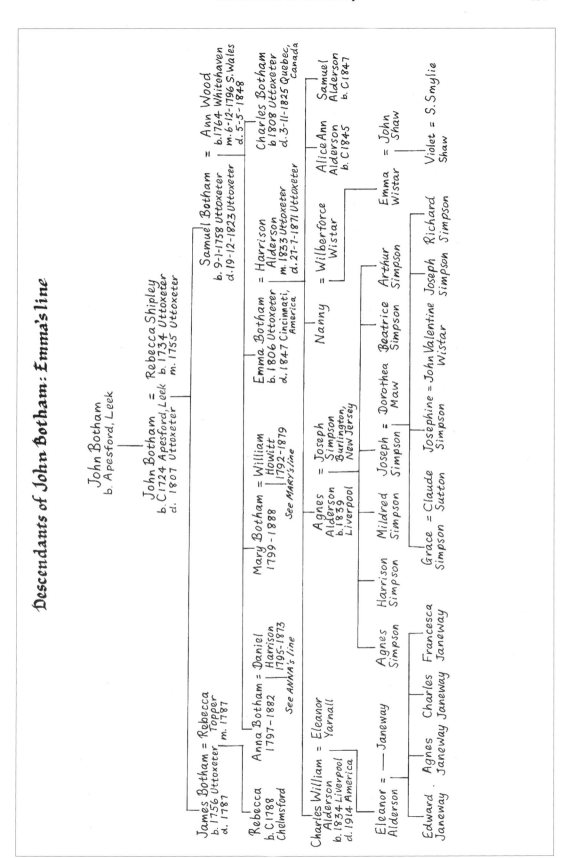

Descendants of John Botham: Emma's line

Descendants of John Botham: Anna's line

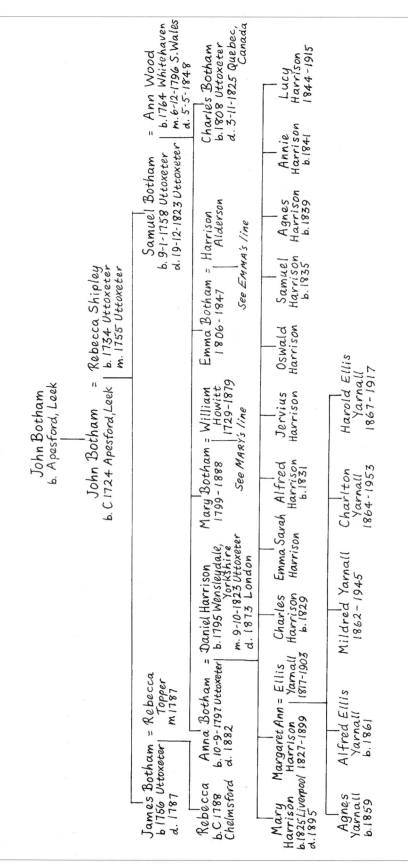

Descendants of John Botham : Mary's line

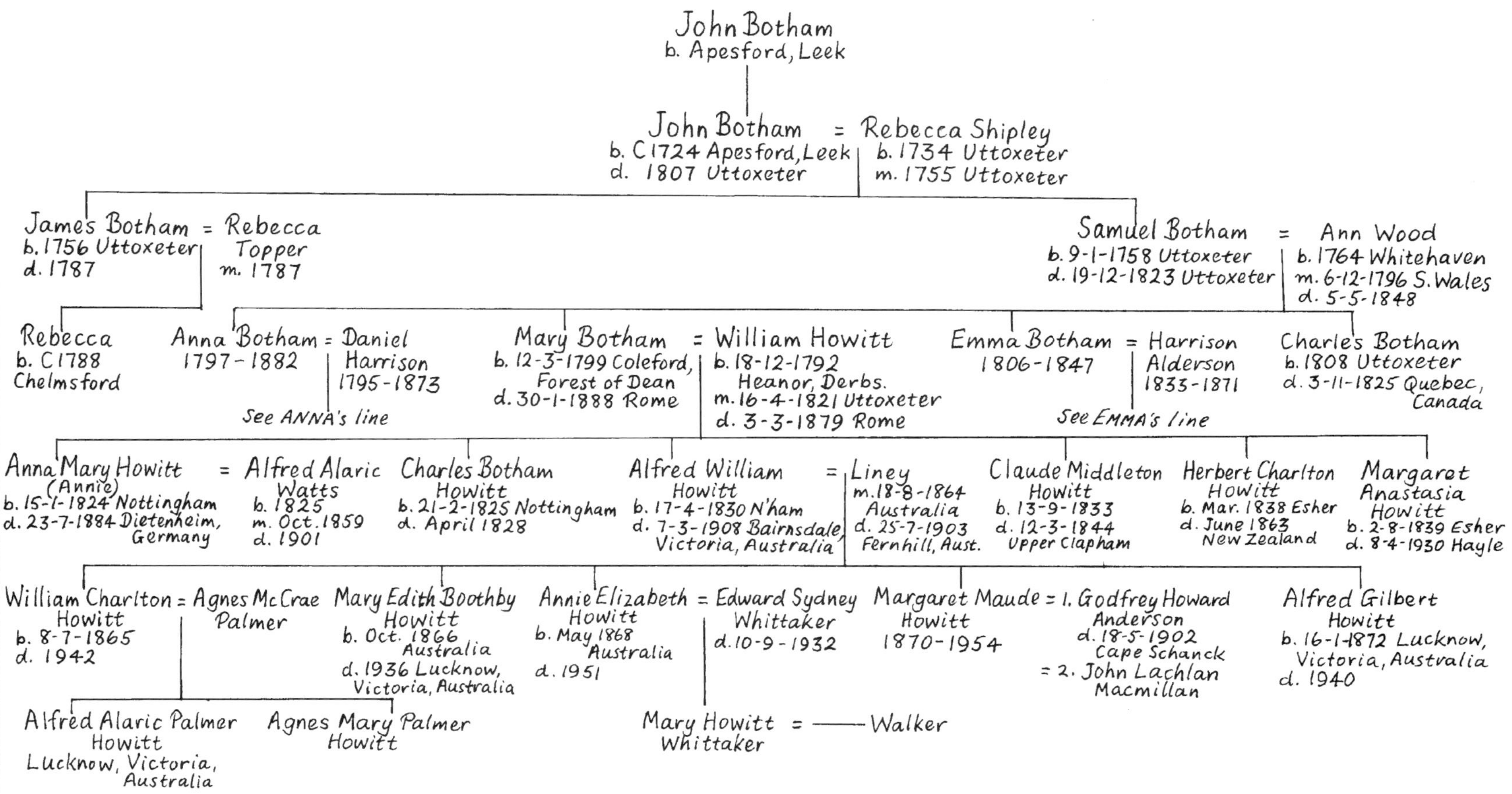

John Botham
b. Apesford, Leek

John Botham = Rebecca Shipley
b. C1724 Apesford, Leek | b. 1734 Uttoxeter
d. 1807 Uttoxeter | m. 1755 Uttoxeter

Samuel Botham = Ann Wood
b. 9-1-1758 Uttoxeter | b. 1764 Whitehaven
d. 19-12-1823 Uttoxeter | m. 6-12-1796 S. Wales
| d. 5-5-1848

James Botham = Rebecca Topper
b. 1756 Uttoxeter | m. 1787
d. 1787

Rebecca
b. C1788 Chelmsford

Anna Botham = Daniel Harrison
1797-1882 | 1795-1873
See ANNA's line

Mary Botham = William Howitt
b. 12-3-1799 Coleford, | b. 18-12-1792
Forest of Dean | Heanor, Derbs.
d. 30-1-1888 Rome | m. 16-4-1821 Uttoxeter
| d. 3-3-1879 Rome

Emma Botham = Harrison Alderson
1806-1847 | 1835-1871
See EMMA's line

Charles Botham
b. 1808 Uttoxeter
d. 3-11-1825 Quebec, Canada

Anna Mary Howitt (Annie) = Alfred William Howitt = Liney
b. 15-1-1824 Nottingham | b. 17-4-1830 N'ham | m. 18-8-1864 Australia
d. 23-7-1884 Dietenheim, Germany | d. 7-3-1908 Bairnsdale, Victoria, Australia | d. 25-7-1903 Fernhill, Aust.

Alfred Alaric Charles Botham Howitt
b. 21-2-1825 Nottingham
d. April 1828

Claude Middleton Howitt
b. 13-9-1833
d. 12-3-1844 Upper Clapham

Herbert Charlton Howitt
b. Mar. 1838 Esher
d. June 1863 New Zealand

Margaret Anastasia Howitt
b. 2-8-1839 Esher
d. 8-4-1930 Hayle

William Charlton Howitt = Agnes McCrae Palmer
b. 8-7-1865
d. 1942

Mary Edith Boothby Howitt
b. Oct. 1866 Australia
d. 1936 Lucknow, Victoria, Australia

Annie Elizabeth Howitt = Edward Sydney Whittaker
b. May 1868 Australia | d. 10-9-1932
d. 1951

Margaret Maude Howitt = 1. Godfrey Howard Anderson
1870-1954 | d. 18-5-1902 Cape Schanck
| = 2. John Lachlan Macmillan

Alfred Gilbert Howitt
b. 16-1-1872 Lucknow, Victoria, Australia
d. 1940

Alfred Alaric Palmer Howitt
Lucknow, Victoria, Australia

Agnes Mary Palmer Howitt

Mary Howitt Whittaker = ——Walker

160   The Traveller on the Hill-top

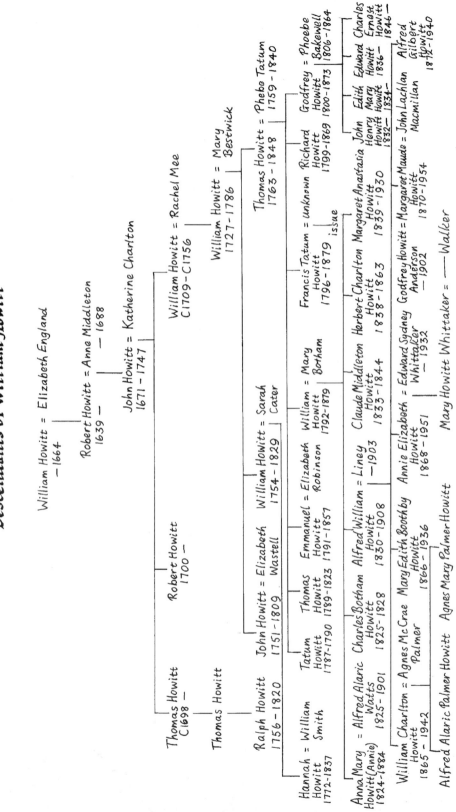